"*Ruse* is a Tale of Two Lives: Kerbeck's acting c[...] life as a corporate con man/spy. If you like cele[...] first, but I prefer the second since it exposes the very dark, greedy, [...] cissistic side of Wall Street and Big Business in general. Kerbeck out-cons the top con-artists — sophisticated CEOs. And he does it over the phone. Wow! In my day I had to fly around the world!"

— **John Perkins, author of** *Confessions of an Economic Hit Man*

"Kerbeck has a very compelling writing style and can pull off humor, too, which isn't easy. I really enjoyed *Ruse*."

— **Bradley Hope, author of** *Billion Dollar Whale*

"I loved *Ruse*! What a crazy story, and believe me, I know crazy. Success-ful spies are great storytellers, and Robert Kerbeck ranks up there with the best of them."

— **Valerie Plame, author of** *Fair Game:*
My Life as a Spy, My Betrayal by the White House

"*Ruse* lives at a truly unique intersection of Hollywood meets Wall Street, and I found myself laughing with and rooting for Robert throughout this book. His personality leaps off the page — he's a great storyteller and *Ruse* is a can't miss best seller."

— **Rob Golenberg, Executive Producer**
of the Showtime series *Your Honor*

"In *Ruse*, Robert Kerbeck reveals himself to be a scoundrel, a raconteur, and a masterful storyteller. In the course of becoming an unlikely corpo-rate intelligence spy, his various masks are so seamless that readers are swept along in his mythic transformation. Sometimes, memoirs become self-involved and forget to give readers a good story. Not here. What other book features a narrator attending a soiree at Paul Newman's Man-hattan apartment, and appearing in an O.J. Simpson exercise video? And that's just for starters. This compelling page-turner is both insightful and an absolute hoot."

— **Sue William Silverman, author of**
How to Survive Death and Other Inconveniences

"Robert Kerbeck's memoir, *Ruse*, is a riveting tale of desire and deception in a world where lies are necessary currency and where con artists can end up convincing everyone, even themselves. *Ruse* offers a fascinating portrait of a life negotiated through a web of fabrications."

— **Lee Martin, Pulitzer Prize Finalist**
and author of *Gone the Hard Road*

"A deliciously outrageous, you-can't-make-this-shit-up caper. Kerbeck takes us on his unlikely transformation from almost-a-star actor to multi-millionaire corporate sleuth. As it turns out, you don't need to climb the greasy rungs of the ladder to make a killing; all you need is a telephone and your wits."

— **Erik Edstrom, author of** *Un-American:*
A Soldier's Reckoning of Our Longest War

Lying the American Dream

FROM

Hollywood to Wall Street

a memoir by

Robert Kerbeck

STEER
FORTH
PRESS

LEBANON, NEW HAMPSHIRE

For information about permission to reproduce
selections from this book, write to:
Steerforth Press L.L.C., 31 Hanover Street, Suite 1
Lebanon, New Hampshire 03766

Cataloging-in-Publication Data is available from the Library of Congress

Printed in the United States of America

ISBN 978-1-58642-316-2

1 3 5 7 9 10 8 6 4 2

To my mother, who always told me to tell the truth.

We have given away so much information that anyone anywhere can become anybody at any time.

— Frank Abagnale, *Catch Me If You Can*

With that little black phone you can achieve anything. That phone equals money.

— Jordan Belfort, *The Wolf of Wall Street*

Is it not monstrous that this player here,
but in a fiction, in a dream of passion,
could force his soul so to his own conceit.

— William Shakespeare, *Hamlet*

CONTENTS

This memoir tells the true story of my life. While I've used the real names of celebrities, I've changed the names and identifying details of many of the other characters and companies to protect their privacy. I've relied on my own memory, such as it is, to reconstruct events and to capture the spirit of what actually occurred. Most of the time I think I've succeeded.

The CEO of Big Daddy's Surf Shack

Phone to my ear, I listen to it ring the way a stage actor, surging with adrenaline, counts the final seconds to his cue. Eyes closed, I breathe in sync with it.

A woman picks up on the fourth ring. I recognize the voice and feel the tension in my knuckles relax a bit. My eyes pop open, and I hit my mark.

"Hey, Zoe, it's Kevin in Compliance."

"Hi, Kev," she says.

"How you doin'?" I ask, my Philly accent like a fist tapping at the window.

"The cancer's back."

It pains me to hear this. I've been calling Zoe for more than a decade, and she's never been anything less than incredibly helpful. I count on her to help me do my job and do it well. Though we've never met, I like her and feel like we know each other. I hate the idea of her getting sick and leaving the company, one of the largest financial institutions in the world. Among other things, it means my work will get much more challenging.

I need her to look up the name, title, and cell phone number for a high-level executive at the bank, plus the names and numbers of everyone who reports to him. She's provided this type of information to me dozens of times over the years. I'm in kind of a hurry, but I'm not an asshole. I need to hear about her illness first.

"I'm sorry to hear that, Zoe. What's the situation?"

"It's not good," she says.

I can tell she is going to say something else, and I'm pretty sure I know what it is. She's going to share with me how much time she has left. I can hear it in her pauses. After so many years working the phone, I've learned to pick out the nuances, the things being said behind what's being said, entire life stories even, in a hesitation or vocal inflection, in blank moments in time.

"Hey, I had a friend who was down for the count, and he's still around five years later," I say. "They're coming up with new treatments every day. You've just got to stick around, and they'll find something."

"I'm on a new chemical now."

"See? Don't you worry. You and I will be having these chats for years to come."

I mean it. She knows I do. I can hear it in the whisper of a smile on the other end of the line.

A few years ago, after she got divorced, Zoe tried to initiate a little flirtation. I was game. Among other things, that kind of rapport would help grease the wheels when I needed help with something.

"Are you single?" she'd asked.

"I am at the moment."

"Do you ever visit Dallas?"

"No," I said. "Working in Compliance, I only get to travel to state capitals to meet with regulators. Austin is as close as I get."

"My daughter has a softball tournament in Austin this weekend. Are you going to still be there Friday? You could stay on. It would be fun to finally meet you."

"I wish. But I'm out of here tonight as soon as we file these docs, then on to the next capital for more of the same."

"Darn it," she said. "Maybe next time."

"For sure."

Zoe didn't stay single long. Once she remarried, our chats focused on my miserable, lonely days traveling around trying to please uptight state regulators. Zoe often reminded me that my life shouldn't be all about work, and she does it again now after my reassurance that we've got a lot of collaboration ahead of us.

"I hope I'll be around long enough to see you getting out there more," Zoe says.

"You and me both," I say, and my tone cues her that we need to get to the real purpose of my call.

"What do you need, Kev?"

I sigh something along the lines of this-may-be-painful-but-we're-in-it-together and give her the name of a senior executive. I need to know his entire organization from top to bottom, every name all the way down to the junior analyst level, plus each individual's location and cell phone number. I need to understand the reporting lines — the company's organizational chart — so I can highlight who's in charge of what and who the heavy hitters are. Zoe knows I'm off-site and don't have access to any of this information at the moment.

"Wow," she says as she pulls up the name on the bank's internal database. "He has over two hundred people in his group. This is going to take forever."

I worry Zoe is going to tell me that she has her own job to do and doesn't have time for this, that she may be dead by the time she gives me everything I need.

Instead, she says, "You ready?"

I smile to myself and nod, pen in hand. "Go for it."

Zoe reads me all the names and titles, tells me who each person reports to, who has teams, and who is on each team. She gives me precise descriptions of what each team does and offers each individual's cell number and physical location. My hand cramps as I scribble everything down. By the time she finishes, more than an hour has passed. I thank her earnestly.

"I've gotta take a break after that," Zoe says. "I'm exhausted."

"You deserve one," I say.

She deserves more than that. An expensive dinner on me or, hell, an all-expenses-paid vacation to Hawaii. But I can't do that. I certainly can't physically go see her in Dallas. I have to keep things professional. Zoe knows that what I do is critical for our multibillion-dollar company to continue doing what it does, so she provides what I ask of her, over and over, year after year, even though it has absolutely nothing to do with her job. Even though it eats up hours of her time. Even though she is not authorized to give me any of that information.

And, most important, even though every single thing she knows about me, and everything I've ever told her, is a lie.

My name is not Kevin, and I don't work in Compliance.

I am not an employee of Zoe's company, let alone an executive.

I've never met a state regulator, uptight or otherwise.

I am not sitting in an antiseptic office in a blocky municipal building in Austin. I've got my feet up on my desk in the converted toolshed that is my home office in Malibu. The sign on the door says, BIG DADDY'S SURF SHOP, though I've always just called it the shack. Shirtless, in board shorts and flip-flops, I gaze out at the Pacific and breathe in its familiar salty musk while I casually manipulate her.

I am not single. My wife's in the house doing yoga.

It's not even true that I'm not an asshole. Well, okay, I'm not. But viewed through the lens of cajoling a woman suffering from cancer into giving me private company information that could get her fired while pushing her to provide it in time for me to catch some waves before the late-afternoon wind comes up, one could be forgiven for thinking such.

My friend who survived cancer? That actually is true. Every good liar knows you need to throw in one big truth to anchor the rest of the bullshit.

But all that internal data about reporting structures and titles and top earners? One of the largest search firms in the world has secretly hired me to steal it. And those private cell phone numbers? My client is going to target the bank's best moneymakers and try to poach them, securing their meaty portfolios as well. It's late 2006, and Wall Street is bursting — year-end bonuses are projected to be 10 to 25 percent higher than last year's, netting the top bankers and traders as much as $40 million apiece. Meanwhile, a couple hundred miles south of Zoe, in Houston, former Enron CEO Jeffrey K. Skilling has just been sentenced to twenty-four years in prison and fined $45 million for his part in one of the greatest bankruptcy and accounting scandals in American history. ("We are the good guys," he infamously said.)

All of which is to say, this seemingly innocuous phone call is taking place in a capitalist ecosystem defined by outrageous, unchecked excess and, yes, rampant deception. The world of corporate spying is shady but lucrative, and I am one of the best. Very few can do what I do. I am the CEO of a thriving underground enterprise that I've been building for almost twenty years. As a professional telephone liar — the last of a dying breed — I operate in a shadow market pursuing corporate intelligence worth billions of dollars to the top firms in the cutthroat world of international finance.

And for a corporate spy, there is nothing on this earth better than a reliable mole. Finding one as good (and as gullible) as Zoe, a low-level paper-pusher, doesn't happen every day. Indeed, she is the longest-running mole I've ever had. Most of my research calls start with someone new. I have to convince them — though it's more like I *hypnotize* them — that I am who I say I am. Then I have to get them to believe I'm off-site, working in a building that's been reinforced with so much steel — because of post-9/11 security concerns — that my cell phone is having trouble accessing our firm's internal directory, which is why I need their help. Often it doesn't go well.

But Zoe? Zoe swallowed the hook the first time I fished and has never spit it out. I want information from her that I have no right to, and she gives it to me. Every time. Her intelligence alone has netted me hundreds of thousands of dollars in fees over the years. Is it any wonder I want her to stick around?

"Anything else, Kev?" she says.

"Nope," I say, "that's everything. Thanks again. Go take that break, yeah? You've earned it."

"Ain't that the truth," she says.

We chuckle and hang up.

The truth. Funny.

CHAPTER ONE

The Biggest Lie

If I told you that you could make millions of dollars, and all you had to do was lie on the phone all day to earn it, would you do it? *Could* you do it? You'd probably start by asking if it was illegal. And if so, *how* illegal. Good for you. You have some kind of conscience. Note that as I flatter you, I'm not answering your question. Or maybe you'd think, *Shit, what's the harm in finagling a few names out of corporations anyway?* After all, Goldman Sachs, Wells Fargo, and the like don't care about us. They've shown repeatedly and remorselessly that they're not terribly concerned about bilking consumers or tanking the global economy. Who cares if they get dinged a little?

While you're pondering that, I'll point out that the job has some serious perks beyond the money. For one thing, you can ruse from anywhere in the world — your car, the beach, your bed or basement (or backyard surf shack), Monte Carlo, the rain forests of Costa Rica. Over the years, I've rused from London, Paris, the *QE2* (those phone calls in the middle of the Atlantic are expensive!), Hawaii, even the boardrooms of Wall Street firms while waiting to meet with their CEOs. All you need is a phone. And you can ruse as much or as little as you like, it's up to you.

There are a few downsides. It's a lot of writing and/or typing since you don't want to leave any kind of electronic trail. If I were a tech-savvy hacker, I'd figure out how to get my marks to send me the intelligence in some encrypted way. But I'm old-school.

So the job's got flexibility, it'll challenge you, and it pays well.

Now for the downside: Not everyone can do what I do. In fact, almost no one can. This is not self-aggrandizement. It's a cold fact. Rusing takes a degree of sophistication and creativity and fortitude (and ethical elasticity) most people can't summon. But by far the most important trait to make it as a telephone criminal is the gift of gab. The talent to improvise and bullshit like a motherfucker. The ability to lie, and lie again, over and over until the lies sound like the truth. If you're as good as I am, the lies sound *better* than the truth. I admit, as a former professional actor I have an advantage, but America is full of top-shelf liars who've never taken an improv class or read Stanislavski's *An Actor Prepares*.

You also need to be an informed citizen. Knowing what's going on in the world is critical. If I'm calling San Francisco and the Forty-Niners won big the day before, I'm using it. If a firm is under scrutiny for some scandalous fuck-up — their executive was accused of sexual harassment or insider trading — it's me who's off-site with the regulators trying to clean that shit up. If I'm on the phone with a European subsidiary, you better believe I know some local news and a couple of foreign-language phrases.

The top headhunters — rather, *search professionals* — don't just "smile and dial" the way less sophisticated recruiters do. My clients want to be very targeted in who they call, so they need to know who the rock stars are. Over the years I've developed proprietary ploys that scored such prized intelligence that my clients believed I was some kind of ninja wraith. I learned to get people to divulge information better than a CIA interrogator.

Still, I'll admit that there were times when I wondered how long I'd be able to do it. I don't mean morally — I could lie forever, and on my most generous days I tend to think of rusing as a crime without a victim: My client does well, my *client's* client does well, the newly recruited do well, I do well, and, well, the Zoes of the world don't have any idea about any of it (until they read this book, I suppose). I mean practically. When I started in the 1980s, there was no internet, no cell phones, no social media or personal websites or digital company directories. Internal personnel data was not readily available to an outsider. With the advent of LinkedIn in the aughts and the disappearance of professional privacy, a good chunk of what I was providing was suddenly free in the public space.

But here's the thing: Not everything valuable can be found online. Even fourteen years after that call with Zoe, in the wake of Facebook and the great wave of digital transparency, the internet still can't tell you who the top producers at a given firm are. Many successful executives aren't even on LinkedIn. They don't want to be inundated with requests from amateur-hour headhunters. They're called passive candidates, and my clients are exclusively interested in these types of individuals. They're not actively shopping around for better deals because they're already killing it where they are, making their firms tens of millions if not *billions* of dollars.

And even if an executive is on LinkedIn, his or her profile frequently isn't up to date, often showing them working for a prior firm in a role they haven't been in for a year or more. My clients are the top professional recruiters in their respective industries — tech, defense, finance — and they're paid big money to know *everything* about their space. How do they stay on top? How do they know about unannounced hirings and firings? How do they know every single name at every single firm? How do they know who's secretly ripe for plucking?

That requires someone with the ability to sneak past the gatekeepers and get up inside the corporate kimono.

That person is me.

$ $ $

How did I learn all this? How did I find this crazy job? Even today, there are only a handful of people on the planet who do what I do. And most of them don't do it half as well. But before I get to the ruse and a lifetime of lying, I have to go back to the beginning, which in retrospect seems prophetic.

You see, I come from a family born of lies.

My father, Bob, and his older brother, Jack, were as close as siblings could be. As a young man, my father looked like Elvis Presley, dark and brooding, his hair slicked back. Jack looked more half-Armenian, which both men were. They bought houses two doors down from each other in the Philly suburbs. Each was the best man at the other's wedding. Together they ran a successful automobile dealership for decades (yes, I am the child of a car salesman; more on that later). At one point they bought *connecting* houses at the Jersey Shore. They talked on the phone every day, often for hours. Their numbers? Dad's ended with 6505 and Jack's with 6504. Even now, I've never met two people more inseparable than they were.

I didn't know it at the time, but there was a very poignant reason for this.

Their Armenian father, JK, was married to an Armenian woman named Haganoush, who discovered she couldn't have children. For JK, not having a male heir was completely unacceptable. But Haganoush had been brought over from the Republic of Armenia as part of an arranged marriage in 1921, six years after the start of the Armenian genocide, and divorcing a survivor was also completely unacceptable. The shame within the close-knit Armenian community of Philadelphia would have been too great.

So instead, my grandfather played around while his wife (and the rest of the community) looked the other way. In the mid-1930s, JK met a woman named Shirley. At a Jewish dance. He told her he was single — and Jewish. Both monumental lies. She was a beauty and no doubt captivated him, at least temporarily. When she became pregnant, JK sent her to live in Atlantic City so no one would find out and agreed to support her financially.

This was almost certainly because the resulting child, my uncle Jack, was a boy. If he had been a girl, I feel sure that JK wouldn't have supported his second family. In Armenian culture, the importance of having a male heir cannot be overstated. This is true in many cultures, but, as a result of the genocide, the need for Armenian men to see their genetic line preserved was powerful. Indeed, when my grandmother — my real one, Shirley, not Haganoush — gave birth to the sons JK wanted, Jack and then my father, Bob, his financial support came with a condition: They had to be raised as Christians. They were to learn nothing of their Jewish ancestry, culture, or traditions. Of course, since my uncle and my father could have no contact with the Armenian side of their family, either, lest JK's secret be exposed, they also learned little of their Armenian heritage.

Put plainly, Jack and Bob were bastards — not the informal definition, but the archaic one, as in children born out of wedlock. The covert nature of their existence and distance from their father's public life meant that they bonded to each other with a special ferocity. They told everyone that JK and Shirley were divorced and, incredibly, they kept that secret until the day Shirley died. Even their wives hadn't known.

I certainly didn't know.

After the truth came out, I did some digging. When JK became infirm at ninety-six years old (the asshole *drove* until he was ninety-three), my father and I came across the letters Shirley had sent him from the Atlantic City boardinghouse he'd set her up in. It was clear that she'd thought JK would leave Haganoush and they'd become a family. Further research revealed that JK's family had left the town of Arabkir, Turkey, after the massacres of 1895, forerunners of the full-scale genocide that took place twenty years later and killed 1.5 million Armenians. On our Jewish side, I discovered that relatives of Shirley had been scheduled to come from Ukraine to live with her in Philadelphia but couldn't make it out in time to escape the Nazis.

So even though my father and my uncle were children of two of the worst genocides of the twentieth century, they knew nothing about their connection to either one because their father had birthed them into a false familial history.

Could I ever tell a bigger lie than that?

Well, no.

But not for lack of trying.

CHAPTER TWO

But I Don't Wanna Be a Car Salesman

My father, Bob, didn't want me to be an actor, a writer, or any other kind of artsy freeloader, let alone a corporate spy. He had his sights set locally, someplace where he could keep an eye on me and make sure I was primed to embrace the version of the American dream he had worked so hard to build and sustain. My mother, Margie, came from a family of coal miners and dockworkers and was only able to attend nursing school because she'd won a scholarship. Having grown up poor, she supported my father's vision for me.

My dad's plan was simple: I would ditch any foolish fantasies of a creative life and take over the Lincoln-Mercury dealership he and Uncle Jack co-owned in North Philadelphia. This was clear my entire childhood — not that it was said out loud. As the eldest son, I knew it as an incontestable fact, just like *hoagie* was the only acceptable word for a long, meat-stuffed sandwich and "Fly, Eagles, Fly" was the best football fight song ever written.

After my Armenian great-grandfather Garabed Kerbeck (originally Kerbeckian) emigrated from Turkey with his family at the end of the nineteenth century, he launched a business selling horse-drawn carriages to well-to-do Philadelphians. When the gasoline engine came along, he switched to selling automobiles — an early example of a key strand in the Kerbeck DNA: the ability to adapt on the fly.

Since I'd inherited another key family trait, the bullshitting gene, I was the best suited of Bob's and Jack's children to take charge and carry on the tradition. Every time I went to visit my dad's office on the lot, I'd walk past the brass placard mounted on the front of the building that proudly declared, SINCE 1899. Which is to say being offered the reins to this legacy was a big deal, and declining them would be an even bigger one.

But by the time I was ready to start freshman year at Drexel University in the fall of 1981, I wanted nothing to do with it, so I was willing to do pretty much anything not to live at home. The school sat a few blocks from the Schuylkill River in West Philly, and I needed some distance from my dad or I feared I'd be conscripted into selling cars whenever I wasn't in class.

"You'll commute from home," my father said. "I'm gonna give you $200 a month. You can use that for spending money."

I didn't want spending money. I wanted escape money.

Against my father's wishes, that fall I got an off-campus one-bedroom apartment with two other guys in Powelton Village, a neighborhood of mostly dilapidated Victorian homes. My share of the rent came to $117 a month. After phone and utilities, I'd eat up $150 of my "spending money" before ever spending a dime on food, drink, or fun. I lived on Kraft macaroni and cheese (three for 99 cents) and never went out.

Drexel was known as an engineering and business school, but the administration paid good money for professors from the University of Pennsylvania, which was just across the street, to moonlight there. In my second semester, I had a Penn professor for freshman English. After reading my first essay, on John Stuart Mill's *The Subjection of Women*, he pulled me aside.

"What the hell are you doing at Drexel?" His tone indicated that no sufficient answer existed. The truth was, I'd been wondering the same thing.

The next day, I was standing with my dad in the showroom of the dealership when I casually mentioned the possibility of transferring schools and switching my major from business to English. My father's nickname was the Bear, partly because of his size (he was six foot one and weighed over 250 pounds) but also because he had a friendly and seemingly easygoing nature — until he felt crossed or threatened. Then it was a life-or-death struggle.

"You can wipe your ass with a liberal arts degree," he snapped, instantly in grizzly mode. Then he berated me about how expensive Penn was.

His words didn't surprise me, but they stung. I thought about the essay, how smart writing it had made me feel. I wanted that feeling again. I wanted the praise of an Ivy League English professor telling me how good my writing was, words that weren't ever going to come from my father.

"*I'll* pay for it," I said, despite not having a clue if that was possible.

"I'd like to see that," my father said with a dismissive snicker.

His skepticism was valid. What did I know about pulling together tens of thousands of dollars for Ivy League tuition? Who was I kidding? All I knew in that moment was that I'd been given a shot at a different life, and I wasn't going to blow it. So with the theme song from *Rocky* crescendoing in my head, I said the bravest words I'd spoken to date:

"You will."

And I did.

I paid my way through Penn by using any means necessary. I worked thirty-two hours a week at the front desk of the Hilton Hotel on the Penn campus in West Philly. I took out loans. I weaseled school grants by charming the sexy older woman in charge of Penn's financial aid department. By that point I was six foot one myself, and I used my blond hair, blue eyes, and gift of gab to full advantage without hesitation.

In my junior year, I was accepted as a resident adviser in one of the dorms. The role gave me free room and board as well as a small stipend, which finally enabled me to have some of the typical college experiences, like going out on a date. I figured the best place to meet girls was the theater, though it was an environment in which I had minimal interest.

My first audition was for an adaptation of Euripides's *Electra*. I had no idea what a monologue was, so I simply recited the lyrics to Bruce Springsteen's "It's Hard to Be a Saint in the City." It may have been incongruous and brazen, but something must have clicked, because when I checked the cast list later I was shocked to find that not only had I been given a part, but it was a part with a character name. Most of the cast were soldiers or chorus. As with my freshman-year Mill essay, I felt pretty proud of myself.

At the first read-through, scripts were handed out. I shuffled through the pages looking for my lines. Then shuffled some more. When I reached the end, I was sweating. I didn't have a single line despite my character's presence in many scenes. Was I some kind of glorified extra?

The director pulled me aside. "You're on stage most of the play," he said.

Yeah, right, I wanted to say. *Without any lines.*

"You're the villain, but you're mute. Your part is critical."

It turned out he wasn't blowing smoke. We performed in the Harold Prince Theatre in Penn's multimillion-dollar Annenberg Center on Walnut Street. Amazingly, Harold Prince himself came to see the show, though at the time I had no idea he'd directed *Cabaret*, *Sweeney Todd*, and countless other Broadway musicals. Even better, when the reviews came out in the school paper, I was singled out for my "charismatic" performance. Apparently standing there and looking dangerous was something I was good at.

Soon after this performance, I was approached by the coolest theater group on campus to join them. Over the years, I played the lead in a number of their productions, always with plenty of lines. My last play at Penn was directed by a professional stage director rather than by a professor or a fellow student. He was casting for a small off-Broadway show and asked me to be in it. Suddenly I was taking the train to New York City every day to act professionally, and I hadn't even graduated yet. It seemed like a career in acting was meant to be, or worthy of a try.

But lacking any support from my father, I didn't go for it, at least not right away.

$ $ $

More than a year after graduating from Penn with a BA in English, I'd spent most of my time selling my father's cars. A lot of them. It turned out I was very good at it. He'd been happy enough to welcome his prodigal son back into the fold when I'd been too chicken to move to New York to take my shot as an actor. He'd even promoted me to sales manager.

One hot afternoon in the summer of 1986, I was at the dealership when my father called to me from across the lot. When I looked up, he waved me over impatiently. The gesture sent a nervous shiver through me, since I was leaving the family business at the end of that day.

I'd finally found the courage to give acting a go, student loan debt be damned. I was heading off to the New Jersey Shakespeare Festival to do *Julius Caesar*, playing a soldier with a short sword, zero lines, and no pay. It was an exciting moment, but the split from my father was giving me anxiety.

We walked into the dealership building and sat down across from each other in his office. Through the fake-wood-paneled wall, my father and I could hear the familiar sounds of my uncle Jack's voice. His office was next door, separated only by the bathroom they shared. My uncle was interviewing candidates to replace me, and my father shook his head in the direction of his brother's voice with a weary combination of sadness and disgust.

"Jesus Christ," he said, his tone implying that I had put the family in a terrible position, since whomever they hired would be neither a Kerbeck nor as talented. Almost absentmindedly, he handed me an envelope. "Here, this is for you."

On the outside was his scribbled writing. It took me a moment to decipher it.

If you change your mind, you can come back.

I hadn't even left and already my father was lobbying for my return. Inside the envelope was a gift of a few hundred dollars.

There was no note wishing me success or good luck.

$$$

While fighting on the side of Mark Antony at the New Jersey Shakespeare Festival, I received a call that a production of George Orwell's *1984* was moving from Philadelphia to the new American National Theater at the Kennedy Center in Washington, DC. They needed a strong thug-like character — my specialty — to play the head henchman of the Thought Police. The production starred a young Tom Sizemore, who would go on to have a major role in one of the most popular war movies ever made, *Saving Private Ryan*. We got to know each other well during the production, and at one point he pitched me on a much more intimate costarring role: He wanted me to fuck his wife while he watched. Method-boning a colleague's spouse wasn't something I had in me. I politely declined.

Addiction and misconduct, including a conviction for physically abusing his girlfriend, the "Hollywood Madam" Heidi Fleiss, would later derail Tom's career.

My parents came down from Philadelphia to see *1984*, but my father didn't say much, and he seemed uncomfortable in the lobby after the show. I hadn't expected him to tell me he was impressed with my talent or proud of me, but I'd hoped for some acknowledgment that getting a job like this meant *something*. I'd gone from being an unpaid summer-stock extra to being a working actor making more than $600 a week in a play at the freakin' Kennedy Center. Hell, a photo of me ran alongside the production's *New York Times* review.

Instead, my father scratched at the collar of his dress shirt as though he'd tied his tie too tight, something I'd never seen him do at the dealership. I'm sure he thought I'd be back on the lot after my summer in New Jersey, hat in hand, dreams permanently dashed. But now strangers from the sold-out show were congratulating me, an indication to him that his plans for me to take over the dealership were probably dead.

When I returned to Philly after the close of the Orwell play, I got a second big acting job that proved the first wasn't a fluke. I received a phone call from a casting director that a famous local band, the Hooters, was searching for someone to play the lead in the video for their upcoming album's first single, "Johnny B." For a Philly native, this was no small thing. The band's founders met at Penn, and after their second album, *Nervous Night*, went platinum in 1985, *Rolling Stone* named them Best New Band of the Year. That summer they'd opened the Philadelphia portion of the Live Aid show at Kennedy Stadium for nearly ninety thousand people. MTV had exploded, making the video at least as important as the song, so visibility would be huge. The director was named David Fincher. He would parlay this gig into two iconic Madonna videos — "Express Yourself" and "Vogue" — and ultimately such films as *Fight Club* and *The Social Network*. But he was my age and at that point almost as unknown as I was.

For the audition, I met David at the casting director's office. He stared at me and hardly said a word, which made me nervous. I'd started to think about maybe breaking into my Springsteen monologue when the casting director abruptly ushered me out of the room for the next actor in line. On the drive home, I berated myself for not doing something, anything, to impress the director. I hadn't even cracked a joke. The entire process took no more than a minute or two. Imagine my surprise then when the casting director called later that day to say that David had hired me to play Johnny B.

In the song and the video, Johnny B is a serious drug addict. I had no experience with hard drugs and wondered if I could pull off the part. Somewhat fortunately for me, David insisted that I smoke for the shoot. Cigarettes had made me sick the few times I'd tried them, and again I was instantly nauseated and white as a sheet. When David saw the effect the cigarettes were having on me, he made me smoke even more — until I looked as strung out as Johnny B.

On the last day of the shoot, during the video's climactic scene, I was supposed to freak out and trash the seedy hotel room where Johnny B was shooting up. David gave me free rein to rip or break anything — with the exception of a TV that had been borrowed from a local appliance company. I was so whacked from all the nicotine in my system that I lost control and knocked the TV over, shattering it onto the ground.

I can't say for sure that this is the reason, but he never hired me again, though the "Johnny B" video was an instant hit and helped launch David's career.

$ $ $

With my face now regularly on TV, even if only MTV, there wasn't much my father could say when at twenty-four I moved to New York in February 1987 to pursue an acting career. I reached out to a high school classmate named Jake who had moved to the city to take a job as an analyst at the brokerage firm Dean Witter to see if I could live with him for a week or two while I searched for a place to live.

Following the recession during the early years of the Reagan administration, Wall Street boomed. The Dow Jones Industrial Average had almost doubled since 1982. When I graduated from Penn in 1985, it seemed that everyone wanted to work there. The extended bull market had created a widespread hysteria to get filthy rich and retire at thirty-five. The same year I moved to the city, Jordan Belfort, of *Wolf of Wall Street* fame, began his infamous career. Eventually, he would open his first brokerage out of a — wait for it — used car lot.

Though we came from the same small suburban town, Jake's family had a lot more money. His father had built a real estate mini empire that was so successful he was considered the Donald Trump of Philadelphia. He even knew Trump. Because of Jake's family's real estate connections I figured his place would be nice, but I was still shocked when I arrived at the luxurious modern building on 66th Street between Central Park and Lincoln Center.

In general, analysts worked two years on Wall Street before they returned to school to get their MBA. Advanced degree in hand, they were rehired as associates and began climbing the ladder to vice president, director, and then managing director, the Wall Street equivalent of a made man. But first they had to survive those years as an analyst. When Michael Lewis, who would go on to write the defining 1989 memoir *Liar's Poker: Rising Through the Wreckage on Wall Street*, started as an analyst at Salomon Brothers in 1985, he was told he was "lower than whale shit at the bottom of the ocean."

A striver in these esteemed ranks, Jake worked six days a week, rarely for less than fifteen hours a day. Unless I was invited to join him and his Dean Witter cronies for a late-night dinner at a fancy Manhattan restaurant, I hardly saw him. Though I appreciated Jake's invitations, the cult of machismo, boorishness, sexism, and homophobia embodied by his compatriots was too much for me. While still in Philadelphia I had starred in William M. Hoffman's *As Is*, one of the first produced plays about AIDS. By the end of the year, nearly fifty thousand people would be dead from the disease. I had many friends taken by it, young and old, some of whom I cared for in their final days. Despite being the same age as many of my theater friends, the Wall Street guys couldn't care less about a pandemic primarily killing gay men. These titans-in-training were only concerned with one thing: the slavish pursuit of money, which they discussed nonstop. There were also subtle echoes of the flimflam men of my dad's car trade, which I was trying to leave behind. After a few dinners, I stopped joining them. Instead, I stayed busy with the acting classes I was taking from a well-known protégé of famous acting teacher Lee Strasberg, who had died in 1982.

I continued to sleep on the comfy sofa bed in Jake's living room, however, for another two months. Each time I told him it was time for me to go, he would ask, "Why? I'm never here. And you stock the fridge, which saves me time I don't have." Buying groceries seemed the least I could do since I had a swanky, rent-free place with a view of Central Park practically to myself. But by staying, it felt as if I were still putting off the decision to fully commit to becoming an actor. I feared that if I stalled any longer in Jake's place I would end up heading back to my father's car business — or worse, apply for a job at Dean Witter.

I finally made my break on one of those hard-pounding rainy summer days and sneaked into the NYU housing office to find a cheap place to live. I ended up in a tiny three-bedroom apartment with two roommates on the border of the West Village and Chelsea at 14th Street and Seventh Avenue, perhaps the noisiest block in all of Manhattan. This was the era before leaning on your horn could get you a ticket. Gridlock on the streets below my window was a daily headache. Horns sounded day and night. But I didn't care. I had my own place on the isle of Manhattan, and I was going to be an actor.

Now with rent and bills to pay, I needed a survival job. I didn't have the requisite patience to be a waiter, the job of choice for most thespians because of its flexibility and reliable evening shifts outside of audition windows. I also wasn't a late-night kind of guy, so bartending was out as well. I reluctantly went around to a couple of Manhattan dealerships to put in applications to sell cars. Fortunately, before one of the dealerships called to offer me employment, I heard about a part-time job with flexible hours that sounded like exactly what I needed. The details were murky, but, really, how bad could it be? I figured any job that didn't require a suit and tie — or an apron — was all right by me.

$ $ $

My college roommate's brother, Paxton "Pax" Freed, lived in Manhattan and had offered to show me around the city. A five-foot-six actor-musician with a mop of wavy brown hair, he was always clad in a black leather jacket like a mini Springsteen. One day, Pax mentioned his new phone job, which sounded like sales to me. If I could sell someone a $30,000 Lincoln Town Car they couldn't afford, I certainly could sell magazine subscriptions or whatever else the product might be. He got me an interview with his boss, Leona, and one afternoon I made my way to the Upper East Side, a section of the city I'd never visited.

Leona's building had a uniformed doorman, which made me nervous, like I was trying to get into a club and unworthy of entrance. I made the cut, however, and was directed to an elevator. Inside, an old man was operating it, something I'd only seen in movies. He didn't say a word to me; he already knew where I was headed. When the elevator reached the ninth floor, the operator opened the gate and pointed at the first apartment directly to the left, which happened to be the only door in sight. I knocked, and after a moment a woman opened it. Leona seemed old to me, though she couldn't have been much more than forty. She wore leopard-print pants, a brightly colored blouse with matching silk scarf, gaudy gold jewelry, and too much makeup, reminding me of Mrs. Robinson in *The Graduate*. I was playing it safe, wearing a suit and tie and carrying a briefcase with my résumé in it. I'm not sure what she was expecting, but she eyed me as if my leading-man looks had made a good first impression.

"Nice outfit," she said. "You look like you should be selling cars."

"Actually, I did sell cars," I said, a little clumsily. "For my dad's dealership."

"I know. I'm teasing you. Pax told me."

She ushered me inside the cleanest apartment I'd ever seen. Everything seemed to be in perfect order, as well as white. The living room looked ready for an *Architectural Digest* photo shoot. On top of the wall-to-wall carpeting was some type of fur rug (polar bear, I would later learn — *polar bear?* — yes, polar bear), the glass-top tables looked freshly Windexed, and the walls gleamed like the painters had just left. Whatever her business was, it was lucrative.

"I didn't think you'd be so . . . tall." Leona gestured for me to sit in a white, padded chair in the center of the rug. I prayed I hadn't stepped in any dog-doo on my trek from the subway.

"Pax tells me you left working for your dad to be an actor."

I nodded.

"How did he take that?"

I was a bit flummoxed by the question. "Uh, not well," I finally said.

"You have siblings?"

"A younger sister and brother."

"Well, maybe one of them will get you off the hook."

I hadn't expected the interview to focus on my father's disappointment with my career choice. I'm sure he would have been impressed with Leona's decor, though. In my head I heard him say *she's loaded* approvingly.

"Why do you want to be an actor?" she asked.

I launched into a rambling monologue about how I'd started acting at Penn and was cast as the lead in play after play. I told her about *1984* and the Hooters video. I explained that these breaks were what gave me the courage to move to New York.

"It's a hard life," Leona said. "Hard to make a living. Hard to keep it going. That's what your dad is worried about."

"I can take care of myself."

Leona sighed. "I have no doubt." She stood and offered her hand to bid me good-bye. "Always keep a survival job, just in case. And take care of your relationship with your father. In case something happens. You don't want to leave things the way they are."

I wondered how much Pax might have told Leona about the tension with my father and how much she just surmised, though I was more focused on the realization that she wasn't giving me the job. She hadn't even asked for my résumé, which I'd forgotten to pull out. Just like that, the Upper East Side fantasia spit me right back out onto the dirty streets of downtown, as unemployed as ever. It was time to pick up a crate of Kraft macaroni and cheese.

Pax called the next day. He said Leona was hiring me at the rate of $8 an hour, and I was to start training immediately. I couldn't believe it. Koo-koo-ka-choo, Leona.

"I guess I blew her away," I said.

"She hires everyone," he said. "Because nobody works out."

"Don't worry. I'll be able to do it."

It was only then I realized that Leona hadn't asked about my phone skills or sales skills — or any skills, really. She'd also not said a word about what the job actually entailed.

For that matter, neither had Pax.

CHAPTER THREE

Luck of the Irish

The following day I made my way to the Williamsburg section of Brooklyn to work with Leona's trainer, Deirdre. In the late '80s, Brooklyn was the antithesis of the Upper East Side; it was dangerous, especially Williamsburg. The crack epidemic was hitting hard. The LL subway train I took over the Williamsburg Bridge was still covered in '70s graffiti. The neighborhood was apocalyptic: no coffee shops, condo complexes, or hipsters with beards, just dirt, decay, and scary-looking human beings. As a strong young guy, I wasn't particularly afraid. After all, it was broad daylight, and my father's dealership was located in one of the roughest sections of North Philadelphia, so I had experience working in downtrodden urban areas. I knew to keep my guard up and my feet ready.

It was unusually hot for late April. New York City seemed to have skipped right to summer with the kind of irritating heat that makes the assault rate go up. I found the building I was looking for and trudged sweatily up four flights of stairs. Along the way, I heard yelling and screaming from inside more than one apartment. I knocked on the door of 4C and a cute young woman with striking green eyes opened it. She was wearing a flowing and flowery Laura Ashley–type dress.

"Top o' the morning," she said with a bright smile. "I'm Deirdre O'Conor. That's with one *n*, not two, the way true Irish people spell it."

"I didn't know."

"I'm American but Irish on both sides. What about you? Are you Irish?"

"Nope."

"Not at all?" She seemed concerned, as if she might not be able to train me if I didn't have some Irish blood.

"I'm part Welsh." I was part a lot of things: Welsh, English, Russian Jew, and, of course, Armenian. Like a chameleon, I could blend into different groups using whichever part of my background fit closest.

"Oh," she said, suddenly happy again. "I love the Welsh. They're almost as nice as the Irish."

She laughed and showed me into her apartment, which consisted of two rooms: a bedroom and a living room with a bathtub in the middle of it.

"You'll work in my bedroom," she said. "Come on."

Her bedroom. What kind of work was she going to have me doing?

Deirdre set me up at a small desk in front of her bed, which was just a mattress on the floor. She pulled up a chair next to me and handed me a writing pad.

"First, you'll need a name."

"What for?"

"For your ploy. You can't use your real name. What happens when you get famous?" Deirdre said this as if it were a given.

"I need a fake name for phone sales?"

"We're not doing sales. Didn't Pax tell you that?"

Pax hadn't told me anything, as if he was afraid to tell people what he did for a living. I had assumed that if the job wasn't phone sales, it was some sort of telemarketing.

"We get non-public information from Wall Street companies."

"What kind of information?"

"Their org charts."

I had no idea what these were. I guess it was obvious by the look on my face.

"Their *organizational* charts," she said slowly, as if I were developmentally disabled. "You know: Who reports to whom?" Deirdre pulled a giant red book from a cabinet and flipped it open. "Like this."

It was some sort of directory. At the top of each page was the name of a bank or financial institution and beneath was a list of the executives working at that company, along with their titles.

"We get information like this for Leona's executive search firm clients. Their headhunters use our charts to identify the best people and recruit them away to *their* clients."

"Why do they need us when they have directories like this?" I pointed at the massive book, which had to be more than a thousand pages.

She scoffed. "This is worthless. It's out of date the second they print it. Half of these executives are gone or in different roles. Wall Street is ultra-competitive. People are constantly moving around to better jobs, often thanks to us. But it's a good starting point, which is why Leona buys it. We use these names as leads to help get us what we want."

"Which is?"

"I'll show you." She grabbed my pad and elbowed me out of my chair. "Always write your name down, so you don't forget who you are." She wrote *Maeve* on the side of a page, picked up the phone, pushed the SPEAKER button, and dialed a number listed in the directory.

"Shearson Lehman," an operator answered.

"Hello, how is your day going?" Deirdre-as-Maeve asked. She seemed to have put on a slight Irish accent.

"It's fine. How can I help you?"

"I'm an exchange student from Ireland writing a paper. You haven't been there, have you?"

"No, I haven't, but I'd like to go. My ancestors were from Ireland."

Deirdre looked at me and raised her eyebrows.

"You must come and visit. I live in Galway. Ask for Maeve O'Shea."

The operator laughed. Her brusque, business-like tone from the beginning of the call had disappeared. "How can I help you, Maeve?"

"Do you have a Ken Monahan listed?"

There was a brief pause as the operator looked up the name.

"I do. He's in Investment Banking."

"Can you see which department within Investment Banking?"

"He's the head of Mergers and Acquisitions."

"Oh golly, that's what I'm writing my paper on. Can you see the list of the people in that department?"

"I can. It's very long."

"Can you read it to me? Please? I'm sending out a survey, and if I don't get enough responses my paper won't count. It's part of my citizenship application."

Her story sounded kooky as well as unbelievable, but sure enough the operator began to read off the names. Deirdre got up and handed me her pen, mouthing *write*. I scribbled down every name, filling seven or eight pages with my sloppy writing, while Deirdre flitted about her bedroom straightening up.

"That was the last one," the operator said after Xavier Zoydius, or whatever name came last on her alphabetical list.

Deirdre returned to the desk and leaned over my shoulder. She smelled great and reminded me of the commercials for Irish Spring soap. "I almost forgot," she said. "Does your directory list titles?"

"It does."

"Can you zip through them real fast? This is the last thing."

I noticed Deirdre had dropped her accent. I wondered if I should warn her.

The operator ran through the list again, this time giving me titles: managing directors and VPs, associates and analysts. I barely understood what they meant.

When the operator finished, Deirdre popped back to her position over my shoulder.

"I'm so sorry, but I need phone numbers, too. I promise, this is it."

"You said that already."

"I know, but I promise this time."

The operator gave me the direct phone extensions for every name on the list. I would later learn the phone numbers made it easier for Leona's clients to contact people, especially if they called after hours when the switchboard was closed.

"Thank you, operator. What was your name?"

"Colleen."

"A good Irish name," Deirdre said.

"I'm not supposed to do that, you know."

"I know, thank you. We Irish have to stick together. Have a great day!"

Deirdre disconnected the call and did a jig, complete with Irish step dancing.

"That's amazing," I said.

"Pretty impressive, huh?"

"No, what's amazing is that she was stupid enough to give you all that. Why? Because you're a student? Oh wait, because you're an *Irish* student? With all due respect, your accent was going in and out the whole time. I don't know how she didn't notice."

Deirdre stopped dancing. "She helped me because the Irish are kind, something the Welsh clearly are not."

"I'm not trying to be mean. It just doesn't make sense that your story worked. You got lucky the operator was Irish."

Deirdre shook her head, as if I'd failed my first test. "Learn this, smarty-pants. The operator is your best friend. I ask every single one if they're Irish. You have no idea how many of them are. Irish immigrants pretty much built this city — that's why they're more than willing to help a young Irish girl new to New York. I always look for Irish names when I call people. By the way, once someone starts giving information, they rarely stop. They're not listening to your accent anymore. They don't even remember the name you gave them. They're under your spell. You should choose an Irish name as your pseudonym." She pointed a finger at me. "Though you better be nice if you use one."

I left Deirdre's apartment that afternoon thinking how similar the ruse job was to selling cars. Both jobs used malarkey (Deirdre's word to describe what we did) to get people to buy what you were "selling." With cars it wasn't enough just to close the deal; I had to extract the most money possible. The greater the profit margin, the more money the dealership made. I was encouraged to add on extras like undercoating, rustproofing, and dealer prep, which were simply ways to charge the customer for filling out paperwork we were required to do anyway. Same with the ruse. Getting the names was great. But job titles and phone numbers . . .

those additional bits of information were of great value. All of that relied on some serious verbal jujitsu. I'd left Philadelphia partly because I didn't want to practice that kind of dishonesty. But just when I thought I was out of the bullshitting game, I was getting pulled back in.

Decades of ruse calls later, I still use an Irish name nearly every time.

CHAPTER FOUR

Preying on the Kindness of Strangers

I trained with Deirdre for two weeks, taking the LL subway every morning to her apartment in Brooklyn. Pax, who'd also trained with Deirdre, said that *LL* stood for "lots of luck," since trains often took forty-five minutes or more to arrive. Deirdre would work in her living room while I rused in her bedroom. She had two separate phone lines, both paid for by Leona. Free long distance — no small perk — was Deirdre's reward for allowing strangers into her home. Leona's deal was she would pay for installation costs, monthly charges, and all long distance as long as you were going to stay in the apartment for more than a year. I made it one of my goals to get my own place so that I could get free phone service, too.

Greenwich Village to Brooklyn was a schlep. I discovered that Leona had another worker, an actress and playwright named Andi, who lived two blocks from me. In Manhattan, that geographic coincidence qualified as a miracle. As much as I enjoyed Deirdre's delightful Irish frolic, I was eager to give up the commute, and Leona gave me the go-ahead to transfer to Andi's place.

When I arrived on my first day to work at Andi's, she buzzed me into the building. I took the elevator to her floor and found her front door ajar.

"Come on in," she hollered. "Set yourself up in the kitchen."

Her kitchen table overlooked Seventh Avenue. Cars drove by in uncountable numbers. There was a phone sitting on the table. I pulled out my notepads and was preparing to make calls when a classically handsome man — tall, chiseled jaw, full head of blond hair — walked out of what I assumed was Andi's bedroom. I immediately recognized him as actor J. T. Walsh, who had just appeared in Woody Allen's *Hannah and Her Sisters*. Later, he would star in *The Grifters*, *A Few Good Men*, and *Sling Blade*.

"Hey," he said. "J.T."

We shook hands.

"Uh, Robert."

"I won't be in your hair long. I know you gotta work. I'm gonna make some coffee and get out of here."

I was embarrassed to meet him under the circumstances. I wanted to be in his shiny shoes, not mine. I wanted to be on my way to an audition, which I assumed he must be. Hell, for all I knew he was on his way to a movie shoot. I reminded myself that the phone job was a means to an end and that serving him in a restaurant would have felt even worse.

J.T. started banging and clanging around the kitchen searching for items, making it clear he hadn't spent much time in Andi's apartment. I wondered if I should mention that my Hooters video was in heavy rotation on MTV.

"Sorry," he said, recognizing he was cutting into my hours. "You want some coffee?"

"Sure."

J.T. finally got the coffee brewing and sat with me at the table. He had twenty years on me, and while he had also done college theater he didn't get his stage career in New York going until he was thirty, his film career at forty. I had so many questions I wanted to ask him: *How did you make it? Do you have any advice? Can you get me a part in a movie?* Before I could open my mouth and say something stupid, Andi came out of her bedroom, her black hair wet. She was in her late twenties, with big brown eyes and olive-colored skin.

"Anything you want," she said, pointing at me and then at the refrigerator. "Help yourself. If you want to bring lunch, put it inside."

"I'm going to grab this and go," J.T. said, pouring coffee from the coffeemaker.

"You don't have to rush," Andi said. "He can bill this time to Leona."

She must have seen the surprised look on my face at the suggestion of billing hours when I wasn't actually working. "Leona is making money hand over fist off our work," she said. "Executive search firms are desperate for our information. They can't recruit without it. You've seen her apartment. She doesn't have any overhead, either. No rent, no payroll taxes, no health insurance. Make sure you charge her for the time you spend eating, too."

"And drinking coffee," J.T. said, handing me a cup. "Gotta go."

He kissed Andi and left, taking her mug with him. I never saw him there again.

I sat at the table while Andi made herself a breakfast that seemed bizarre to me: granola and yogurt. She took her time cutting up fruit. Was I billing Leona for this, as well?

When Andi completed making her concoction, she sat next to me at the table.

"Let's hear what you've got." She pushed the SPEAKER button on the phone.

Doing a ruse call was hard enough without someone judging me as I did it. Plus, the firm I was calling was Goldman Sachs, by far the most difficult bank to research. Pax said getting information out of them was like robbing the US Bullion Depository, otherwise known as Fort Knox.

"Hello, this is, uh, Kieran O'Shaughnessy," I said, making a feeble attempt at an Irish accent, which was far worse than Deirdre's. "I'm a student at NYU."

"Who?" the operator asked.

I went further with the accent, channeling the leprechaun in the Lucky Charms commercials. "Kieran O'Shaughnessy. I've just come from Ireland. I be a student at NYU."

"NY who? I can't understand you. Who are you calling for?"

"What be your name, operator?" In my head, I was obsessively repeating the tagline from the commercials — *They're after me lucky charms!* — to help me get the accent right.

"We don't give out names at the switchboard."

"Ah, but you sound Irish."

The woman sounded less Irish than any voice I'd ever heard. She hung up.

I picked up the phone, made a few more calls using the same lame script, and got nothing. Not a name, not a title, not a direct extension. I rationalized that I was nervous with Andi listening, but during my training with Deirdre I'd found that less than half my calls were successful. What worked consistently for Deirdre didn't work for me. I'd spend hours and hours on the phone yet often end up with only three or four names from groups that had dozens of people. Even in the beginning, I knew there had to be a better way, a better story, for me to get the intelligence Leona's clients wanted so badly.

I went to pick up the phone again, but Andi put her hand over mine.

"Relax. You need to find your voice."

It sounded a lot like the advice my acting teacher was giving me.

"Look," Andi continued. "Deirdre is great at training people because she's a sweetheart. But right now you sound like a poor imitation of her. A couple of times your accent was more Scottish than Irish."

She laughed, and because it was true as well as funny — I was terrible at accents — I laughed with her.

"Do you know how many actors Leona has hired to do this job? Hundreds. Everyone sees her ad in *Backstage* and thinks how great it would be to have a flexible, part-time job. Do you know how many people have worked out? Three: me, Deirdre, and your buddy Pax. You could be the fourth. But you've got to find your own style. Oh, and pick a shorter pseudonym. One-syllable names generally work best."

Andi picked up the phone and hit the SPEAKER button. She dialed and the same operator I'd spoken with earlier answered.

"I'm sorry to bother you," Andi said. "I'm the assistant of an executive that does business with your firm, and like an idiot I lost the Christmas card mailing list you guys sent us." Andi's voice slipped as if she might cry. "I'm going to lose my job."

"Sorry to hear." The operator's tone seemed different.

"Me, too. I've got a kid, you know." Andi's voice cracked now like she actually was crying.

"I've got two myself."

"Is there any chance you could check this one name for me? Gus Walraven? I think he's in Structured Finance."

"Sure, no problem." There was a brief pause as the operator looked for the name in her directory. "Got him. Yup, Structured Finance."

"What floor is he on? I need that for the card."

"He's on seven, but if you are sending something you'll need the mail stop. The code for the Structured Finance group is 7B36."

"You saved my life."

"Happy to do it."

"One more thing. Can you read me the other names in the mail stop? That's the list I lost."

I waited for the click of the operator hanging up, or for her to explain that she couldn't possibly release such information, particularly since the holiday was months away. Instead, she started reading the list of executives along with their titles, which Andi scribbled down.

When she was done, the operator asked, "Anything else?"

"I need their phone numbers."

I wondered what the hell Andi was going to say when the operator asked her why she needed phone numbers for a Christmas card list, but the operator simply started reading them. Clearly, it was better not to ask for everything you needed up front, when it was more likely someone might balk. As I was also learning, once someone was under the spell of a ruse they'd tell you just about anything.

When the call ended, Andi had a list five pages long. I couldn't believe her ditzy ploy had worked. She didn't even give a fake name. It seemed illogical to me that an operator who was trained not to release such information had done so simply because someone said they lost a Christmas card list. Andi's ploy relied on the kindness of strangers, something I didn't believe in. I'd made my way to New York despite knowing practically no one. I was used to doing things on my own. I wasn't comfortable begging people for help. I needed a ploy that played to my strengths.

$ $ $

I worked out of Andi's place through the summer of 1987 and into the fall, struggling to obtain the kind of intelligence she regularly did and generally failing. One Monday in October, I was having a particularly rough day. No one would give me a thing, not a single name. It was as if all of Wall Street had gone on full lockdown.

On my next call a trader picked up, and I started in on my ploy. "Fucking unbelievable," he said, cutting me off. But he didn't hang up, as usually happened when someone busted me. There was a strange note of fear in his tone. I wasn't sure what was going on, so I remained quiet.

"It's like the world is ending," he added. While I knew some might object to the morality of the ruse, I was pretty sure no one thought it meant the end of civilization. Something else was happening. "They're already calling it Black Monday. The Dow's dropped over 20 percent. It's gonna go down as the worst trading day in stock market history."

There was no omnipresent stock ticker listed at the bottom of every TV channel. There weren't umpteen smartphone apps to track the price of every single stock across the globe. It was October 19, 1987, and this trader was telling me what was happening in real time, when most of America didn't know yet. The stock market was crashing, and billions of dollars were evaporating by the hour. I knew only one other person who would know what was going on.

My father.

He was in the stock club in high school and had always been an investor. When he answered the phone that day, he seemed short of breath. I imagined him in the living room I knew so well. I could hear escalated financial chatter in the background on the new big-screen TV he was so proud of.

"You okay?" I asked tentatively.

I hadn't told my father yet what I was doing for money since I was afraid he might laugh at the irony. So I didn't let on about the crash because I was worried he would wonder how I knew. I certainly didn't follow the stock market. The only numbers I paid attention to were how many sacks Reggie White had and how many goals Rick Tocchet had scored. But my father had greater concerns.

"Merrill Lynch just gave me a margin call," he said, and I could hear him sweating. "If I don't put enough cash in to cover my losses, they're going to sell me out of every position I hold."

I barely knew what a margin call was despite now working (sort of) on

Wall Street, but essentially my father had been buying stocks on credit. With the market plummeting, Merrill Lynch was afraid he wouldn't be able to cover those losses since they were so great. To avoid being stuck holding the short straw, Merrill would immediately sell every stock my father owned. While I wasn't a student of US equities, even I knew the bottom of the market was the worst possible time to sell. I had no idea how to respond so, again, I remained silent.

"I can't talk right now, I gotta figure something out. I'm gonna call Jack." He hung up abruptly.

When the smoke finally cleared, Black Monday would be the worst single-day loss in Wall Street history, with half a trillion dollars vanishing mostly via unstoppable automated sell-offs. The Dow dropped an astonishing 23 percent (a record it held until March 12, 2020, when it became clear that COVID-19 was going to destroy the economy). The '80s expansion was officially over.

On top of my leaving the dealership, my father was experiencing an even bigger financial loss. Again, I felt as though I'd let him down. If I were still working at the dealership, at least sales would be good. But rather than wallow in hypotheticals, the only thing I could really do was prove that I'd made the right choice. So I got back to work — not by making another ruse call, which seemed pointless given what was going on, but by opening my dog-eared copy of Tennessee Williams's *The Glass Menagerie* and preparing the scene I was doing for my next acting class. As Andi had taught me, I could bill the time to Leona. It didn't mean I was getting paid to act, but it was something.

The winter was relatively mild (for New York), as Tom Wolfe's satirical Wall Street novel *The Bonfire of the Vanities* became a bestseller. At the end of the year, Oliver Stone's *Wall Street* was released featuring Gordon Gekko's iconic "greed is good" speech, which seemed less pithy than pathetic following the crash. It had filmed all over the city, including on the floor of the New York Stock Exchange, with input from advisers such as financiers Carl Icahn and Asher Edelman. Meanwhile, Andi and I had settled into a comfortable routine, and since the walls of New York apartments are generally thin I ended up hearing a lot of her calls, both ruse and personal.

One day in February 1988, she started shouting with joy on the phone. Her acting coach, Olympia Dukakis (cousin of Massachusetts governor Michael Dukakis, future Democratic nominee for president), had just been nominated for an Oscar for her role in *Moonstruck*. Olympia would go on to win the Academy Award for Best Supporting Actress that year (and Michael Douglas would win Best Actor for playing Gekko). Her costar in *Moonstruck* was a part-Armenian, Cherilyn Sarkisian, a.k.a. Cher, who was also nominated and who later won the Oscar for Best Actress. Standing in the tiny kitchen, I was almost as ecstatic as Andi as she whooped and hollered.

After all, if one Armenian half-breed could score an Oscar nomination, why not two?

$ $ $

In the spring of 1988, I moved to a marginally better apartment on the Upper East Side where the rent was actually cheaper than what I'd been paying in the Village. I found that rather strange, as the area was ritzier than the rest of Manhattan. Every building seemed to have a uniformed doorman, except, of course, for mine. I wasn't complaining. I'd gone from two roommates to one, which was a step in the direction I wanted to head. Still, my room wasn't much larger than a closet.

Because my new place was closer to Leona's, I started working out of her apartment instead of Andi's, using the makeup table in her bedroom as my desk. One day I opened a drawer while searching for a pen and found an erotic novel, *The School Boy and the Naughty Teacher*. Leona was single and desperate for a boyfriend, so working in her bedroom was already awkward. I started to wonder if she was planning to get naughty with me, which would make it even more awkward since I wasn't attracted to her in the least. Either way, what I needed was my own apartment, but that dream was financially far out of reach. I didn't know what Deirdre and Andi were making, but I was sure it wasn't much more than the $8 an hour I was getting. I would need a major raise to get my own place, something I couldn't imagine the job ever affording me.

Five days a week I'd arrive at nine, work for a few hours, break for lunch, and then work again until three. Six hours or so of rusing was the most I could handle. The concentration required to keep my stories straight was exhausting. More than a few times I went home with a migraine. Sticking with the student ploy — even after I'd given up my Irish accent — meant my success rate was low, around 50 percent on a good day.

One day after a morning audition I arrived at noon and worked late. I made a call after five and got a major executive on the line. Often, after their assistants (and gatekeepers) had gone home for the day, executives would answer their own phones. This one wasn't buying the story I was selling.

"Who are you? Who are you working for?" he demanded.

"I, uh, told you, I'm, uh, doing a paper."

"Bullshit. I want to know who you are. I want your real name right now."

"Uh, Fred," I said without thinking.

"Fred who?"

A crazy notion came into my head.

"Fred *who*?" he yelled.

"You have a pen?" I said. "It's a little tricky."

"Of course, I have a pen. Give me your name right now!" He was screaming so loudly I had to pull the phone away from my ear.

"Relax, I'm going to give it to you. I'm even going to spell it out so you have it correctly." I started saying letters. "F-L-I . . ."

I could hear him scribbling the letters down.

". . . N-T-S . . ."

The Wall Street honcho grunted with what sounded like satisfaction at having cowed me into getting his way.

". . . T-O-N-E."

When he finished writing the last letter, I heard him groan.

"Yabba dabba doo," I said and hung up.

Of course, most calls didn't end like this. If someone *was* busting us, the last thing we wanted to do was make that person angry. We didn't want them warning anyone else. Pax said we were like brain surgeons. Our job was to extract the intelligence we needed as efficiently as possible, without causing tumult or harm. Leona's clients would often ask us to go into the same areas again and again for more information, so keeping things calm and unmemorable was critical to having any chance of going back.

Working out of Leona's for well over a year gave me the opportunity to hear her on the phone with her clients. She had set up an office in her kitchen area, though she didn't use it much. Indeed, she hardly seemed to work at all. Leona didn't do any rusing herself, and she had Deirdre do the training of the actors who reached out from her ad. All Leona did was handle her clients.

More than once when I went to the kitchen for a glass of water, I heard her discussing project costs. Coming from a business family, it didn't take me long to figure out that her researchers earned a fraction of what she made. The evidence of money was everywhere. Leona wore a new outfit every day and was always buying tickets for the theater or other pricey cultural events. At the time, it didn't bother me. I was young. I wasn't going to be doing this forever. I was going to be a successful actor, maybe even somewhat famous like J. T. Walsh, who'd just costarred in *Good Morning, Vietnam*, *Tequila Sunrise*, and David Mamet's *House of Games*. In fact, by late 1989 I'd been hired as the lead in an off-Broadway production of Willy Holtzman's *Bovver Boys* opposite a young Calista Flockhart. When it opened in February 1990, we received a rave review in *The New Yorker* that claimed our play was better than anything currently on Broadway or the West End.

An extremely wealthy middle-aged woman who went by Dame Judy saw *Bovver Boys* and loved the show so much that she contacted me, offering to host an expensive dinner for the entire cast. I thought that anyone called Dame was supposed to be British — Judy was from Connecticut — but who was I to question a free party? I accepted her offer without realizing there would be a second. On the night of the dinner, after plying the cast with bottle after bottle of fine red wine, she pulled me aside.

"You could have this every night," she said. "My ex left me well provided for."

While I was grateful to be feted like a Broadway star, I didn't want to be anyone's boy toy. "I'm seeing someone," I said, just trying to be polite since in reality I had recently broken up with a girl I'd been dating.

"That's okay," Dame Judy said, leaning in to nuzzle me the way I sometimes feared Leona wanted to do. "I'm sure there's plenty of you to go around."

Fortunately, one of my *Bovver Boys* castmates picked up on my delicate situation and stepped in to rescue me. I have to admit, it was exhilarating to have a complete stranger spend $5,000 on a dinner just to woo me, which never would have happened if I hadn't landed a role in the hottest play in town. Rumors were flying that we were about to make the leap to Broadway. Was this a taste of what it was like to be a star? Of what my future held?

Leona was a big supporter of our work as performers, as she, too, had once been an actress. With the exception of Andi, who was mainly a playwright and later had plays produced on Broadway, we were all actors. Indeed, Leona only hired actors because we had no qualms about pretending to be people we weren't. She attended pretty much any play we were in. This included more than a few shows I did in church basements and tiny theaters in run-down neighborhoods. Once, she attended a production Deirdre had cast me in that was staged in the basement of a single-room occupancy hotel. SROs, as they were commonly known, were a form of housing for individuals with minimal income. Residents rented single rooms but shared kitchens, bathrooms, and toilets. Conditions ranged from the relative comfort of an extended-stay hotel to complete squalor.

Deirdre had of course selected a play by an Irish writer: *Misalliance* by George Bernard Shaw. She and I played siblings, which summed up our relationship perfectly. The drawing room comedy was set in the conservatory of an aristocratic British family. Deirdre's choice of material seemed odd to me given that many in the audience were one step from homelessness. But the opportunity to hone my craft while playing the lead in a Shaw play had been too much to pass up.

On opening night, Leona showed up wearing designer scarves and lots of lipstick despite the dingy basement location, which was full of SRO residents who all seemed in need of a bath. Deirdre's accent kept slipping from British to Irish, while mine careened back and forth across the Atlantic. At one point, I even thought I sounded Jamaican. But the SRO residents loved the show, cheering as if Deirdre and I were on our way to Broadway.

Afterward, Leona was positive about our performances, but she also offered some advice.

"Don't ever stop doing this job, you might need it someday," she told me. "Oh, and no more accents."

$ $ $

In the spring of 1990, Leona announced that she was getting an office in Midtown. She wanted more space to be able to hire additional researchers, even though no one had worked out since she hired me. The word was getting out on Wall Street about her firm's ability to penetrate even the most secretive companies. A few search firms tried to do what we did, but, since none of their employees were actors, they struggled to get the results we obtained on a regular basis. There were also a handful of cases where rusing calls were traced back to search firms, causing major reputational damage and prompting threats of lawsuits and arrest. Someone in the search business wrote a book titled *Why Not Ruse?* that detailed the myriad reasons not to do so. God forbid anyone on Wall Street would act dishonestly — junk bond maestro Michael Milken (one of the models for Gordon Gekko) had just pleaded guilty to six counts of securities and tax violations as the result of a huge racketeering and insider trading investigation, but sure, rusing was beyond the pale.

The upshot was that every reputable search firm started outsourcing the down-and-dirty work to us, as we had no public reputation to damage. If calls *were* traced to us, our search firm clients would bear no responsibility. Even if we tried to implicate them, which we would never do, they could claim they had no idea how we obtained our information. Hiring us gave them plausible deniability.

I didn't think much at the time about the legality, let alone the morality, of what we were doing. We were actors. We needed a job to support our art. What was the harm anyway? We weren't stealing trade secrets. We weren't dumpster-diving or hacking. We were simply obtaining lists of employee names. Those people were then called and offered better jobs. How could that be a bad thing? It seemed to be a victimless crime

— if it was a crime at all. Selling overpriced used cars to poor people at my dad's dealership had felt much worse to me.

The news about the new office was great for me, as working at Leona's apartment was uncomfortable. I was constantly worried I would spill something on her white carpets, or that her naughty side would emerge and she'd spank me with a ruler. Also, the new office location was more convenient for my auditions and theater work since it was within walking distance of Broadway. I got my own apartment in Hell's Kitchen so that I could walk to work. The landlord offered me a break on the rent since there was a drug dealer living next door, which was the only reason I could afford the place.

But the main thing the office gave me was the opportunity to work with Pax. Because we had both been renting rooms in crappy apartments, we'd never had the chance to listen to each other work the phone. Each of us hearing the other ruse on a daily basis ultimately led to us elevating the game. It would inspire us to come up with better (and more dangerous) techniques that would change our lives, make us wealthy — and bring us into the crosshairs of the authorities.

CHAPTER FIVE

Born to Ruse

Pax and I started to work together regularly in the new office. Every morning he'd bring the *New York Daily News*, and I'd bring the *New York Post*. Buying two newspapers was too great an extravagance for either of us. We each had our own roughed-up copies of *Backstage*, however, so we could track all the acting jobs we thought we were right for.

"Such bullshit," Pax said one morning, throwing his into the trash can next to our desks. "Not one audition in there if you're not at least five foot eight."

I leaned back in my chair to glance around the flimsy partition that separated us. He wore his usual all-black outfit: jeans, T-shirt, leather jacket, and motorcycle boots, which made him seem five foot eight to me. Sometimes it felt as if he used his height as an excuse for why he wasn't getting hired — and mine for the reason I was.

"You see the Rangers last night?" I asked. "They won in OT." I passed him my *Post*, since I was done with the sports. After he snatched it from me, I held up my hands to show how black they were.

One of Pax's many pet peeves — besides being too short — was that the tabloid papers couldn't come up with an ink that didn't smudge. Another one that got him going was the lame student ploys Deirdre taught us, and how we often had to make dozens of calls to find a single person willing to take pity on us — if we were lucky. Andi and Deirdre utilized the fact that most operators and assistants were women. They bonded with them in ways Pax and I couldn't, which meant they obtained more information.

Pax was actually the first man Leona had ever hired, since she thought women were better at the job. He was determined to prove her wrong. He wanted to make one call and get hundreds of names the way Andi and Deirdre did, which is how he came up with the transfer agency ploy. We had no idea what a transfer agency did but noticed there was one listed for every firm in our directories. Posing as a job seeker, he called the personnel department at one of the agencies. He learned that they were service companies responsible for the maintenance of clients' records and documents. Pax believed that by pretending to be an executive from a firm that had an existing relationship with the company we were calling, it would *require* those at the company to give us what we wanted.

I scooted my chair into Pax's cubicle as he tested his hypothesis. He opened up a directory, looked up Bear Stearns, an investment bank we researched often, and wrote down the name of its transfer agency. He called the Bear switchboard and got transferred directly to the executive we wanted information on — something Deirdre and Andi taught me never to do. The women were big on getting the operator to help you or, at the very least, to tell you the name of the assistant of the executive you were calling. Pax skipped all of these steps.

"Hi, this is Pete De Niro, no relation to Robert," Pax said, adding a phony-sounding laugh as he hit the SPEAKER button. To my surprise, the executive's assistant laughed back.

"You tawkin' to me?" she said, doing her best Robert De Niro impression. (*Taxi Driver* was still a big movie in New York in the early '90s.)

Pax laughed even louder. "I'm an executive with First Manhattan. As you probably know, we're the transfer agency for Bear. I've got to list your boss on one of my documents and I just need his exact current title."

"Oh sure. He's the SVP of Institutional Sales."

Pax didn't need that particular piece of intelligence — the executive's title was listed in the directory we had. He was setting up the assistant. Once she answered his first question, which was harmless by design, she'd be much more likely to answer the critical ones.

"Perfect," Pax said. "That's what we had. Oh, one last thing, I need to list the names of his direct reports."

"His sales team?"

"Exactly."

"It's a pretty long list."

"Good thing we only do this once every two or three years," he said and manufactured another belly laugh.

The assistant read the twenty-five or so names on the team. When she finished, Pax said, "I noticed the list is in alphabetical order. I'm supposed to put the names in order of rank."

"What do you mean?"

"You know, who is the number one salesperson, who's number two . . . ?"

There was a pause on the line. In the silence, I could hear the assistant questioning the request. I was doing the same thing. It seemed to me that Pax had pushed it too far. Suddenly it was like the tension in that scene from *The Grifters* where Cole — played by . . . J. T. Walsh! — is adding unnecessary bluff, pulling the mark right to the edge of blowing the whole con. Most times, silences like these were followed by objections that were usually insurmountable: *Who are you again? What do you need this information for? What's your direct contact number?* The key to being a great corporate spy was to keep the mark from getting suspicious in the first place.

Pax must have sensed this, too. "I have no idea why my bosses want it that way, but when they say 'jump' I say 'how high?'"

"I'm with you," the assistant said. "Hold on, I have their production on a different sheet."

Pax smirked at me. But I wasn't convinced he'd closed the deal. I gave him a we'll-see smirk in return.

When the assistant came back on the line she was breathing heavily, as if she'd run a marathon to get the ranking list. More likely, it was because her adrenaline was pumping. Some part of her was aware that she shouldn't be doing what she was doing, but she did it anyway. There's a fascinating psychological phenomenon known as the Ben Franklin effect (yes, that Ben Franklin), which basically observes that a person who has already done you a favor is more likely to do you another one than if you had done *them* the initial favor. Dale Carnegie cites the effect in his classic book *How to Win Friends and Influence People*, suggesting that when we ask someone to do us a favor, we are signaling that we consider them to have more knowledge, more skills, and more — ahem — intelligence. The request becomes "a subtle form of flattery" that actually makes the person more willing to help us again because they have "genuinely started to like us." The other phenomenon in play is induced compliance, a form of cognitive dissonance whereby a person tries to resolve the contradiction between their values and a requested action by bending their values to the action so as to alleviate the psychological discomfort of refusing the favor.

As the assistant rattled off the rankings, Pax grinned at me and scribbled away on his pad. His new ploy had worked, yielding the kind of difficult-to-obtain non-public intelligence for which we would become famous. I was genuinely impressed. Our search firm and corporate clients dreamed about lists like these. They were *actionable* because the rankings told them who the top revenue producers were — and who they should target for poaching. Which meant they were also worth serious money.

Of course, we had no idea what Leona's clients actually paid. We were just two young guys trying to one-up each other. There was major competition between us as to who was better at the ruse — as well as who had a better acting career. I was currently ahead in the latter category. I'd recently booked my first major on-camera role since the Hooters video four years earlier. This time I had lines. I played the lead in an episode of the horror anthology TV series *Monsters*. While the series was fun, especially the special effects, the stories were weak, if not hokey. Still, I was in good company: Matt LeBlanc, Gina Gershon, Steve Buscemi, and Lili Taylor all appeared on the show. And because my episode, "Bug House," was adapted from an award-winning short story by Lisa Tuttle, it was better than most.

I played a sexy bug man who had impregnated one woman and was working on doing the same to her sister. It was my first on-camera sex scene, and it did not disappoint. The actress who played the sister, Karen Sillas, was as sexy as she was talented. I was nervous about being practically naked in front of the crew, but Karen had no inhibitions and played the scene as if there weren't twenty others in the room watching us gyrate and grind against each other take after take. The simulated snogging got both of us so worked up that on the limo ride home we made out nonstop. When we arrived at her place, though, she didn't invite me in. I guess she felt like we'd already gone to bed. Either that, or she liked a crowd.

Pax watched the show with me when it aired in October 1990 and said I reminded him of John Malkovich in *Dangerous Liaisons*. I could tell he thought I wouldn't be rusing for much longer, which made him envious since he, too, didn't want to be rusing forever. But as he hung up with the assistant from Bear holding a fresh batch of high-end intel, it was clear that while I may have been forging ahead on the acting beat, in terms of the ruse he was kicking my ass.

$ $ $

What I learned from training with Deirdre, and then working at Andi's, was that what worked for them usually didn't work for me. Deirdre relied on the luck of the Irish, Andi on the kindness of strangers. I was neither Irish nor especially sympathetic. Working full-time to pay my way through an Ivy League education had put a chip on my shoulder — and an edge in my voice. Pax's transfer agency ploy was similarly difficult for me to pull off. It required Orwellian doublespeak, which sounded to me like gobbledygook. Because we were friends, he tried to teach me the ploy by putting people on speakerphone so I could see how he handled them when they questioned him.

"Why do you need these names again?" someone would ask.

"Our records," Pax would say.

"What records?"

"The ones we keep for you."

"But what are they for?"

"To ensure you're in adherence."

"Adherence to what?"

"The required documentation."

"Required for what?"

"For our records."

Pax's nonsensical, circular responses somehow convinced people to give him what he wanted. Most days, he would obtain huge swaths of names, enabling him to kick back and read the sports section or peruse *Backstage* for roles he was tall enough for.

It was remarkable how much the ruse job was like acting. If you didn't believe in your character (and your ploy), you stumbled as you spoke, which was the kiss of death on a call. To this day, I start talking before the person on the other end has even answered. The phone is still ringing and already I'm speaking as the person I am pretending to be.

It's called getting into character.

The truth is, I wasn't terrible at the job. Leona wouldn't have kept me around if I weren't obtaining critical information. But most days my research was 50 to 70 percent accurate. At notoriously difficult firms like Goldman Sachs, my success rate was close to zero. Sometimes the ploys I copied from the others worked, other times they were worthless. I tried combining their approaches. One day, I was an Irish guy working at the transfer agency. The next day, I was the same guy *and* I'd lost the Christmas card mailing list. At one point my confidence started to dip, which was scary since I needed the job. I certainly wasn't going to make a living doing off-Broadway theater. Most of the shows I did paid little, glowing reviews in *The New Yorker* notwithstanding.

I needed a ploy that worked every time, or almost every time, one that got me all the names in a department, not a few. I figured that if I could get close to a 100 percent success rate, well, that would make me more valuable to Leona. Comprehensive, current-to-the-moment intelligence like that would definitely be worth more than $8 an hour — maybe even as much as $10.

Never once did I think it would be worth millions.

$ $ $

Pretending to be from the transfer agency didn't work for me, but I realized that I needed to find a similar type of firm, one that would have, or seem to have, a legitimate purpose for the information I wanted to extract. I studied the directories in Leona's office. Listed beneath the transfer agency was the name of the law firm that repped the company. Undoubtedly, a law firm would have a compelling reason for obtaining sensitive information, but this ploy was too scary for me. The ruse job was about paying the bills, not going to jail. Pretending to be from a transfer agency was one thing, pretending to be from a law firm seemed like a quantum (and dangerous) leap, one I wasn't ever going to take.

Indeed, Pax and I had become more concerned about the legality of what we were doing since we abandoned the student ploy. We asked Leona to consult an attorney. She made us each pay a third of the cost, which seems ridiculous now knowing how much money she made on our work. The upshot from the attorney was that what we were doing was "in a gray area." No shit, Sherlock. I didn't need to pay hundreds of dollars I couldn't afford to be told that. Reading between his legalese lines, it appeared that as long as we didn't impersonate a *real person* we were somewhat safely in the gray. After all, it wasn't against the law to lie. As far as I was aware, none of us had ever pretended to be someone who actually existed.

Leona had ordered annual reports for the companies we called the most, and I started reading them. There was a huge collection in the office. In the back of each report, there was a list with the names of the firm's senior executives, almost always with a picture of nine or ten white guys in suits. I used these reports to generate leads from which to begin my research.

I noticed that in every annual report, there was an entire page devoted to the independent auditor. On that page, the auditor made guarantees that the firm's financial numbers were accurate. Obviously, the auditor needed to have access to tremendous amounts of information to be sure that what they were attesting to was, in fact, the truth. I figured if they had access to numbers, why wouldn't they have access to information about people, as well?

By accident, I discovered that these firms were given office space at the headquarters of the company they were auditing. I called Chase Manhattan looking for an Andrew Anderson. I was supposed to obtain his entire team. The operator heard *Arthur Andersen*, which was the name of one of the Big Eight public accounting firms, and transferred me there by mistake.

Sometimes it's better to be lucky than good.

"Arthur Andersen," a man answered.

Though I recognized the name, I thought it was a coincidence and that the company had an employee with the same name as the auditing firm. "Oh, sorry to bother you," I said. "I was calling for an Andrew Anderson."

"Yeah, we've gotten calls for him before. He's at extension 6282."

The man's use of "we've" seemed odd to me.

"Okay, thanks," I said. "You know you have the same name as the accounting firm."

He snorted. "This *is* the accounting firm. My name's Matt Biello, by the way."

"Kevin Slater," I said. "I'm with the transfer agency for Chase."

"Good to meet you, Kev."

I could tell right away that Matt was one of those nice guys who made the world a better place. Which made *him* an ideal target for pulling information.

"What's your role with Arthur Andersen?" I asked now that we were telephone buddies.

"I'm the audit manager."

"Doesn't sound like a lot of fun."

Matt chuckled. "You got that right."

"Is it normal for the auditors to have an office at their clients'?" I asked.

"Nothing in the audit world is normal." Matt snorted again. "But, yeah, we have a permanent office here. During audit season, we have a couple. It makes it a lot easier to get the information we need."

That's what I was thinking, too.

"Are your names listed at the Chase switchboard? Or just Arthur Andersen?"

"Nah, just the firm name. We get a lot of turnover from week to week, so listing who's over here on any given day is impossible. Sometimes it's just a couple of us, but during the audit there are dozens."

This was important intel. Since there was no listing of the audit firm's individual team members at the switchboard, Chase executives would have no idea who was a legitimate Arthur Andersen employee. But because Arthur Andersen had an on-site office, most executives and assistants would recognize the name of their outside auditor. This gave me an advantage over Pax and his transfer agency ploy since most employees hadn't heard of a transfer agency and would never recognize the name of theirs.

At the time, the Big Eight accounting firms were Arthur Andersen, Deloitte Haskins & Sells, Touche Ross, Coopers & Lybrand, Price Waterhouse, Ernst & Whinney, Arthur Young, and Peat Marwick Mitchell. We could look up in the annual report which of these firms handled the audit for the company we were researching. When Leona didn't have the report for the company we were calling, the operator would usually have the name of the auditor listed at the switchboard; again, because they had an office there.

"Hi, this is Kevin Slater with Arthur Andersen," my next call began. "As you know, we do the audit for Chase." It never hurt to remind people of your relationship with their company — and to give them credit for being smarter than they were. Once I'd made a bunch of calls using this new ruse, I discovered that about two-thirds of people recognized the name of their auditor. But when they didn't know, they didn't want to admit that. What were they going to say, *I'm sorry, I've never heard of Arthur Andersen?* Even if they weren't positive that I was who I said I was, the ploy sounded legitimate. But then, what purpose would accountants have for lists of names? Numbers, maybe, but *names?* Do you know how many times people questioned me about why accountants wanted so many names? Not once.

"It's that time of year again," I continued.

I noticed Pax had rolled his chair into my cubicle space. He'd overheard me testing the new ploy and wanted to see if I could pull it off.

"Uh, what time?" the female assistant asked.

Pax leaned over me and pushed the SPEAKER button so he could hear both sides of the call. I shot him a dirty look but forced myself to stay focused.

"Tax time. Fortunately, you guys do a great job with your records. I wish my other audit clients were as organized. Pretty funny I'm from Arthur Andersen and I'm calling Andrew Anderson." I forced a laugh to show how crazy the corporate coincidence was. "I just need the title of your boss to list on one of my documents." The subtext being that if she answered one question, I'd go away.

But I never wanted what I asked for in that first question, a technique I'd adapted from Deirdre. To this day I start every conversation with a softball question, one I know the answer to. Typically, I ask for the title of the person's boss or the senior executive of their group. The person usually gives it to me easily; after all, what's the big deal about one senior exec's title? Even back in the day, that information was listed in directories and annual reports. But I was establishing an important rhythm: I asked and they answered, my version of call and response. I was also putting them under my spell. After they'd given me what I wanted *once*, why not a second time? Or a third?

"Sure, he's the SVP of Loan Restructuring," the assistant said.

"Perfect. That's what we had. I guess you'll keep Arthur Andersen around for another year." I forced another belly laugh. "Oh, one last thing. I need to list Andrew's direct reports and we're done."

"He's got a pretty big group, over thirty people."

"Good thing we only do this once a year. And we don't need titles for his reports, just the names."

The woman hesitated but then began to read the list. When she finished, I said, "You know, I better get titles."

I could hear the woman balking, though she didn't utter a word. I heard it in the silence on the line, but she'd come too far to stop now. She should've done that before she gave me the names, which were the most important part of the research. The titles just tied it up with a ribbon.

With a grumble, she read me the titles. I could tell I'd pushed her as far as I could. I stopped there in case I wanted to come back to her at a later date for more information. Perhaps she'd turn into a long-term internal mole.

I slapped the SPEAKER button to end the call and hopped up from my chair, raising my hand for a high five. Pax jumped to make contact but missed. He glared at me like I'd put my hand too high to make fun of his height. He ripped his chair from my cubicle and yanked it back behind his desk. If he'd had a door, he would've slammed it. We didn't speak the rest of the day.

$ $ $

My success ratio immediately shot higher than it had been using the student ploy, which now seemed like a joke. More important to me, my audit ploy yielded better results than Pax's transfer agency ploy. He tried appropriating my ploy a couple of times, but, again, what worked for one researcher often didn't work for another. He sulked back to his transfer agency gobbledygook.

Almost instantaneously, he and I became Leona's best researchers. We started turning around research projects faster than ever and with unprecedented accuracy. Pax put the kibosh on sharing our ploys with Deirdre or Andi. Since we'd done the homework to develop them, he felt we should be the ones to benefit. While I was grateful to them both, I hardly disagreed.

Not long after, Leona threw us the most difficult project we'd had to date: We were tasked with researching defense industry conglomerates such as Lockheed, McDonnell Douglas, Martin Marietta, and Rockwell. These were the firms that built nuclear bombs and missiles, that designed F-16 fighter jets and Trident submarines. Suddenly, I had to learn terms like *AWACS* (Airborne Warning and Control System) and *JSTARS* (Joint Surveillance and Target Attack Radar System). The Reagan presidency had ended, but billions in government money was still pouring into the defense industry as part of the decade-long spending spree that included his Strategic Defense Initiative (a.k.a. Star Wars). Change was in the air, but as far as anyone knew the Cold War was still raging. The profit rates of the top defense contractors far exceeded those of comparable non-defense-related companies. I was to learn that whenever we were asked to research a certain industry, it was often because that area had become "hot," which meant there was serious money at play — usually hundreds of millions, if not billions, of dollars in profits and personnel.

At first, I thought the crazy project wasn't even doable. And that Pax and I would surely be arrested for espionage — or treason. After all, wasn't every weapons program these firms handled top secret? Wasn't every person who worked at these firms trained never to release any information under any circumstances?

Because we'd never called any of these firms before, we had no old research to guide us. Fortunately, Leona's client had access to directories

published by the Janes Information Group, the closest thing to a defini-
tive source for information on intelligence and warfare systems. Like the
Wall Street directories, the Janes ones were out of date and, more often
than not, completely wrong, but they were our proverbial foot in the
door. Once we had a sliver of information, it was much easier to slip
inside.

Over several months, we obtained every name we wanted at every
firm. Even today, I'm shocked that Pax and I were able to call major
defense contractors and learn anything we wanted about their organizations and the top-secret projects they were handling for our country. It's
a damn good thing we weren't actual spies. Christopher John Boyce and
Andrew Daulton Lee, the protagonists of Robert Lindsey's 1979 book,
The Falcon and the Snowman: A True Story of Friendship and Espionage,
both served more than twenty years in federal penitentiaries after being
arrested in the 1970s for selling classified military documents to the
Soviets — secrets not dissimilar to those Pax and I pried loose in our
research.

What did Leona give us for our efforts? For taking on so much risk?
Eight dollars an hour.

CHAPTER SIX

The Color of Money

After the major success of the defense industry assignment, Pax and I made a decision to squeeze Leona for a raise. If she was being hired by headhunting firms that worked for defense contractors — the biggest companies going — we knew she had to be making more money than ever. Pax was supposed to come in early one Monday morning so that we could approach Leona before the workday started, since neither of us could afford to lose any hours on the phone. But he didn't show up until nine forty-five, looking disheveled and a bit panicked. His eyes were wide, and he carried no newspaper. Perhaps he'd been mugged on the subway.

"You okay? Where've you been?" I'd been rehearsing my pitch all morning for why we deserved a raise to $15 an hour. I knew we were shooting high, but our new ploys had radically improved the quality of our research. I figured Leona would split the difference and we'd end up with around $12 an hour, which would still make a huge difference to our bottom lines.

"I don't know, man," Pax said. "I don't want to get fired."

"What are you talking about? She's not going to fire us. We just figured out who designed the missile launch system on nuclear submarines. She needs us. And we need more money."

I had somehow finagled a line of credit and was already a couple of thousand in debt. I didn't have a house, a car, or kids. I didn't go out to dinner or on vacation. I was living in an apartment where prostitutes gave blowjobs outside my door. I needed a raise — or a movie role — to have any chance of continuing my acting career.

"Maybe you should go in on your own," Pax said.

"We're a team, remember? She has to be afraid she could lose both of us."

"But where else are we going to find a job like this with flexible hours?"

"Will you stop? She's not going to fire us. I promise you."

My reassurance seemed to calm him down. He knew my family's history in the automobile industry and had faith in me as a businessman.

"Come on." I slapped the back of his motorcycle jacket. "Buck up."

He moved toward Leona's office door like he was about to step into a haunted house. I stayed close behind him in case he decided to turn and run.

"Knock," I said.

"You knock. This is your idea." He was sweating, which could've been the leather jacket, but he was also breathing heavily.

"Jesus Christ." I gave the door a light tap.

Leona's voice called from inside. "Come in."

She was seated behind her desk and wearing a leopard-print blouse and a red scarf, already perusing the newspaper's personal ads. She was trying to get a jump on any potential candidates to be her boyfriend.

On the wall next to her was a bulletin board where she posted all the research projects we had in-house. The board was completely filled. I made a mental note to remind her of that fact during the negotiations.

"Ohh, my boys look so sexy this morning. Auditions? Or did you dress up for me?" She smiled and batted her eyes like she was Amanda Wingfield and had not one but two gentlemen callers.

I wasn't sure what she was talking about. Pax was wearing the same thing he wore every day. I was wearing jeans and a Genesis T-shirt.

"We dressed up for you," Pax said and gave his hips a shake like he was onstage at Chippendales and working for tips. He seemed to think we needed to win Leona's affection to score a raise. For me, it was strictly a business proposition.

"Uh, we'd like to discuss a raise," I said.

Instantly her flirty demeanor disappeared. Leona was all fun and games until money was involved. She reminded me of my father that way. Her eyes narrowed and appeared to turn black. Her jaw tightened. She pointed at the chairs opposite her desk. We sat.

"As you know," I said, "Pax and I have recently developed —"

"The nerve," Leona said.

"What?"

"The nerve of you." She glared at me. "The nerve of you both." She glared at Pax, who shrank down in his chair. Everything I had planned to say went out of my head.

"If you wanted a raise, you should've just knocked on my door and come to me."

I was thinking, *Isn't that exactly what we just did?*

"But no, after all I've done, you approach me together like this." She wagged her finger as if Pax and I were trying to start a corporate intelligence union. "It's not right, not right at all. But I'm going to be generous. I'm going to raise you to $9 an hour. But don't you ever come in here together again."

Pax jumped out of his chair. "Thank you." He came from a family of teachers, so apparently he was used to getting the short end of the financial stick. He turned and left.

But I was devastated. "Uh, thanks," I muttered, and limped toward the door.

I'd been positive our hard work and ingenuity would be rewarded since we were making Leona more money than ever. With the new ploys, Pax and I were able to get names more quickly, so we could research firms faster. And what did we get?

Basically nothing.

$ $ $

The only way to make more money was to work for another firm, but I had no knowledge of others existing. The idea of starting my own firm never occurred to me. Why would it? I'd recently gotten my first agent and was auditioning regularly for lead roles in major films such as Robert Redford's *A River Runs Through It* and Quentin Tarantino's *Reservoir Dogs*. My agent said I'd gone down to the wire for the Brad Pitt part in *Thelma & Louise* that made him a star. I was doing a play, *Lloyd and Lee*, at the legendary Actors Studio where, in the spring of 1988, I'd been made a lifetime member.

Founded in 1947 by film director Elia Kazan (*On the Waterfront, A Streetcar Named Desire*), Robert Lewis, and Cheryl Crawford, the Actors Studio was created as a laboratory to train American actors using the system developed by Constantin Stanislavski at the Moscow Art Theatre in the 1920s. This method was honed further by renowned acting teacher Lee Strasberg, who served as artistic director of the studio from 1951 until his death in 1982.

Twice a week, on Tuesdays and Fridays, members would present scenes, which were then critiqued by the other members in attendance, many of whom were famous. In the forty-plus years of its existence, the Actors Studio had developed some of the finest actors in cinematic history: Marlon Brando, Marilyn Monroe, Al Pacino, Robert De Niro, Ellen Burstyn, Dustin Hoffman, Dennis Hopper, and Jane Fonda, to name a scant few.

After the closing-night performance of *Lloyd and Lee*, the Studio's most famous member came backstage to congratulate me.

"Nice work, kid," Paul Newman said.

His eyes were so blue I couldn't look him in the face. "Thank you, sir."

"Call me Paul. I look forward to seeing more of your work." He patted me on the back and left. Had the star of *Cool Hand Luke, Butch Cassidy and the Sundance Kid*, and *Slap Shot* (my favorite of his films) just complimented me on my acting? It happened so fast it seemed like a dream — or a fantasy.

A couple of days later I came home from a night out with my eighteen-year-old brother, Dave, who was visiting from Philly. I hit the PLAY button on my answering machine and waited for the little cassette inside to rewind. A series of loud clicks followed as the tape switched from reverse to forward, and the messages began to play.

"Hello, Robert," a woman's voice said, "this is Joanne Woodward. Paul and I loved your work in the play at the Actors Studio. I was wondering if you might come up to our apartment for a reading."

She left her phone number and hung up.

I looked at my brother, who appeared to be as stunned as I was.

"The 'Paul' is Paul Newman, right?" Dave asked, gesturing toward the answering machine like he was afraid of it.

I nodded and gulped.

"Maybe they want to put you in a movie!" He lunged at me with a high five.

"I'm sure it's nothing like that." Though I was silently praying that my brother was correct. I'd heard stories at the Actors Studio about how a few years earlier Tom Cruise was brought to their apartment to read for *The Color of Money*, which he ended up starring in for director Martin Scorsese opposite Newman (who finally won his first Oscar). Could something similar be happening to me?

I had a restless night's sleep and returned the call the next morning. It was all I could do not to dial before 9:00 A.M.

"Good morning, Robert," Joanne said like she'd been up for hours. "We're having a little reading at our apartment on Sunday morning. If you're not busy, I'd love for you to attend."

"Sure," I said, trying to mask my disappointment that they weren't asking me to star in *Cool Hand Luke 2: Back in the Box*.

She gave me their Fifth Avenue address and ended our call.

"What did she say?" Dave asked. "What did she want?"

"She wants me to come to a reading at their place."

"For a movie?"

"I don't know."

"Are you gonna be in the reading?"

"I didn't ask."

"Why not?"

"Because she would've told me if I was in it."

"Oh." Dave looked as crestfallen as I was pretending not to be. "Well, hey, you're going to their place. That can't be bad, right?"

True. Though I figured if it was something really good, Joanne would've told me. Still, to be in the audience for a salon-type event at their home was thrilling and unexpected.

"Think of the networking," my brother said, trying to buck me up. "Think of the people you'll meet."

He was right, of course. Twenty hours earlier, I would've killed for the opportunity. But I wanted to act, not watch others do it. I wanted to be in a movie with Paul Newman, not merely in the audience at his apartment.

That Sunday, I had difficulty finding their building since the street was called Museum Mile on that stretch and not Fifth Avenue. Joanne and Paul lived opposite Central Park smack dab in the middle of the richness and diversity of the city's major museums. Their building was sentried by uniformed doormen, whereas mine was crawling with chatty crack addicts.

When I exited the building's elevator at the penthouse level, I entered directly into their home. The foyer, which was larger than my entire apartment, was filled with statues, vases, and paintings. Some of the artwork looked familiar to my untrained eye. There appeared to be a number of high-quality Monet knockoffs. Or at least that's what they would've been had this place been in Philly. I blinked at the realization that the paintings were authentic, that Paul and Joanne were the owners of millions of dollars' worth of art, as if they didn't have enough to brag about. Before I could abscond with one of the smaller pieces, Joanne found me.

"There you are," she said with a smile both kind and genuine. "Welcome to our home."

I wanted to ask about the paintings, but I couldn't move my mouth. Good thing I wouldn't be reading.

Joanne led me into a long and sumptuous living room where a small group of people sat around holding scripts and chatting. The decor was vaguely southern — Tennessee Williams meets the Upper East Side. Chairs with flower prints mingled with traditional sofas that held classic hard lines. Paul Newman reclined in a lounge chair drinking Budweiser from a can. It wasn't quite 11:00 A.M. on a Sunday. Through a bank of windows I could see Central Park — all of it.

"Everyone, this is Robert Kerbeck. He was wonderful in a play Paul and I saw at the Actors Studio. He's going to be reading the lead role of the race car driver."

I wanted to protest that I wasn't prepared to read, but Paul jumped in. "Hey, wait a second," he barked. "That's my part."

"A hundred years ago," Joanne scolded and laughed.

Everyone in the room got quiet, as if we were about to witness a marital quarrel, since actors generally didn't like to be reminded about their age.

Instead, Paul grumbled to me: "When the hell did I get so old?" He took a swig of the Budweiser. I swear his blue eyes twinkled at me.

Someone handed me a film script and moved over to make room for me dead center on the couch. I tried to take in the movie memorabilia and photographs that tastefully cluttered the room, but Paul Newman was staring at me, beer in hand, the rest of the six-pack waiting at his feet. I did note a shot of him playing Ping-Pong with Robert Redford on the set of *Butch Cassidy*, and I was half tempted to challenge him to a game of beer pong — they had to have a table somewhere in the giant apartment — to avoid doing the cold reading.

"This is a casual table read," Joanne said, obviously noticing the panicked look on my face. "That's why I didn't send you the script. I didn't want you to get nervous."

Thanks a lot, lady.

At first, I didn't recognize the other actors gathered around me because I was too freaked out to pay much attention. I eventually realized that future *West Wing* breakout Allison Janney sat next to me, and *Raiders of the Lost Ark* star Karen Allen was playing my love interest.

The reading went by in a blur, though I was aware throughout that all eyes were trained on me. While the others had a scene or two in the script, I was in every one, so when they weren't reading their lines they were studying me. Was this what it's like to be a movie star? To carry an entire film? Everyone else's fortunes rising or spectacularly falling based on your performance? Paul laughed at a couple of my lines, though those may have been burps, which he let fly occasionally. At the end, Joanne thanked me for my time. She told me they were going to have a reading of the script for the entire Actors Studio and that she would be in touch.

As I left their luxurious abode, I wondered what Paul and Joanne would have thought of me if they'd known the illicit way I made my living. I reminded myself that soon the only rusing I'd be doing would be in front of a camera. It was just a matter of time before I didn't need the support job.

A week later, however, the Actors Studio called to tell me I'd been replaced in the reading by Kevin Bacon, star of *Footloose* and *Diner*. They said that Joanne and Paul had something else in mind for me: They wanted me to read the stage directions, which is the equivalent of being invited to an A-list party and having someone hand you a valet's vest when you show up. *Ouch*. Of course, I said yes.

Good thing I hadn't quit my day job.

$ $ $

Because she had finally opened an office, Leona was hiring more researchers. She asked Pax and me to be in charge of the new people. We didn't bother asking if we'd receive additional compensation. We already knew what her answer would be.

Since there was no financial incentive to help the trainees, Pax and I were reluctant to give out the ploys we'd worked hard to develop. We felt proprietary about them. They were our creations, so we kept them to ourselves. Unsurprisingly, none of the people Leona hired worked out, though as I would learn later when I launched my own firm, the success rate at the ruse job was infinitesimal. It was the rare individual who could lie on the phone all day for a living.

Something else got under my skin. Because Leona had extra office space and no researchers to fill it, she hired a recruiter, Paula, to work there. Leona's search firm and corporate clients used our research to recruit the executives we found, but occasionally they needed help with the initial screening of candidates. Leona was too busy scouring the classified pages for a boyfriend, so it fell to Paula.

One day, I spotted a pay stub on Paula's desk and saw that she was getting $60 an hour while I was getting $9, which made no sense to me. I could do *her* job, but she couldn't do *mine*. If I didn't obtain the hard-to-get names, she wouldn't have anyone to call. Why was she the one making more? I estimated that Leona had to be making double what she was paying Paula. I did the math on a solar-powered calculator. Leona had four full-time researchers, so she was billing approximately 160 hours a week. If her rate was $120 an hour, she was grossing nearly $20,000 a week. I gulped when I multiplied that number by fifty-two. Leona was making well over a million dollars a year, which didn't include what she was earning from Paula's recruiting calls. I was creating millions of dollars in value — first for Leona, then for her search firm clients (who made even more), and then for Wall Street itself (which benefited the most from our work). Yet like most workers in America, I was receiving pennies.

Around then, Deirdre called me to say that she needed help on a project, which wasn't uncommon. Often, when one of us struggled with a certain firm, we would give it over to another researcher whose techniques were different. Most times, the new researcher would get the information, which gave them crowing rights.

"Sure," I said, manufacturing enthusiasm since I knew the firm would be difficult. I reminded myself of how kind Deirdre had been to me when I was starting out. "Happy to help."

"Can you keep a secret?" she asked.

"Uh, yeah."

"The project isn't for Leona."

Suddenly it was like I was Redford in *Three Days of the Condor*. I glanced around the office furtively to see if anyone was watching me. This seemed scandalous. Theoretically, I would be two-timing Leona, though I was only a part-time employee. I received no benefits. I wasn't even guaranteed full-time employment, only twenty hours a week. Fortunately, work was booming, so that was rarely an issue. But I remembered how she'd reacted when I'd asked for a measly raise. Who knew what degree of dressing-down this type of betrayal would provoke.

"It pays $20 an hour," Deirdre added. "Obviously, you'll have to work from home when you do it."

Twenty? The prospect of doubling my pay made any doubts vanish instantly. As for location, I'd do it from the crack den across the street from my apartment in Hell's Kitchen for that money.

It turned out that Deirdre had been working for John Smith Associates and the husband-and-wife team of John and Kelly Anne Smith for a few years on the side. *A few years!* Oh, sweet, sneaky Deirdre. Apparently, most of their clients were industrial firms, so the projects were looking for technical types: engineers, general managers, and product managers. After my success with the defense industry, I knew I could pull that intel.

As I left that afternoon, I told Leona that I had a bunch of important auditions the next day and so needed to work from home.

"Break a leg," she said.

Little did she know, I would never work regularly in her office again.

CHAPTER SEVEN

Inside the Actors Studio

When I was accepted as a member, the Actors Studio was in dire financial straits. There were even rumors of bankruptcy. Since the Studio charged no fees, the organization was completely dependent on donations from famous members like Al Pacino and Paul Newman. Indeed, it was the success of Paul's salad dressing that had kept the Studio going for many years. Though all profits from the Newman's Own brand, which he'd launched in 1982, were supposed to go to charities, somehow the Actors Studio counted. I'd heard that Paul was worried, however, that it wouldn't look good if the press found out. Giving company proceeds to sick kids was one thing, giving them to a group of professional actors was something else.

The artistic director of the Actors Studio in the early 1990s was Frank Corsaro, a prolific director of opera and theater, including the 1961 Broadway premiere of Tennessee Williams's *The Night of the Iguana* starring Bette Davis. Paul was a big fan of Frank's — he'd directed Frank as an actor in the 1968 film drama *Rachel, Rachel* that starred Woodward and had gotten him the position — but other powerful Studio members (Ellen Burstyn and Estelle Parsons, to name a few) were upset when Frank let in a large group of new members, myself included. Normally, the Studio admitted only a handful of actors each year. When Frank came on board in 1988, he let in close to fifty. He was trying to bring in fresh blood to reinvigorate the Studio, but many of the older members weren't having it. There was tension between the new "Frank members," most of whom were in their twenties, and the older generations.

Whenever new members presented their scene work, whether in one of the regular Tuesday or Friday acting sessions or in the Thursday Playwright/Directors Unit, they were harshly critiqued by the older members in attendance. The critique was supposed to help the actors better understand their craft and improve their work, but, more often than not, it seemed merely a way of settling scores or proving how knowledgeable the person speaking thought he or she was. Often it was some combination of the two.

Many times, new members broke down in tears at the level of vitriol cast their way. A good friend of mine, an actress in her early twenties, presented a soliloquy from *Romeo and Juliet*. When an older male member asked whom she was imagining as her Romeo, the actress said, "Marlon Brando." The older member snickered and then ripped into her: The reason her speech had failed so miserably was that her person- alization wasn't specific enough, since she had certainly never met Brando. Shelley Winters then piled on. "I fucked Marlon so, trust me, I know," she said. "Girl, he would've chewed you up and spit you out." The actress fled the stage sobbing. Which seemed to be the entire purpose of the critiques. Others handled the viciousness differently. Taking a tack truer to future roles, James Gandolfini once threw a chair at the audience.

For years, I'd seen Jimmy do plays in the basement of the Theater for the New City on the Lower East Side, often with only a handful of people in attendance. Invariably, somewhere in the production, he threw someone against a wall. Watching him onstage was fascinating because while you *knew* an outburst was coming, it always took you by surprise when he exploded. I did a play with Jimmy at the Actors Studio, a comedy called *One Day Wonder* about the making of a '70s pornographic film. Jimmy played the director of the film while I played Willie the Poke, "the biggest bone in the business." A sort of theatrical predecessor of Paul Thomas Anderson's *Boogie Nights*, the play took place entirely in the dressing room of the film set, so all the sex scenes were offstage — though one actress with impressive breasts did the entire play topless. I had a great time working with Jimmy, who was equally adept at comedy, something many fans may not know. He did not throw me against a wall, however, which was strangely disappointing.

The possibility of bankruptcy — as well as fisticuffs — at the Studio kept things interesting during my time there. Actors were naturally melodramatic; we didn't need an excuse to be even more so.

Shortly after I became a member, I went to see Ellen Burstyn in the one-woman Broadway play *Shirley Valentine*. Afterward, I waited outside the theater — in the rain — to express my admiration for her performance. Ellen shared her umbrella with me as I raved about her work, beaming as if my praise had made her night. "Are you an actor, too?" she finally asked.

I'd been waiting for the opportunity. "Yes, I recently became a member of the Actors Studio."

A member since 1967, Ellen had been the artistic director before Frank, so she instantly knew that I was one of the new members. "Oh." She stepped away from me, taking her umbrella with her and ending our conversation.

There was so much stress about the future of the Studio (and whether there was a future) that Frank agreed to hold elections to create a committee that would give members a voice, though it really seemed to be a way for the older generation to express their bitterness and resentment, as if the new members were somehow responsible for the financial downfall. On the day of the elections, the Studio was packed. Most of the famous members were seated in the front row. I sat a few rows back and watched as Shelley Winters (*Lolita*) ogled Christopher Walken (*The Deer Hunter*) while he chatted with Tina Louise (*Gilligan's Island*). The Studio had a way of bringing together the most incongruous individuals.

Frank sat onstage, looking miserable. He was a short man, but he seemed even smaller on the stage, which was empty except for a handful of chairs. He knew the membership committee would be filled with anti-Frank members, all of whom wanted him fired even though it wasn't his fault the Studio was going under. Those problems long predated his arrival. Letting in a larger group of new members had had zero effect on the bottom line.

Paul Newman got up from his ringside seat to join Frank onstage, looking like he could use a beer.

"Let's get this over with," he said like someone was about to be guillotined, which was in a sense the truth. "Nominations?"

Someone called out Ellen Burstyn's name. The crowd murmured positively. There were even shouts of "hear, hear," as if we were on the floor of Parliament settling matters of world importance. Ellen got up from the front row and took the farthest chair from Frank.

Another voice shouted, "Estelle Parsons!" There was a round of applause. Estelle walked onstage and sat next to Ellen.

"Anyone else?" Paul said, peering around the room like he was on the *Titanic* and searching for a lifeboat. He knew Ellen and Estelle were dead set against Frank. He likely suspected that many of the older members had met beforehand to come up with the plan to nominate them.

From the balcony of the theater, a voice muttered meekly, "Robert Kerbeck."

Paul lifted his hand like he was staring into the sun. "I'm sorry, who was that?"

Silence.

One of the new members had gotten the courage to nominate me, but with the eyes of the Studio on them they chickened out. They were afraid to make enemies and perhaps sabotage their career.

But Frank was desperate for a friendly face on the committee. "They nominated Robert Kerbeck," he said. "Robert, where are you?"

I seriously contemplated sneaking out. I wanted no part of the battles waging, but I was surrounded by fellow new members who were not going to let me escape. They nudged me out of my seat and pushed me toward the stage. Frank patted the chair next to him, which I took. I smiled over at Ellen to see if she might remember the nice things I'd said about her work. She glowered at me like it wasn't going to make any difference.

Paul took a few more nominations, most of which were older members, then passed out ballots. I figured I had little chance of being one of the top vote-getters, which was fine by me.

While Paul counted the ballots, the members filed down the theater's narrow stairs toward the lobby. On the staircase, I was directly behind Estelle.

"Who the hell is Robert Kerbeck?" I heard her say.

I prayed no one would turn around to spot me hovering over her shoulder. Thank God people were too focused on not falling down the stairs. As soon as I reached the bottom, I headed home rather than wait for the results.

When I entered my apartment, the phone was ringing. I thought about picking it up, but my Spidey sense said to let the answering machine get it so I could screen the call.

"Hello, Robert, this is Estelle Parsons. Congratulations on being elected. I'm looking forward to working with you. I've heard a lot of great things about you and your work."

Yeah, right.

I wanted to throw up. All I wanted to do was act, learn from the masters, and embrace the art with like-minded creatives. Instead, I was now stuck on a committee I didn't want to be on, working with people who didn't want me on it — notably a pair of middle-aged Oscar winners who could crush me at a whim.

It was almost enough to make rusing look good.

$ $ $

Into this financial stress and internal turmoil walked a strange guy in his sixties named James Lipton, who had received an invitation to join the Studio's Playwright/Directors Unit. While playwrights and directors couldn't become lifetime members (unless they were also actors), they were allowed to present plays or direct scenes within the context of the weekly PD Unit, held every Thursday.

Shortly after the elections, Jim approached me at the Studio. He had an odd, vaguely European-sounding accent that reminded me of Peter Sellers as Inspector Clouseau in the *Pink Panther* movies. He'd seen my work and wanted me to play the lead in a production of the French farce *A Flea in Her Ear* by Georges Feydeau that he was directing.

The Actors Studio was known for Method acting, which usually meant realistic, gut-wrenching performances like Marlon Brando's in *On the Waterfront*, Ellen Burstyn's in *The Exorcist*, or Al Pacino's in just about every movie he's ever done. The Studio wasn't known for comedy, let alone French farce. Even Strasberg, in his book *A Dream of Passion: The Development of the Method*, foresaw the issues Actors Studio members would encounter when trying to express themselves in creative works that required a heightened theatricality such as Shakespeare, Molière, or musical comedy. Besides, I wasn't classically trained. I had a bit of a Philly accent. Jim's choice of material seemed odd — as well as pretentious.

"This is how you will show your range," Jim said, attempting to woo me. "When you approach the Pearly Gates, what do you want God to say about you as an actor?"

I wasn't concerned about my range, let alone God. I just didn't want to get ripped apart by the older members, who were looking for the "Frank members" to fail as proof that they weren't Actors Studio quality. I had no interest in being French farce red meat.

"It's a question often asked by the French television interviewer Bernard Pivot," Jim continued.

"Huh?" The only French names I recognized were those of Canadian hockey players like Mario Lemieux and Mark Messier.

"Bernard Pivot," Jim said, emphasizing the French pronunciation like that might jog my memory. "Though the question originally came from Proust."

I had no idea what he was talking about.

"What profession other than your own would you most like to attempt?" he asked.

This conversation was without a doubt the strangest I'd ever had. "Uh, a rock star, I guess. Or a professional ice hockey player."

He beamed up at me. "I'm good friends with the general manager of the New York Rangers. If you like, I could get you backstage to meet the players."

"That would be awesome!" I reflexively enthused, hearing my Philly accent come out. Certain words triggered it, so I painstakingly avoided them. But my exuberance over the possibility of meeting some of my childhood heroes took me back to the time before I'd spent thousands on speech classes.

Jim had me. I accepted both of his offers.

$ $ $

We rehearsed for weeks at Jim's Upper East Side apartment. While it wasn't as posh as Joanne and Paul's home, it wasn't far behind. I wasn't sure what Jim did to afford such a nice home. There was a sense of mystery about him. We chatted often about the turmoil within the Studio as well as the financial difficulties. Paul Newman had apparently written a check for $1 million to prevent the Studio from entering bankruptcy but warned that it would be the last time he would come to the rescue.

"They need to monetize the brand," Jim said during one post-rehearsal conversation.

Because I was the lead in the play, I was usually the last to go home. "What do you mean?"

"The Actors Studio is world famous. Their members are celebrities. They're not utilizing that to their advantage."

"What are they going to do? Offer tours?" I chuckled.

"No, a TV show. With the famous members discussing their careers and their craft." Jim at least acted as if he were getting an idea in that moment. "An interview show with the host pressing the actors for the secrets behind some of the most important moments in cinematic history. Wouldn't that be riveting?"

I nodded. Indeed, it would.

"And if it's worth watching, then it's worth money. I just need to find a way to sit down with Paul and Frank to pitch the idea. You don't know Paul well, do you?"

I thought of mentioning the reading I'd done at his apartment but reminded myself I'd been replaced in that project. I shook my head.

Jim was a good director, both kind and encouraging. He gave me the confidence I needed to handle the sophisticated role. He had me wear a tuxedo for the performance, which helped me get into character. I'd worn a tux only once before in my life — for my senior prom.

On the day of the performance, the Actors Studio theater was filled, even the balcony. I'm not sure why, but Bob Dylan was there. He wore sunglasses and looked bored. Sally Kirkland, who'd been nominated for an Oscar a few years earlier for her work in *Anna*, was next to Bob, fawning all over him. She completely ignored Norman Mailer, who sat on her other side. He was stewing and sitting caveman-style with his elbows on his knees and his legs spread wide. He wore a rumpled frown as if he wished he were somewhere else, a boxing match perhaps.

I felt enormous pressure, and not just because of the legendary celebs in attendance. If I failed in the role, I would be letting the new members down. Fortunately, I didn't allow my nervousness to affect the lightness the farce required. To my surprise, the audience laughed uproariously. It can't be overstated how uncommon that reaction was at the Studio, where the work was nearly always treated with extreme reverence — and harshness.

Afterward, Jim joined the cast onstage. We received a critique that amounted to a lovefest with unanimous praise for the actors — and Jim's direction. The members — old and new — lauded his choice of material. Many expressed the feeling that the Actors Studio had been unfairly pigeonholed as only being able to present realistic, kitchen-sink dramas. They were ecstatic to see Studio members breaking that mold and tackling not only comedy but French farce, and with such resounding success.

When the session was over, Jim was given the ultimate honor: He was invited into the artistic director's office to meet with Paul Newman. While I wasn't included, that was the beginning of Jim's high-level involvement with the Actors Studio. He presented his idea of monetizing the Studio's reputation and created the *Inside the Actors Studio* television show, which launched in 1994 on Bravo. The program featured Jim interviewing celebrity members of the Studio about their careers. Of course, his first guest was Paul. Along with the show, Jim created the Actors Studio Drama School MFA program. With the moneys earned from these projects, the Actors Studio was saved. Jim became world famous and was even spoofed on *Saturday Night Live* by Will Ferrell. He never did get me hockey tickets, let alone "backstage" with the players.

I earned no money for being in the farce, since the Actors Studio paid no salaries. The theory was that if you did great work there, one of the famous members would notice and get you into a film. The only TV show shooting in New York was *Law & Order*, so series roles were hard to come by. I'd recently starred in the world premiere of two Joyce Carol

Oates plays at the prestigious Long Wharf Theatre in New Haven, Connecticut, and received reviews comparing me to a young Marlon Brando or a more handsome John Malkovich. Yet still no film roles.

I certainly couldn't imagine Ellen Burstyn or Estelle Parsons recommending me for anything. At the first meeting of the membership committee I felt pressured to come over to their side. But Frank had been kind to me, and I was a loyal guy. After the meeting, I started looking for a way to get off the committee so I could avoid the political intrigue and backstabbing, which seemed to intensify daily. At one point the FBI was brought in to protect a new member who'd received written death threats for speaking out against the old guard. I don't think the agents ever analyzed the handwriting in the letters, but if they had, my money would've been on Estelle.

In the midst of this drama I received a call from my father, a rare occurrence. His business had gone downhill after I left, as if I'd taken the wind out of his sails (and plans) by moving away. I didn't like hearing about his troubles — some financial, others legal — since they felt like efforts to pull me back in. I hadn't told him the exact truth of what I was doing for money, describing the ruse job generically as "headhunting," which was the same thing I told my friends. I was afraid even my car salesman father wouldn't approve of me lying for a living.

"They're revoking the franchise," he said.

This was the worst thing that could happen to a car dealer. I had figured that my father and my uncle would eventually sell the franchise to another dealer. Instead, Ford, the parent company of Lincoln-Mercury, was taking it back. For no compensation.

"I need to borrow some money." His voice was tight, the words fast.

I was a struggling actor and had no money. But he was my father, and I knew that asking me for money — even if it came out like a demand — had to be the hardest thing he'd ever done. For a moment, I thought he was going to cry. Young men don't often feel sorry for their fathers, but hearing him in a panic about losing everything — when a few years earlier things had been good — had me feeling sorry for him then. I knew he wouldn't be in this position if I'd stayed at the dealership. He knew it, too. I could hear the resentment in the silence on the other end of the line.

The Armenian in my father had taught me that family always came first. To help him pay his bills, which included the mortgage on my childhood home, I wrote him a check for $5,000 off my credit card, which tripled the debt I already had. I couldn't pay my own bills as it was, and to cover the loss I'd now be forced to do months of extra rusing calls, which I'd have to dive back into the moment we got off the phone. To make that kind of money on the lot we'd only have to sell three or four cars, which I could pull off in a week. Meanwhile, fucking Leona, and every Wall Street firm she did business with, could underwrite the whole enterprise in an afternoon without skipping lunch. If I were making *that* type of money, running my *own* show, this wouldn't even be an issue.

I wasn't angry with my dad, though. I was angry at myself. I felt I'd failed him as a son. The least I could do was help him keep the lights on.

Even so, shortly thereafter Kerbeck Lincoln-Mercury folded forever.

CHAPTER EIGHT

Killing Clooney

With the additional financial pressure, I resolved to work both of my ruse jobs as many hours as possible. My agents wanted me to go to Los Angeles for pilot season, but I'd need to get an apartment and buy a car. The second job with John Smith Associates gave me hope of getting out of New York — and debt — since they were paying me double what Leona was. Because of this, I often found it difficult to get motivated to work for Leona, whose firms were just as challenging to research, if not more so.

John Smith and his wife, Kelly Anne, were sweet midwestern folks. They'd come to New York so John could get his MFA in directing. Because he was busy with school, he no longer had time to ruse for the Rust Belt client base he'd developed over the years, so Kelly Anne had taken over the business. Needing help, she'd put an ad in *Backstage*, but she was unable to train potential researchers since she didn't know how to do the ruse herself.

Somehow, Deirdre saw the ad and presented herself as the answer to all of their problems. Because of the workload, however, she became over-whelmed and reached out to me. I found it flattering that she hadn't called Andi or Pax. Maybe it was because I was part Welsh. And while John Smith wasn't Irish, Kelly Anne was. Her maiden name was O'Malley.

All of our research reports were still handwritten. I had thought Leona would eventually hire someone to type up our work and make it more presentable for her clients, but apparently they didn't care. They just wanted our nitty-gritty intelligence. So each day when I was done making calls, I'd walk from my Hell's Kitchen apartment to the newsstand two blocks away that had a fax machine. I'd fax over to Leona and Kelly Anne the research on the firms I'd done, grab a cup of coffee, and head home to read a play or work on a scene.

One day I returned home to find that I'd been robbed, even though I had locked my door and was away for less than fifteen minutes. I was sure it was my next-door neighbor, a drug dealer and crack addict. Often, he played music as loud as possible, driving me out of my apartment on numerous occasions. The sole reason I was able to keep living in the place (besides the dirt-cheap rent) was that he slept most of the day, enabling me to get my rusing done in relative peace. But he knew my schedule, and I suspected he'd somehow stolen a copy of my key from the building's elderly super.

The only thing missing was my father's jewelry box, which he'd given me.

It held sentimental value for me, but there was nothing valuable inside, unless you counted the ticket stubs from all the rock concerts I'd attended. Imagine my surprise when I received a call from the NYPD a week later saying that my father's box had been found in *another* robbed apartment. When I went to pick it up, the ticket stubs were still inside. The thief was probably disgusted I'd actually gone to the trouble to see REO Speedwagon live.

The theft made me uncomfortable about living where I did. Because of its low rents and proximity to Broadway, Hell's Kitchen was a popular destination for aspiring actors, but its grittiness had only marginally softened with the beginnings of gentrification in the early '90s. Drug addicts and half-naked prostitutes roamed along my street day and night, and many mornings I found used condoms outside the door to my apartment. At the same time, I felt like I'd gone as far in the theater world as I was going to go without some film or TV credits to my name, and there were just too few shows shooting in New York. By the end of 1992, the only on-camera work I'd done was the lead in the *Monsters* episode and a couple of small recurring parts on the soap operas *One Life to Live*, *Another World*, and *General Hospital*. I sensed, too, that Frank Corsaro was losing his battle for control of the Actors Studio to Ellen Burstyn and Estelle Parsons. His protector, Paul Newman, seemed tired of the ordeal and had stopped attending the biweekly acting sessions. Without Frank in our corner, I wasn't sure what would happen to the new members. Maybe we would be kicked out — or killed. Also, the concept of stunt-casting had taken over Broadway. I saw Madonna in Mamet's *Speed-the-Plow* and couldn't hear or understand a word she said. But ticket sales were through the roof, which justified the celebrity fluffing for cowardly producers.

Finally, I did catch a break, though not the one I wanted. An older actor from the Actors Studio was heading out to LA to try his luck and needed someone to sublet his apartment, which happened to be on 44th Street directly across from the Studio. It was still in Hell's Kitchen but on a far nicer block than mine. The ground-floor one-bedroom was spacious, with a large backyard rare for Manhattan. A woman I was interested in, in fact the sexiest woman I'd yet to meet, Shannah Laumeister, came by to check it out after I bragged about the size of my patio. She said she wanted to go Rollerblading on it, which sounded spectacularly kinky. Shannah had been discovered skating in Central Park at age thirteen by the famous photographer Bert Stern (who shot the iconic Sue Lyon promos for Kubrick's *Lolita* and the last sitting photos of Marilyn Monroe) and grew up skating around the city with her pal Drew Barrymore. Watching Shannah in her short shorts twirling in circles made me dizzy. When she finally pirouetted into my arms, we began ripping each other's clothes off. I carried her inside and we went at it on the kitchen floor, her skates still on, wheels spinning wildly. Not long after, Shannah started appearing in movies such as *Bullets over Broadway* and *The Brady Bunch Movie*, though her most memorable appearance would be sitting topless at a strip poker game with Paul Newman and Bruce Willis in *Nobody's Fool*.

In LA a fancy car might turn a woman's head, but in Manhattan it was all about the apartment. Maria Bello, who would go on to star in the movie *Coyote Ugly* because she was anything but, told me I had the sexiest bedroom she'd ever seen. Vanity, who'd already had a fairly successful music and film career by then (and a classic *Playboy* spread), also spent some time there, which weirdly put me in a category with rock star royalty Prince, Adam Ant, and Nikki Sixx.

The sexual performances weren't going to pay the bills, however, and they didn't land me any acting jobs, either. So I sublet the sublet to the most famous ballerina in America, Gelsey Kirkland, and seriously considered my options. The crime, the lack of opportunities, the mind-numbing Studio politics and movie-star infiltration of Broadway — it all seemed to be sending me the same message.

In the words of REO Speedwagon, it was time for me to fly. To Los Angeles.

$ $ $

As a parting gift, Leona bought me a fax machine. Which was as much a gift to her, since it meant I could continue sending her the killer intel she needed to keep that Bergdorf wardrobe stocked with fresh scarves. I was grateful, though. I'd be able to ruse the second I landed, which was critical since I was spending everything I had to make the move.

I hit the sand in LA in February 1993. My first West Coast home was a tiny room in a shared apartment in Santa Monica. An actor buddy had found the place and told me about it. He didn't tell me there was one bathroom for four people, or that I had to pass through a woman's bedroom to use it. Still, the neighborhood was a huge step up from Hell's Kitchen. Each morning on the way to the 10 Freeway, heading into Hollywood for auditions, I'd drive alongside the Pacific Ocean in the minivan I'd scored from Rent-a-Wreck.

"I'm so lucky," I'd say out loud.

And for those first few years, it turned out I was. Right away I started booking TV jobs, including *Chicago Hope*, *Star Trek: Deep Space Nine*, *Melrose Place*, *Boy Meets World*, *Nash Bridges*, *Judging Amy*, and my mother's favorite show, the NBC drama *Sisters*, which shot on the Warner Bros. lot in Burbank.

My first day on the *Sisters* set, in the summer of 1994, I was hovering over the craft services table admiring an assortment of junk food — Twizzlers, M&M's, potato chips, all a bad idea for an aspiring leading man — when a woman with jet-black hair and the brightest smile I'd ever seen glided toward me.

"Hi, I'm Sela Ward."

I knew who she was. After all, I'd been hired to kill her.

"Uh, hi, I'm Robert Kerbeck."

"So nice to meet you. Have you met George Clooney yet?"

I shook my head. I didn't know who he was since I didn't watch *Sisters*, but I knew Sela from her work as Harrison Ford's murdered wife in *The Fugitive*, which had been one of the biggest big-screen hits the previous year. She was the friendliest person I'd met since moving to Los Angeles. Her beauty and kindness were making me sweat.

"Come on. I'll introduce you."

She linked her arm in mine and promenaded me onto the soundstage, which was set up for the outdoor scene we were about to film. The lighting created a full-moon effect on the facade of the home of Teddy Reed, the character Sela played on the show. In a few moments, I, as the hitman John McCormick, would knock on the front door, and Sela, playing a blind Teddy, would open it. I had earlier set off a bomb that temporarily blinded her and killed her boyfriend, Detective James Falconer, a.k.a. George Clooney. In the scene we were to shoot, Falconer's ghost had come back to prevent me from finishing the job on Teddy.

"George! George!" Sela called to a man standing by himself in the set's living room. He looked like a Teddy, too — a teddy bear, dark-skinned with big brown eyes. He was a bit thick-waisted for an actor.

"Howdy," he said, extending his hand to shake. "George Clooney."

"Robert Kerbeck."

"You go by Bob?"

"Robert. I'm a junior," I said. "My dad goes by Bob, so it was easier to keep us straight if I went by Robert."

This was a lie. I'd been Bobby as a kid and then Bob throughout high school. It was only after I started acting that I "changed" my name, when I no longer wanted to be a copy of my father. But I wasn't letting this guy know that.

"Where do you hail from, Bob?" George asked.

"I just moved from New York."

"New York Bob." George slapped me on the shoulder like he was christening a ship — or had sold me a crappy car. "Thanks for killing me on the show," he said, laughing.

I laughed back. "No problem."

"You know *why* they're killing me?"

I didn't. I hadn't even thought about it. I was just happy to get the gig.

"George is doing the new Michael Crichton series that Steven Spielberg is producing," Sela told me.

"Great," I said, glad to recognize at least one of the Hollywood names. I was a theater guy, after all.

"It's called *ER*," he said with the kind of car-dealer grin that would've made my father hire him, too.

Later, during our lunch break, George and I exited the interior sound-stage together and traipsed across the huge studio lot under a typically perfect Los Angeles sky. I was still getting used to the glamour attached to coming in through the gates of a major Hollywood studio. Scenes from *Casablanca*, *The Big Sleep*, *Rebel Without a Cause*, *Bonnie and Clyde*, *Blade Runner*, *Basic Instinct*, and hundreds of other iconic movies were shot on the Warner Bros. lot. Even though I was only there for a one-week shoot, it felt like I'd been given the golden ticket to access my wildest dreams. George insisted on showing me the *ER* set, even though we were given only an hour to eat (I'd been warned the lines at the commissary were long). One or two people said hi to him, but otherwise he was as un-notable as I was.

He led me into a building that was quite dark. It took my eyes a moment or two to adjust, but when they did I found myself standing inside a hospital corridor, looking into a perfect replica of an emergency room. It dawned on me then that his new show, which wouldn't premiere until September, was called *ER* because it stood for "emergency room." Here I'd thought E.R. were the initials of the main character, like an abbreviated version of *T. J. Hooker* or *Magnum, P.I.*

George morphed into a studio tour guide and began to show me every room on the set, explaining this and that, all while telling me the struggles of his career. Apparently, *ER* was the fifth or sixth pilot he'd done. None of the previous ones had been picked up as a series. Though *Sisters* had been on the air for a few years, George had only recently landed a recurring part on the show — and now I'd killed him. (He didn't mention the handful of films he'd done, most of them B horror flicks.) He was a working actor, but barely. And he was no kid, either: He was thirty-three, which is geriatric by Hollywood standards. He joked that hiring him meant the pilot was doomed. I could tell he felt the clock ticking on his career. He was praying that *ER* would break his curse before he stopped getting phone calls.

I felt no similar sense of desperation despite being just a few years younger. I was getting a steady stream of jobs. Surely, it was just a matter of time before I no longer needed to ruse because I had my own series.

I hardly had time to dwell on it either way because George would not shut up — or let me go to lunch. It seemed he would've been content to discuss the set and the series (and his hopes for it) indefinitely, or at least until the *Sisters* crew tracked us down. Finally, given no other choice, I did what I had to do.

"George," I said. "I'm fucking starving." I turned and walked away without looking back.

Three years later he was Batman and *People*'s Sexiest Man Alive.

CHAPTER NINE

In Which I Spend Two Days Dancing with the Man About to Commit America's Most Infamous Double Murder

By spring of 1994, I had my own place in Santa Monica: a rent-controlled studio apartment with a sliver of ocean view. I thought I'd hit the jackpot. I was four blocks from the beach, and my best friend from New York, Richard Joseph Paul, whom I'd followed out for pilot season, was living next door. Richie had scored me the apartment and found another one in the building for our friend Mike Mahon, also an actor. The three of us spent our afternoons Rollerblading on the beach path or playing pickup basketball. While we auditioned frequently, we always found time to work in our sports. Being in shape was a requirement for thirty-year-old leading-men types.

We considered working out to be a part of our career, but I never expected our obsession with fitness to result in an actual job. Being a TV guest star didn't pay as much as I thought it would. Not that I was complaining. I usually received around $5k for a week's work, but after a 10 percent agent commission, a 15 percent manager commission, and exorbitant payroll taxes, I would take home about a third of that. Still, I could see the day coming when I no longer needed to ruse for a living.

One morning in late May, I got a call.

"It's Bobby," as if I didn't know my manager's voice. Bob McGowan worked both coasts and carried a roster of up-and-comers such as Teri Polo, Dylan Walsh, and Jesse Martin. He'd steered Julia Roberts's career through the *Satisfaction–Mystic Pizza–Steel Magnolia*s climb that resulted in her breakthrough with *Pretty Woman* in 1990. I liked him. He'd done well by me so far, and he repped Mike and Richie, too. "Wanna make some money? Nancy's directing an exercise video. She needs a couple of guys."

Nancy was Bobby's wife. For some reason she was a fan of mine, telling him I was the one who was going to hit it big. I flashed to the dreadful aerobics exercise classes I'd taken in New York wearing my skintight nut-hugger shorts. I always stood in the back because I was so pathetic. For a fairly athletic guy, it was embarrassing how uncoordinated I looked.

"It pays $750 a day for two days," he continued.

"Jeez, I don't know." This one would pay my rent for three months, and I couldn't admit to my own manager that I sucked at dancing. Besides, if I wanted to stop rusing I couldn't afford to be picky.

"Mike's doing it, too," Bobby added, continuing with his dance video sales pitch. "You get to keep the clothes. You get to keep the sneakers, too." Perhaps he thought I was holding my nose at the "not really acting" job, but the free sneakers got me. I'd been using shoe glue to cover the holes in my own.

"Uh, it's just . . . don't you have to know how to dance?"

Bobby laughed. "Nah, nah, nah. They're not gonna do any of that stuff. It's an exercise video for men. She's gonna shoot you playing basketball and doing push-ups and stuff. She wants real guys. It's for O. J. Simpson."

"Wait — O. J. Simpson?"

This was a game changer. I'd grown up idolizing the Juice, watching him set the NFL record for most yards rushing in a season. I'd seen him in countless rental car commercials and as a *Monday Night Football* commentator in the early '80s. I'd loved him in the movie *Capricorn One*.

"Yeah, it's his video. It's gonna be called *O. J. Simpson: Minimum Maintenance Fitness for Men*."

"I'm in."

$ $ $

Two things struck me immediately when I met O.J. on set a week later: how big he was and how friendly.

"Hey, Rob," he said after Nancy introduced me. I shook his massive hand and felt small even though I cleared six feet and weighed 190 pounds. He was years from his playing days, but I could still feel the strength that had propelled him to the Heisman Trophy and five NFL All-Pro designations. Mike, who was my size, described us as "twigs standing next to an oak." Besides us, there was a lean and muscular black woman named MaDonna, a voluptuous white woman named Desireé, and a white man named Richard Walsh, who would be choreographing us on camera.

I'd been so caught up in the excitement of meeting my hero that I hadn't paid much attention to the room in which we were about to film. It had a wooden floor — a *dance* floor. I began to sweat. Where was the basketball court? And why was Richard being referred to as the *choreographer*?

I pulled Mike aside. "Are we gonna have to dance?"

"Nah," he said. "Probably do some jumping jacks and calisthenics."

"Then why are there women here for a men's workout video?"

"Kerby," he said, using my nickname. "If they want guys to buy the video, they need hot girls." Mike pointed at MaDonna and Desireé.

"Okay," Richard called out. "Let's get started."

Short and thin, he reminded me of Richard Simmons. He lined us up and demonstrated an energetic sequence of moves that made my aerobics class in New York seem like amateur hour. MaDonna and Desireé executed the sequence perfectly on the first try. Even O.J. handled it well. Mike struggled a bit but quickly figured it out.

I, on the other hand, was lost.

Richard came over to me, looking pale, obviously wondering how the hell I'd been hired. "You all right?" he asked, like maybe I had food poisoning.

"Yeah, it's just I'm not a dancer."

"Clearly," he said, making sure the others could hear.

"Hey, I'm glad Rob's here," O.J. said, cackling and slapping his thigh. "He's making me look good." Everyone else laughed, too, except Richard, who stared at me like if it were up to him, he'd fire me. But O.J. had spoken. Rule number one in Hollywood: Make your star look good.

"Well," Richard said to me, "you're going to stand in the back. Make sure I don't notice you."

The rest of the day, Richard taught us the routines we would be doing on camera while O.J. pattered incessantly, cracking jokes and singing Isley Brothers songs.

"Hey, Rob, don't slip in that puddle," O.J. hollered when he saw the pool of sweat at my feet. The physical challenge was pretty intense, but mostly it was Richard glaring at me that literally made me sweat.

On a break, O.J. grabbed me. "Rob, come here." He took me to a corner of the large room where filming equipment was stacked and popped a videocassette into a VCR that sat underneath a small TV.

"This is the trailer for the pilot I shot. It's about a team of ex–Navy SEALs. It's called *Frogmen*."

"Cool," I said, meaning it. I was thinking maybe O.J. could get me a job if the show went to series.

O.J. beamed while the trailer played. It seemed rough to me, the story disjointed and hard to follow. It appeared that O.J. recognized this because he kept filling me in.

"I play John 'Bullfrog' Burke, the leader of the team," he said.

After a slow-motion shot of him coming out of the ocean in a wet suit, he added, "We had to undergo military training for the pilot."

Later, during a fight sequence, he told me: "My character's a knife expert."

"Cool," I said over and over, like I was eleven and watching him break tackles on TV. It was exhilarating to be so close to the superstar, who seemed to have taken a liking to me. He wasn't showing anyone else the *Frogmen* video, though he did keep staring in the direction of Desireé. She was the prototype of the Southern California dream girl, blond, buxom, and tan. I followed O.J.'s gaze, and we took her in together for a moment, then he turned back to me.

"Wanna watch it again?"

"Sure," I said, thinking it would be a good way to further bond.

"Just hit REWIND."

O.J. rolled out of his chair like he was going off tackle and making a beeline for the hole.

I watched as he hustled over to Desireé.

$ $ $

Later that day, while filming a routine that simulated boxing, O.J. said, "Don't want to get too close to the wife when you're doing this."

We all chuckled uncomfortably.

"Better get your spacing if you're working out with the wife, if you know what I mean."

Nudge, nudge. Wink, wink.

"You could always blame it on working out," O.J. added, in case we hadn't figured out he was making jokes about domestic violence.

This was on camera, in front of the female director and the entire crew. I was shocked but didn't say a thing. No one did. We all let O.J. continue saying whatever he wanted. On break between shots, O.J. started in on Desireé.

"Mmm, mmm, mmm, what I'm gonna do to you tonight," he said, looking her body up and down. "How many children we gonna have together?"

O.J. did everything but lick his lips. Sometimes he would silently leer at her for up to a minute. Desireé didn't say a word, just gave him a tight-mouthed half smile in return.

At one point when O.J. was preoccupied, I approached her.

"You okay?" I asked.

"Yeah, I'm fine."

"You sure? We can get the union down here with one phone call. They'll put a monitor on the set. He'll have to stop right away."

"No, it's fine," she said, like his behavior was no big deal. I sensed she was afraid to speak up out of fear for what calling the union could mean to her career. I understood her reluctance. I'd been told that O.J. was best friends with the president of NBC, Don Ohlmeyer.

"You can call anonymously," I said.

"It's all right."

"I can call. I'll call for you."

My *in*tention had as much to do with winning her *at*tention as it did with doing the right thing. For if it had only been about doing the right thing, wouldn't I have called anyway? O.J.'s behavior was inappropriate regardless of whether she objected. It was offensive, I suspect, to everyone in that room. But no one did a thing.

Including me.

$ $ $

A week later, on the evening of June 17, I sat on my apartment futon gape-mouthed as O.J. made a run for the border, taking my chances of a role on *Frogmen* with him. I couldn't believe he'd murdered two people, including his ex-wife. But why else would he be trying to escape? I stared at the TV as his friend and attorney Robert Kardashian read a letter O.J. had written that sounded to me like a suicide note. Pictures of the victims flashed on the screen. It struck me how much Nicole Brown Simpson looked like Desireé. The news reported that O.J. had been harassing his former wife and, a few years earlier, had pleaded no contest to a charge of spousal abuse.

I felt sick.

All that week tabloids phoned me. They'd found out about the video and wanted to know what it had been like to work with O.J. right before the murders. But what was I going to say when they asked if I thought he'd done it, or if he'd done anything on the set to suggest he was capable of such an act?

I didn't return their calls. I did, however, call the district attorney's office.

They never called me back.

For years, I played do-overs in my head. What if I'd called the union and convinced them to send a monitor? Could the events that were to occur have been changed?

Certainly, with a monitor on set O.J. would've stopped harassing Desireé, at least openly. He wouldn't have made any more comments about punching his wife, words later entered at trial via the subpoenaed video footage. But really, I was the one most likely to suffer consequences — and potentially Desireé. At the very least, O.J. (and Nancy) would have stopped talking to me, since they would have learned that it was me who called. I probably would have been fired, then dropped by Bobby as a client as well as blackballed from NBC and any upcoming dance videos.

I spent the next few months (years, really, since O.J. never seemed to go away — or get *put* away, until 2008) auditioning while ignoring the tabloids that wanted to pay me big money to tell them what happened on that set. Meanwhile, O.J. went on to spend most of 1995 peddling the gravest lie anyone can tell: "I didn't kill her." A jury of his peers ultimately believed him — or at least that the prosecution had not proved its case beyond a reasonable doubt — while a hundred million people listened in on the verdict.

Today, you can view the exercise video footage on YouTube. Outtakes from the shoot with much of O.J.'s inflammatory language are there for all to see and hear. You can judge for yourself whether my saying something might've made a difference.

I'm the one hiding in the back.

CHAPTER TEN

The Darth Vader of Hacking

Through the fall of 1994, I continued to score TV guest-star roles. I was featured in the ads for the *Sisters* episode in which I killed George Clooney, and an actor friend of mine called from New York to say he was proud of me for making it in Hollywood. I declined to tell him that my acting income, after commissions and taxes, wasn't much above the poverty line.

Fortunately, I still had ruse work from a number of clients, which enabled me to buy a black Nissan 240SX convertible, a car I couldn't have afforded otherwise. I nicknamed it the Batmobile and once used it to squire a pre-fame Jennifer Lopez to a Dodgers game. I'd met the TV producer Glen Larson (*The Six Million Dollar Man, Battlestar Galactica, Magnum, P.I.*) at a party at his Bel Air mansion. He had four season tickets behind home plate and offered them to another couple at the party. The husband was a friend of mine, and he invited me to join. His wife asked JLo, whom I'd met at the party. I could tell she didn't consider it a double date, but I did. She was engaging and present in a way few people are, and even momentarily had me convinced she was into me when she was really just into baseball. At the time, she'd been a Fly Girl on *In Living Color* and danced on tour with New Kids on the Block and Janet Jackson but hadn't yet broken through in films.

Executive search firms were beginning to find me, though I often had no idea how. Unlike with my acting career, I didn't have to do anything to get work. Pax and I shared some of the larger clients, including one woman, Donna DiLeo, who ran her own firm. Her targets were always difficult ones — technology firms, consulting organizations, phone companies — but she paid top dollar.

In February 1995, Pax and I were working on a particularly challenging assignment from opposite coasts when he called me in a panic.

"They're after me!" Pax's normally strong voice was shaky. "They came to my apartment."

"What? Who?"

"The police. My neighbor said they were banging on my door. They told my landlord they're looking for me. I'm going to be arrested." He sounded like he was hyperventilating.

"Whoa, calm down," I said. "Where are you now?"

"In my apartment. They were here an hour ago. They just missed me."

"Hang up right now and call me from a pay phone."

While it was possible that law enforcement was after Pax, it seemed strange to me. I'd assumed that if we got caught it would be by the company we were researching. Someone from the firm, probably in its legal department, would threaten us never to call them again, and we would simply "cease and desist" and move on to other targets. It wasn't until that moment that I realized I may have misjudged the threat completely.

Suddenly, preparing for the audition I had that afternoon was no longer a priority. If the authorities had found Pax, it meant they were listening to his calls. If they'd tapped his phone, they had my number, too. For all I knew, the police — or the feds — would show up at my place in Santa Monica any second. Before I could start hyperventilating, too, the phone rang and I answered it.

"I'm going to turn myself in," Pax said.

"Whoa, don't be stupid. Just hang on a second. Let's think this thing through."

If Pax did turn himself in, what was the crime? Clever improvisational skills? Pretending to be someone who didn't exist? I recalled the attorney who'd warned us that what we did was in a "gray" area of legality. He said it was conceivable that an aggrieved corporation, sick of losing its top executives to rival firms, which could cost it tens of millions, even billions, of dollars, might take action against us for the theft of names that led to those losses. Since Pax and I were using the telephone (as well as fraud-ulent pretenses) to obtain the information, we were susceptible to the charge of federal wire fraud, which under Title 18 of the United States Code was defined as devising "any scheme or artifice to defraud, or for obtaining money or property by means of false or fraudulent pretenses, representations, or promises . . . in interstate or foreign commerce." It was punishable by a hefty fine or up to twenty years in prison, and *if the violation affected a financial institution* the potential penalties went up to $1 million and thirty years. To further underline the possibility of grave consequence, apparently each ruse call could be considered a separate crime. Pax and I had made *thousands* of those calls. String them together and we could be sentenced to prison for the rest of our lives.

"Wait," I said. "They left an address?"

"Huh? No."

"How do you know it was the police? Were they wearing uniforms?"

"They told my landlord they were investigators. Holy shit, maybe it was the FBI!" Pax's voice slid higher than I'd ever heard.

"Did they show ID?" I asked.

"Uh, no."

"You gotta hold it together, man. Any agency would show ID or a badge. If these guys didn't, that means they aren't the law." I had no idea if I was right, but I needed to calm Pax down. If I didn't, I feared what he might do — and how that would implicate me.

"Who are they then?" he asked.

"That's what we have to find out. In the meantime, you've got to lay low and keep your mouth shut. Can you stay someplace else for a few days?"

"You want me to go on the lam?" Like we were in some kind of crime caper. Though maybe we were and just didn't know it yet.

"I want you to calm the fuck down. What about that girl you met? Can't you stay at her place for a few days?"

"I guess."

"Go back to your apartment — five minutes max — and grab enough stuff to last for a couple of days. Call me in ten minutes." I hung up before Pax could protest.

My thoughts were whirling back and forth from deep skepticism to genuine fear. I couldn't imagine that the NYPD — let alone the FBI — would care that much about what we were doing. But what if I'd been dangerously wrong?

Fifteen minutes later, Pax called back.

"They left a message on my answering machine earlier today. They were telling me to come outside, that it would go easier on me. Oh my God, I'm gonna go to jail for the rest of my life."

"Are you on the pay phone again?"

"Yeah."

"Listen to me. Did they identify who they were?"

"They're investigators. With the phone company."

"Wait, what?" I wondered why the hell the phone company would give a crap whether Pax was researching Goldman Sachs or Price Waterhouse or whatever firms he'd been calling. It didn't make sense to me.

"They said they know what I've been doing. They left a number for me to call."

"Do not call them," I shouted. "Do not tell them anything." I remembered the project we were doing for Donna. I'd taken the consulting firms on her list, and Pax had taken the telephone companies. Was it possible he ruffled some feathers with his recent calls? "Did the investigators say what firm they were with?"

"Sprint."

"Wasn't that one of the firms on Donna's list? Did you research them yet?"

"Yesterday."

"Well, duh, that's why they showed up. You must have pissed somebody off and they called their internal security."

"I don't think so. Nobody busted me. Nobody gave me a hard time. The Sprint research was way easier than I thought it would be."

I knew Pax would have a good sense of whether he'd aroused suspicions — or hackles — with his calling. But if his research went smoothly, why the hell had investigators shown up at his door? "Who is your long distance with?" I asked.

"Sprint."

"That explains it. Someone got suspicious *after* you called, and they ran a trace on your number since your account is with them."

"No, dude," Pax said. "The guys told my landlord that they've been after me for a while."

I wanted to ask Pax to play the voicemail but didn't dare risk sending him back into his apartment. Had they been monitoring his phone and tracking him for months? Years? Were they tapping my phone, too? A few times I'd heard strange clicks on my line but thought it was my imagination — or paranoia. Now it appeared Pax, at least, was under investigation.

I was already taking a chance talking to him on my line. I rationalized that I wasn't the one who'd called Sprint, so their investigators shouldn't (I prayed) have any interest in me. But there was something odd, not to mention frightening, about investigators just showing up. After all, Sprint had Pax's telephone number. Why not call and threaten him over the phone? Why go to the trouble — and expense — of sending two guys all the way out to Pax's crummy apartment in Brooklyn? And if they'd been after him for a long time, why only now had they shown up?

"Those investigators have no authority to talk to you," I said, "let alone arrest you. Ignore them. They're just trying to scare you." I heard the confidence in my voice, and it wasn't mine. It was my father's. He had a saying for whenever someone in the family was threatened: "Let them kiss our Kerbeck ass." As the child of two genocides, he knew something about being tough.

"Easy for you to say. They didn't come to your house."

"You gotta trust me. Go to your girl's place. Call me from a pay phone in a few days. It's gonna be okay, I promise."

I had no idea if that was the truth, but I needed Pax to believe it was. For his sake and, possibly, mine. I feared Pax would give me up without being asked. I also imagined the authorities getting a much bigger kick out of busting me, an actor who'd recently worked with O. J. Simpson. Hell, maybe they'd even question me about the murders.

After I got off the phone, I called my agent and canceled my audition. I told her I had the flu. It was the first and only audition I've ever walked away from.

$ $ $

I needed to clear my head, so I went out for a walk to grab coffee. As I headed toward Main Street and the Pacific Ocean, I caught myself checking for unmarked cop cars and glancing over my shoulder to see if I was being followed.

While I'd been rusing for seven years without any major trouble, I'd once received a letter from a Swiss investment bank after I'd foolishly given out Leona's fax number in a fit of desperation. A kind secretary had offered to fax me what I needed, but instead a fax came through from the deputy head of the firm's US legal department warning that if I ever called the firm again he would forward the fax number to the authorities. I knew that would lead to Leona, who'd simply claim she had no idea what we did to get our information. After all, Leona didn't ruse, nor had she trained us to ruse. If the authorities showed up at her door, Leona would suffer no consequences. The only one to go down would be me. Yet it was impossible for me to refuse to research a particular major investment bank. There were only ten of them. Our clients specifically wanted intelligence on those ten firms, minus one — the one that had hired the search firm to do the poaching. As much as I'd wanted to drop that firm from any future research, it wasn't an option, so from then on I simply proceeded with extreme caution whenever I called them.

Inside the Coffee Bean, I stared at the other actors reading scripts and preparing for auditions, oblivious to my impending arrest as a white-collar criminal. I went crazy and ordered a White Chocolate Dream Latte — not a good idea if I had to take off my shirt at an audition anytime soon, but the call with Pax had freaked me out. I rationalized that if the FBI came calling I could just quit the ruse, promise I'd never do it again. Perhaps the situation was my wake-up call. Maybe I didn't need the money. I'd been reading the self-help book *The Artist's Way* and doing the exercises in the workbook that came with it. The author, Julia Cameron, wrote, "Leap and the net will appear."

I walked back up the hill to my place, resolved to wind down the ruse — if I didn't get arrested first.

$ $ $

The following days I was on edge as I waited to hear from Pax. Hour after hour passed with no word. I didn't have his new girlfriend's number, so I couldn't call him. In the shower, I noticed clumps of hair coming off in my hands. Was I going bald as a result of the stress?

One week later, I returned from an audition for film director Ridley Scott and the phone was ringing — an insistent type of ring. Had Ridley been that impressed with me? He hadn't done much since his Oscar-nominated helming of *Thelma & Louise*, but he was gearing up to shoot the action drama *G.I. Jane*. Was he calling to offer me my first major film role?

"Dude," Pax said when I answered. "They think I'm that computer hacker, the one being hunted by the Secret Service and the FBI."

"Who?"

"Kevin Mitnick. Remember the article I showed you in *The New York Times*?"

I recalled reading the article the prior summer. Mitnick had been described as the Darth Vader of the hacking world — a.k.a. the Darkside Hacker — and a threat to national security. Our rusing was essentially identical to what Mitnick did, though we just tricked people into giving us lists of names for recruiting purposes. Mitnick got passwords and codes so he could hack into corporations to gain access to trade secrets worth billions. He claimed it wasn't for financial gain, that it was all just a game to him, but law enforcement wasn't amused. The feds and representatives of the major phone companies had met to come up with ways to stop him. The internet was only just becoming commercially accessible to individuals and corporations — online banking had gone live the previous fall — and a computer emergency response team (CERT) was created to prevent it from being shut down, which is what they believed Mitnick was trying to do via telephone lines.

"Wait, how do you know this?" I asked.

"One of the Sprint investigators called again."

"You answered your phone?"

Pax may have been good at the ruse, but he was a terrible criminal.

"It's all good. I told them it wasn't me. That I'm not Mitnick. I told them I don't know anything."

"What did they say?"

"Uh, that they're keeping an eye on me. They said they'll be in touch."

I'm sure one phone call with my panicked friend had made it clear to the investigators that Pax didn't possess the skill set — or the balls — to escape a parking ticket. Mitnick had been on the run from the FBI, the US Marshals Service, the Secret Service, and an alphabet soup of other federal organizations yet *still* hadn't been captured.

A few days later, however, on February 15, it was all over the news that Mitnick had been arrested in North Carolina as a domestic terrorist. He was placed in irons and put in solitary confinement in a federal prison on a laundry list of charges related to his use of the telephone: damaging computers, gaining access to proprietary intelligence, and intercepting passwords, as well as committing hundreds of counts of wire fraud — many of which Pax and I were guilty of, as well. Was this what awaited me? Leg irons and twenty-three hours of darkness a day in a three-by-six cell?

I immediately made a few moves to protect myself. First, I decided I would never research phone companies again. It was way too risky. Second, I told Leona that I couldn't work for her anymore. I explained that I was getting paid a lot more working for her competitors. If I was going to go down, it may as well be at the higher hourly rate my other clients were paying me. With all of the acting work I was getting, my availability to ruse was limited anyway. I figured I should get as much as I could before my acting career fully took off.

Leona went ballistic when I gave her the news. She accused me of being a taker. I wasn't sure what she was referring to since she was paying me a fraction of what the others were. Kelly Anne at JSA had raised me to $30 an hour without me even asking, something Leona had never done. But I still felt bad about how things seemed to be ending between us since I genuinely liked Leona. I respected her as a businessperson, as well — the same way I respected my father.

After our tense call, I contemplated Leona's words. Maybe I *was* a taker. Maybe I had been duplicitous working for JSA and others. Right when I was about to call her and apologize, the phone rang.

"Dude, thank you!" It was Pax.

"For what?"

"For the raise Leona gave me right after she got off the phone with you. She's pissed, by the way."

I was surprised by Pax's enthusiasm. A few days earlier he'd sworn he was done with the ruse, that he'd gotten religion after the close call with Mitnick's pursuers.

"Congrats on the extra dollar an hour," I said with a chuckle.

"Did you tell Leona what you were making?" he asked.

"Sure, I wanted her to know how underpaid we've been." I figured that Leona would understand, even agree, that yes, of course, I should work for the highest bidder. After all, her clients were financial institutions. Wasn't the whole point of capitalism to make as much money as you could? Besides, she'd heard about the Mitnick caper and understood the risks we were taking.

"She matched your salary," Pax shouted. "She's going to pay me $30 an hour!"

Part of me couldn't believe it, but Leona had lost one of her best researchers. There was no way she was going to chance losing another one. While I was happy for Pax, the news of his raise stung. Leona had made me feel like a crappy person for wanting to be paid a fair wage when all along she could afford to pay us more. She took advantage of us because we wanted to be actors and were desperate for any reliable income that would keep that dream afloat. She knew we didn't want to ruse for the rest of our lives.

$ $ $

A few months after the call with Leona, John and Kelly Anne offered to sell me their business. John had finished his degree and was offered a teaching job. They wanted out of the ruse game. I couldn't blame them. Kelly Anne sent me information about how much I could expect to make. They billed their clients between $60 and $80 an hour, which meant they were paying me almost half of what they received, leaving $70,000 or $80,000 a year for them. As much as I appreciated their honesty, I didn't have the money to buy any business. I'd recently moved from my studio into a one-bedroom apartment that cost $100 more per month. Finding that extra money was a supreme challenge. Where was I going to find the $80,000 they wanted?

But even if I had been able to come up with the money — or some of it, since John and Kelly Anne offered flexible payment terms — I didn't want to run a business, let alone an illegal one. The problem with turning down their offer was that the amount of work they had to give me began to decrease. Some weeks I had none. As an actor, I was earning more than 98 percent of the members of the Screen Actors Guild, and it still wasn't enough to support a meager lifestyle. How would I ever buy a house or go on vacation when I couldn't even afford to go out to dinner?

I realized that the only way for me to make a true living as an actor was to get on a TV show — and not as a guest star or in a recurring role, which I'd already done, but as one of the stars. I resolved to get a series, but in the meantime I still needed the ruse, which meant eating some crow.

I had to go back to Leona.

CHAPTER ELEVEN

Queen of the Hags

Leona readily accepted me back — and at $30 an hour. She was over-whelmed with work and desperate for my corporate intelligence skills. I dove back into the work but kept telling myself the ruse would soon be coming to an end.

I felt sure I would book a series, though the number of auditions I was getting had started to dwindle. I was no longer the new kid in town every Hollywood casting director wanted to meet. If I'd been an actress, agents would've already told me it was too late, that I should've come to LA when I was sixteen, not thirty. Still, I was getting hired to do guest spots on shows such as *Nash Bridges* with Don Johnson and *Star Trek: Deep Space Nine*. (My Cardassian Soldier character from the latter was immortalized in a collectible card, which you can buy online today; I think it goes for two bucks.) I also continued to be cast in lead roles on the stage. LA theater often gets a bad rap, but the plays I was doing were as good as anything I did in New York. A production of *The Pink Triangle* won the award for Best Play in Los Angeles, and my work in Tom Jacobson's *The Beloved Disciple* earned me a best actor nomination that year. Because of these accolades I remained confident in my talents, even if my film and TV career was losing momentum.

On the plus side, my romantic life revived in unexpected ways. Over the summer, Richie had roped me into coming along on his blind date with a Czech woman named Petra. My date turned out to be his dog, Safta. As the four of us walked down toward the beach in Santa Monica, I realized I needed some cash and ducked into the ATM vestibule of my bank. Unfortunately, it was out of order. When I walked out, a pretty woman in jeans, a white T-shirt, and no makeup was waiting for her turn.

"Oh," I said, startled by how attractive she was. "The machine's out of order."

Where's a screenwriter when you need a good opening line? I hoped my wince went unnoticed.

"Okay." She started to walk away.

"Wait, uh, do you know where the closest ATM is?"

"Venice Circle." She pointed south and started away again.

Couldn't she tell I was trying to flirt with her? Didn't she find me attractive?

"I'm on foot because we live up the street," I said, gesturing toward Richie, Petra, and Safta. All three of them were staring, waiting for me to get her phone number or invite her to join us — or slink back to them defeated. The crowd was making her nervous, though. I could tell she was going to leave. I had to go big.

"If I give you my ATM card and code, will you pull out five hundred bucks for me?"

That got her attention. She stopped fidgeting and let me approach her.

"Where can I bring it to you?" she asked, smiling coyly. I was making progress.

"How about World Cafe? I'll buy you dinner for your trouble."

We glanced across the street to World Cafe. A giant sign read CLOSED FOR PRIVATE PARTY.

Fuck.

If I'd been selling an elementary school teacher on a Mercury Cougar — a feat I actually accomplished in fifth grade — or sweet-talking a phone receptionist at J. P. Morgan, I'd have charmed them. But here I was at a loss. Tongue-tied. Deirdre and Andi would have been appalled. The beautiful woman and I looked at each other, said nothing, and she walked off.

Fifteen minutes later, Richie, Petra, Safta, and I were squeezed into a tiny outdoor table at Joe's Diner on Main Street. Because of the dog, we couldn't sit inside. Suddenly, I heard shouting.

"Hey! Hey!" someone was yelling. "Hey! Hey!"

I looked up from my menu and saw a car blocking traffic in front of the restaurant.

"Hey! You!" It was her, ATM woman. She was pointing at me. "Come here."

I got up from the table and walked toward her car, a funny feeling in my legs. People on the sidewalk had stopped to watch. They were wondering what was going on. So was I.

"I got your money," she said, even though I hadn't given her my ATM card.

"You did?"

"Yeah, and if you want me to give it to you, you'll have to meet me at Lulu's for a drink."

"How long are you going to be there?"

"As long as your money holds out," she said and drove off.

After finishing dinner, I showed up at Lulu's to find the woman, whose name turned out to be Gardia, sitting with her best friend Sharan. Gardia worked for Madonna's record company, Maverick, and in addition to being brazen, she was Southern California through and through. She'd even been part of an all-girl punk rock skateboard gang called the Hags. Things clicked, and we started going to shows and premieres together. By fall, I'd been cast in the role of her long-term boyfriend.

$$$

Even as things were going well with Gardia, I weathered a series of near misses and unlucky breaks in the TV world. I booked my first pilot, playing the sidekick to actor Daniel Baldwin, younger brother of Alec. Right before I was to fly to Atlanta for the shoot, my agent informed me that the producers wanted me to play a different character — one that was *not* a series regular. Apparently, Daniel wanted a buddy to play his sidekick and forced the producers to dump me, despite the fact that he'd never seen me act. Fortunately, the union required the production to pay me in full since they'd already committed to hiring me.

Thank God for the Screen Actors Guild.

But while the pay was good, I didn't want money for nothing. I wanted to work as an actor. I wanted to be a series regular. I wanted to have a career in the business, which for the first time was seeming less than likely. In a nice twist, after the producers paid me for the original role they still wanted me for the smaller part. Because my sister lived in Atlanta and had just had a baby, I accepted the job. This meant they had to pay me *twice*.

On my first pilot set, I saw firsthand how the lead of the show ruled the roost. Daniel, who'd starred on the first three seasons of NBC's *Homicide: Life on the Street*, was hostile and confrontational with just about everyone. One night, he had a drunken fit and threw chairs at people. I remember standing there thinking that if one hit me I'd punch him so hard he'd wake up back in Baltimore. The next day, he apologized to the entire cast and crew. After filming, he went into rehab. To this day, I've never seen the pilot. I don't think it ever aired.

My second experience with booking a pilot was actually worse.

When you're down to the wire for a role, producers hold a screen test. They bring in three or so finalists and have the actors do scenes, often on the same set they will eventually be working on. I was up for a sci-fi show called *Earth: Final Conflict* based on notes Gene Roddenberry's widow had found after his death in 1991. Kevin Kilner from *Almost Perfect* had been hired to play the lead, and I was "testing," as they called it, to be his rival — basically, the lead bad guy. Kevin was an energetic and positive guy. He made the screen test easy for me, and after I'd returned home my agent called to say I'd booked the show.

I drove straight over to Gardia's office at Maverick Records to give her the great news, but she was less than enthusiastic.

"Congratulations," she said without offering me a hug or a kiss, let alone jumping up and down. Where was the passion of the adventurous woman who'd tracked me down on the street?

I knew the reason for her apprehension, though. One thing no one tells you about going in for a screen test is that they require you to sign the contract (and your life away) *before* the actual test. That way, if you're hired you can't hold out for more money. I was now committed to the show for as long as seven years. The series was shooting in Toronto, which meant I was moving there. Because of Roddenberry's popularity and legendary status as the creator of *Star Trek*, there was a high likelihood the show would run for many seasons. Gardia had never lived outside LA. She also had a pretty cool, if stressful, job working for twenty-six-year-old wunderkind Guy Oseary, the head of A&R — artists and repertoire; in other words, scouting and development — for Madonna's record label. If Gardia wanted us to be in the same city, she would have to quit.

I was ready to commit to her, but she was hesitant to do the same. She assured me it was only the thought of moving to Toronto that gave her doubts, but we had a number of difficult late-night heart-to-hearts that left me fearful I was about to lose a really good thing. In the acting life you're so often made to believe you're on the brink of something — an important meeting, a killer agent, a role, a breakthrough, a series greenlight, a solid foothold to the next level, even stardom. The constant psychological tension between that potential for success and the much more frequent disappointment is stressful. And it takes a toll. Would I have to give up something lovely for my latest and best shot at a successful acting career?

One morning, I woke up and found a card from Gardia that said she would go anywhere to support me and my career. I read it four times. Endorphins flooded my body. Everything I'd ever wanted was coming together. I was even counting on finally getting those free hockey tickets Jim Lipton had promised me, since the Toronto Maple Leafs would want the public support of a "local celebrity." Could life get any better?

Not long after, I received a panicked call from my agent. There was a problem, a big fucking problem. Had Kevin Kilner decided that he, too, would rather have a buddy in the show? At least I'd get paid for doing nothing again. But there was to be no silver lining this time. The one and only out in the contract I signed had to do with immigration. The Canadian government didn't want too many Americans coming north to do the Roddenberry series. They'd agreed to accept Kevin but insisted that my part be played by a Canadian actor. The government was forcing the producers to replace me.

It was a gut shot, a heartbreaker, a soul killer. The series also would have, even with marginal success, created a mostly passive income stream for me for the rest of my life. Science-fiction shows have such a devoted audience base that even actors on second- and third-tier series can make money by appearing on the fan convention circuit, which has grown exponentially with the internet, social media, comic-cons — first in San Diego and now in several major cities — and superhero culture. But even before the internet, in the mid-1990s, a guest star showing up to a weekend convention could make amounts equivalent to a week's work on the show. Leads could walk away with tens of thousands of dollars.

But then I watched the series.

It was as bad as television could be. I love Gene Roddenberry and the *Star Trek* shows — I'd had the pleasure of appearing in the *Deep Space Nine* episode "Defiant," which Den of Geek labeled one of its best — but *Earth: Final Conflict*, which premiered in October 1997, sucked. Reflecting on the equally bad Daniel Baldwin pilot I'd done, I realized I'd somehow fallen into the TV gutter. I'd started my career doing Euripides and Brecht. I was a lifetime member of the Actors Studio. My picture had been on the front page of the Sunday *New York Times* arts section. Now I was lucky to get, and then lose, jobs on crummy genre shows that failed.

$ $ $

Unfortunately, I wasn't done with terrible television.

I did two pilots with Glen Larson, the successful producer whose Dodgers tickets had led to my baseball date with JLo. A big fan of mine, he said I reminded him of a young Richard Widmark, the rugged actor who'd played so many great villain roles on radio and TV, and in film noirs such as *Kiss of Death* and *No Way Out*. By the time I came along, the career of the man Harlan Ellison nicknamed "Glen Larceny" for his tendency to steal film ideas and convert them to TV shows (*Star Wars* into *Battlestar Galactica*, for example) had seriously waned. The kind of wholesome, aw-shucks humor predominant in his hit shows of the '70s and '80s — *B.J. and the Bear*, *The Fall Guy* — seemed dated in the irony-saturated '90s. Both pilots I did with Larson were oblivious to the trend toward darker, grittier fare. The jazz-musician-turned-superhero show *Night Man* went to series without me and ran for only two seasons. The sci-fi thriller series *The Darwin Conspiracy* wasn't picked up; Paramount released it as a widely panned TV movie in 1999.

I was getting fewer and fewer auditions. My TV career was dying. My acting income had gone down for the first time since I moved to LA in 1993. I was hired as the lead for a play, Rick Cleveland's *Home Grown*, but there was as much drama offstage as there was on. It was double-cast, a common technique in LA, where actors often get other jobs on a moment's notice and have to miss performances. It was my first time in a play that used the tactic, and there was competition between the two casts as to which was better. Unfortunately, this was egged on by the director, Paul McCrane, who was also a well-known actor (he'd just been hired as a recurring character on . . . *ER*).

On top of this, live theater in LA paid miserably. I was doing the play for love but found myself standing in the shadows engaged in petty whispering about which actor was better. The other actor playing my role was Brian Cousins, who'd done some of the same TV shows I had and looked nearly identical other than being an inch or two taller. It was like staring at myself in the mirror, which besides being uncanny had disturbing implications for my career. It was hard enough to get an acting job without having a virtual double running around Hollywood. That said, he was as nice a guy as I'd ever met. Others weren't so kind. One of the actresses in the show told me, unsolicited, how much better she thought I was in the role than Brian. My father taught me long ago that if someone is bad-mouthing others to your face, they're doing the same to you when you're not around.

The experience ruined the theater for me, which had been one of the great loves of my life. As an exchange student in London, I'd sobbed watching Judi Dench in Brecht's *Mother Courage and Her Children* at the National Theatre. John Malkovich took my breath away in Lanford

Wilson's *Burn This* when I was a young actor in New York. After a career of more than one hundred plays as a member of Actors' Equity, starring opposite talents such as James Gandolfini, Calista Flockhart, and Maria Bello, this two-faced production would be the last play I'd ever do.

CHAPTER TWELVE

Partying with the Yakuza

In 1998, I was hired by Michael Mayer to play the lead in his short film *The Robber*. I was in nearly every frame of the fifteen-minute film. For the first time in my acting career, plays aside, I was tasked with carrying an entire project. I played a rather hapless burglar who breaks into a woman's home and gets caught by her. She happens to be a martial artist and security nut, so she kicks his ass, escapes the apartment, and locks him inside. The film details my character's attempts to get out before the police show up. Along the way, he befriends the woman's dog.

The Robber was a hit at film festivals in the United States and around the world. In 1999, I was invited to the prestigious Clermont-Ferrand film festival in France. Right before I was to fly to the festival, I read Frank Abagnale Jr.'s 1980 autobiography, *Catch Me If You Can*, which details the financial scams he pulled off in the 1960s by posing as a pilot, a lawyer, and a doctor, meeting scores of women and passing thousands of bad checks along the way. I found the book exhilarating — until I got to the part where Frank is arrested in France and sent to jail. For nearly a year he lived on bread and water with no sunlight and a bucket for a toilet.

While rusing, I called Paris regularly since it was the financial capital of France, and now I was scheduled to do French television and radio as part of the film festival. In bed at night, I imagined someone identifying my distinctive Philly accent and calling the authorities, who would then throw me in the same Perpignan dungeon where Abagnale had nearly died. It was paranoia on my part, but these are the types of thoughts that haunt the minds of people who commit crimes.

Shortly after Clermont-Ferrand, *The Robber* was accepted into a Tokyo film festival at which George Lucas was the honored guest. I spent a week with the creator of *Star Wars*, attending events with him that included a gala dinner at the residence of the US ambassador Tom Foley, former Speaker of the House, and a party thrown by the head of the Yakuza, the Japanese equivalent of the Mafia. Lucas was so shy and reserved, however, that eventually I gave up trying to chat with him.

The Yakuza godfather was a different story. He attended the festival because his mistress was a wannabe actress, and they both fell in love with *The Robber*. A member of the festival staff contacted me and told me in broken, and breathless, English that the godfather — and his mistress — wanted to meet me. More than that, he'd offered to host a celebration in honor of *The Robber*.

On the day of the event, the staff member took me and a handful of other filmmakers to what seemed to be a street fair. The director of *Star Wars* had not been invited, but in fairness, Lucas didn't have a film in the festival for the godfather or his mistress to fall in love with.

In Philly, we would have called the celebration a block party. Instead of kegs of beer, however, there were huge barrels of sake. Colorful banners waved in the air. I had no idea what they said, though, and no one translated for me. Very few Japanese spoke English, and even communicating with the festival staff relied heavily on facial expressions and hand gestures. In my lack of comprehension I started to wonder: *Had this entire event been put together just for my film?*

It appeared so.

A retinue of bodyguards greeted us, each one wearing only a white loincloth. My attention was drawn to their tattoos, which covered every inch of their bodies. Even their shaved heads had dragons, mountains, and, of course, women inked on them. The men said nothing as they escorted us to a long wooden table. At the head a man in his midfifties wearing an all-white suit leaned back in his chair confidently. Next to him sat an attractive woman in a see-through white dress who looked less than half his age. Her skin was as white as any I'd ever seen, as if she'd never been outside before. A bodyguard stood behind her holding a parasol.

The godfather smiled at me and directed me to take the seat to his right, which I would later learn was the seat of honor. The problem was that his mistress was currently sitting in it. She smiled at me, too, raising her index finger to place it on her bottom lip. He barked something at her and she got up, bowing first to him and then to me. I bowed back. The godfather frowned and waved for me to take her seat, which I did. The mistress plopped herself in the chair to my right so that I was sandwiched between them. She didn't seem pleased about the new seating arrangement and scowled back at him.

The godfather gave what sounded like an order, and three or four bodyguards took off in different directions. He spoke to me for the first time. I smiled and nodded but had no idea what he'd said. He looked at his mistress as if she was supposed to translate, but she just smiled and nodded, too. He threw up his hands in disgust. Under the table, I felt her leg rub against mine.

Uh-oh.

The bodyguards also served as waiters. When they returned, they placed copious amounts of food and sake in front of me, and I noticed that many of them were missing their little fingers. I later learned about *enko-dzume*, having a finger cut off for hurting or shaming the Yakuza family. I liked my pinkies and wanted to keep them. To make sure I kept my hands to myself, I squeezed my thighs tight.

As the meal went on, the godfather became what my father would call Jersey Shore drunk. He began slurring his orders and gave up attempting to communicate with me. By the end, he couldn't sit up straight. I was pretty buzzed myself despite not drinking that much sake, which was unbelievably strong.

The mistress, though, was completely sober, as well as totally focused on me. I felt her eyes stroking me through most of the dinner, though she didn't touch me again. I wasn't taking any chances and kept my eyes straight ahead. When I was about to leave, I thanked the godfather profusely for hosting the event even though he was nearly unconscious. Then I made the mistake of giving his mistress a cursory glance. She was staring at me as if she wanted to leave with me. If she had spoken any English, I'm sure she would have whispered something or written me a note about where to meet up. I got the hell out of there, fingers intact.

Experiences like these were exhilarating, if a tad nerve racking. At festivals in Asia and Europe, and often at regular movie screenings there, too, feature films are usually preceded by a short film, as opposed to a barrage of previews. *The Robber* once "opened" for *American History X*, starring Edward Norton, at a major festival screening with Steven Spielberg and Catherine Zeta-Jones in attendance.

I felt that my acting career had been rejuvenated, but when I returned to the States no one cared about an award-winning short film. It was the best work I'd done on camera, and I didn't get a single audition from it. Here I was confident that people would *hire* me off the performance when they wouldn't even *meet* with me.

$ $ $

The same year *The Robber* had me globetrotting, a British search professional named Peter McBee contacted me. I don't know how he found me, but it had to have been via word of mouth since I wasn't exactly advertising my unethical services. Peter wanted me to do all the intelligence work for the global headhunting firm he was starting. He was on vacation in LA with his wife and three kids and insisted we meet in person, a get-together I refused to take seriously. I still believed I had an acting career ahead of me and Rollerbladed to meet him outside a restaurant in Santa Monica. Because of my skates I couldn't go inside, so we chatted on a sunny street corner for a few minutes. Throughout, he appeared to be eyeing my sweaty, shirtless body.

The interaction with McBee reminded me of an encounter I'd had with Kevin Spacey a decade earlier. We were doing a backer's audition for a Broadway show at Sardi's, the theater district's most iconic restaurant. Kevin was playing the lead, while I was reading stage directions. Afterward, Kevin approached to compliment me on my acting, though I hadn't done any.

"You're something," he said, eyeing me like I was a steak on the Sardi's menu. "I want to introduce you to my agent."

In the late '80s, Kevin wasn't a movie star yet — he'd appeared in a couple of Mike Nichols movies, but *Glengarry Glen Ross* was still a few years away. He was a well-known stage actor, though, with Broadway leads in *Hurlyburly* and *Long Day's Journey into Night* on his résumé. He certainly had a powerful agent, whereas at the time I had none. The idea that he would get me a meeting was tempting.

"Give me your phone number," he said.

I hesitated, since I sensed where he wanted this to lead. "Uh, why don't you have your agent call me? He can contact me through the union."

Kevin looked at me as if I were being silly and didn't appreciate what he was doing for me. "Don't you want an agent?"

"I do." *Desperately*, I might have added. "Why don't you give me the name of your agent and I'll call him?"

Now he looked at me like I was stupid. "That's not how these things work."

I was pretty sure I knew how it would work. Kevin would invite me over late one night to "discuss my career" and corner me in his bathroom.

"Come on," he added. "Don't you trust me?"

I didn't and passed on the offer.

To the public, Kevin was straight. I understood why he — and his big-time Hollywood agents — thought he needed to maintain that image: They believed, justifiably, that audiences wouldn't buy him in leading-man roles if they knew he was bisexual or gay.

Peter McBee likely had similar reasons for hiding his sexuality, assuming my instincts about him were correct. He was one of the leading recruiters in the executive search industry and, as such, part of the old-boys' club. I was fairly certain none of its members at that time were openly gay. The world of high finance was a repository for high school jocks, humiliating pranks, and fag jokes. It was not an accommodating place for a gay man — or anyone, really, other than a straight white male. If Peter was pretending to be something he wasn't, I felt sorry for him.

"I'm going to make you rich," he said. "And you're going to make me richer."

That was a proposition I was open to. Without hesitation, I went to work for Peter. He doubled what I was making and had more research work than I could handle.

For the second time, I told Leona I was leaving. I dialed her office in New York prepared for her once again to lambast me and call me a taker, but she seemed pleased by my announcement.

"It's time for you to go out on your own. If I can ever help in any way, please let me know."

As a master telephone listener, I could tell something was off about her voice and heard her sniffle. She was becoming emotional about my leaving, something I would never have expected. The word that came to mind was *verklempt*. Leona's research business was her life. She had no husband or boyfriend despite trying for years to find someone. I realized that Pax and I and Deirdre and Andi were as close to children as she would ever have.

I was unable to speak for fear I might cry, too. Leona had given me a job that enabled me to survive in Manhattan, train and develop as an actor, move to Los Angeles to do TV shows, and now start my own research business. Yes, she had made a lot of money from my work, but I owed her a debt of gratitude. I wish I could've expressed that to her. I thought of my father and what it must have been like to let me go and realized that he, too, had likely shed tears. Tears he wouldn't have let me see — or even know about. All I could say to Leona was "Thanks."

"You've taken this job further than I ever could have imagined," she said like a proud parent.

Little did she — or I — know how much further I would take it.

Or how many millions I was about to make.

CHAPTER THIRTEEN

The Inside Ploy

I'd finally given my research business a name: RK Research, Inc. Up until this point, I had been an actor who did research. Now I was the CEO of a research company who hadn't quite given up acting. I hired my first employee when Gardia showed up at my apartment one afternoon in the middle of the week, her face flushed. I could tell she'd been crying and gave her a hug.

"He fired me," she sobbed into my shoulder.

I knew the "he" was Maverick Records A&E executive Guy Oseary.

"Because I wouldn't pick up his laundry."

For years, Gardia had been the number two person at Lindy Goetz Management. Lindy's main client was the Red Hot Chili Peppers, whom he'd discovered at a Hollywood club in 1983. Following the release of their breakthrough record, *Blood Sugar Sex Magik*, in 1991, the band became one of the biggest acts in the world. Gardia was involved in all aspects of their management, including scheduling concerts, recording sessions, interviews, and photo shoots, and coordinating cover art, liner notes, and other key album elements. But when Lindy unexpectedly decided to retire, the Chili Peppers switched to a new management company based out of New York. Oseary then wooed Gardia to take a new job working for him at Maverick.

Now he wanted her to pick up his underwear.

Oseary regularly had Gardia run personal errands, none of which had anything to do with the music business. Making the situation worse was the toxic environment Madonna had created at her firm. The pop star didn't talk to most of the people who worked for her, ignoring them whenever she passed them in the halls. She came to Gardia's desk daily (some days multiple times) to meet with Oseary, but she never acknowledged Gardia's presence, never even said hello. Oseary must have figured that if Madonna was going to treat people like crap then he could, too.

Although I knew Gardia was devastated to lose the job, particularly because she was living paycheck-to-paycheck, I also believed it would be better for her sanity to be out of the malignant culture of Madonnaville.

"You can come work for me," I said without thinking about it. She'd been willing to move to a foreign country for me. The least I could do was help her in a time of need.

She pushed me away and smiled like I was being kind but silly. She had a real job with a pension and health benefits; mine wasn't even legal. She had perks like free CDs and concert tickets; I had an office in my bedroom and a filing system in a broom closet.

"No, I'm serious," I said. "I'll match what you were making. I'll even pay you under the table so you can collect unemployment."

Much like at the ATM machine, my cash offer got Gardia's attention. She was practical when it came to money, but noncommittal. "Okay, but only temporarily," she said.

As a high-level assistant in the music industry, Gardia had accumulated the expertise and experience to turn my survival job into a thriving enterprise. She bought filing cabinets and developed a detailed filing system. She began typing up the research to make it look professional, as well as legible, since my handwriting was atrocious. By taking over the parts of the business I sucked at, Gardia enabled me to focus on what I did best: rusing.

Instantly, our revenue increased. *A lot.*

Gardia wasn't fazed by the ethics of what I did, either. During her time with Madonna, she had seen music business dealings that made lying on the phone seem quaint. She was sick and tired of being undervalued and underpaid, something we had in common. She and her fellow workers weren't paid much more than the $8 an hour Leona had once paid me. Just like on Wall Street, a lucky few in the entertainment industry made tens of millions while the rest were supposed to be simply grateful they had a job — and were lucky enough to have Madonna pretend they didn't exist.

Gardia and I moved together into a rented house in Santa Monica and set up an office in the basement. Gardia even tried to make some ruse calls when the work from Peter McBee first began to pour in, but, like nearly everyone before her, she wasn't able to handle the constant lying.

By the summer of 1999, Peter McBee was giving us so much work that Gardia and I were going to need to hire another employee, this time a fellow ruser. Gardia's best friend, Sharan, felt like I owed her a favor because she'd been with Gardia the night we met. Her boyfriend, Shen "Shenanigans" Stephens, needed money. His gigs as a bongo player in various Venice and Topanga Canyon hippie bands weren't covering his expenses. He sounded like the worst possible candidate ever to ruse Wall Street firms, but I agreed to meet him to keep the peace in my home.

On the day of the interview, Shen showed up thirty minutes late riding a skateboard like a teenager, though he looked to be about my age. I wasn't even going to let him in, let alone offer him a job. I walked outside to lecture him about punctuality, but he ignored my frown and greeted me with a hug as if we were drum circle buddies.

"What's up, brother?" With his slightly thick build, dark-brown eyes, and mop of brown hair, he reminded me of a teddy bear, in the way George Clooney had.

"You're late," I said.

"Car trouble." He pointed at his skateboard like it was evidence.

"You broke down?" Maybe I'd judged him too harshly.

"No, I don't have one!" He laughed and hugged me again. I had to force myself not to crack a smile. I would learn that Shen was a hard guy to stay mad at — or say no to.

Training Shen was an eye-opening experience for me. In the twelve years since I'd started rusing, it had become much harder to obtain information. Almost every Fortune 500 company now used executive search firms for all of their mid- and senior-level hiring. As a result, the demand for top-quality research had never been higher — or more lucrative. This brought more researchers into the industry, which meant more individuals calling firms for intelligence, often using cockamamie ploys. Companies started training their employees never to release information over the phone. The ploys I'd used in the past with such success were no

longer effective — or efficient. Because of this, I never considered starting Shen with the student ploy. I took him straight to using the audit
firm. To reduce the pressure on the newbie, I gave him random dummy
firms to call — they were real companies but not firms I'd been assigned
to research. That way, if Shen got busted it didn't matter.

As I sat listening to him, I was shocked at the hostility he encountered.
Even when he switched to an Irish name, people had zero interest in
helping the outside auditors. They kept telling him to call his contact
within the company for the information. Maybe it was because the
industry had gotten jittery in the wake of Jordan Belfort's spectacular
implosion. After his pump-and-dump outfit Stratton Oakmont was
shut down in 1996, Belfort moved out to Beverly Hills (I was nearby
playing a desk clerk on *Melrose Place*). He'd been indicted in 1998 for
money laundering and securities fraud, then pleaded guilty in 1999 to
defrauding mom-and-pop investors to the tune of $200 million or so.
And he did most of it through a phone line with nothing more than
some masterful motormouth bullshitting. Were we experiencing collat-
eral blowback?

"Why don't we say we're an internal person?" Shen asked after a couple
of days of getting beaten up. "Someone that really works at the firm we
want?" The second most important quality for a researcher was the willingness to get back on the phone after being shut down. Shen had that
kind of persistence. The most important skill, of course, was the ability to
lie like a motherfucker. With aggressive enthusiasm and a nimble mind.
Somehow the bongo player had that, too.

"No, no, no, that's an inside ploy," I said. "We don't do that." The truth
was there had been a few times I'd made the executive decision to employ
it at particularly difficult firms. Pax and I called it "the nuclear option."

"You'd get the information a lot faster," Shen said, which was true. I
had hired him because I couldn't keep up with the workflow and meet
the deadlines on my own. The bulletin board in my office was covered
with assignments that would last for months. Faster would certainly be a
huge plus. But it was too risky, and I said so. Up until that point — for
the most part — I had used made-up names like Chris Ryan and Michael

Sullivan. I feared that someone would record me impersonating an actual person and then turn it over to the FBI or the SEC.

"You don't have to say you're a real person at the company, you just make it *seem* like it," Shen countered. His father had been a stockbroker, which explained why Shen understood so much about Wall Street. But Shenanigans had also proved himself a natural at coming up with ploys. By that time, I had tried to train scores of people in the ruse: dozens of Leona's actor recruits and just about every one of my friends who was curious about the corporate spy game. Who didn't want a flexible, high-paying job you could do from home? But none of them worked out. Most gave up within an hour. Morals and ethics were rarely the issue, it was more the inability to lie and improvise on the phone. They would freeze up the second someone questioned why they were calling. But not Shenanigans. It was too early to tell, but he was showing signs of the potential to be as good as I was.

"What do you mean?"

"Say, for example, the guy who heads the tax department is Bob Jones. You say you're Bob in the tax department. You don't even need to say the name of the company, because if you really work there you're not going to say the company's name." He paused and then wagged his finger at me. "There's no way that saying, 'Hi, it's Bob in Tax,' can be illegal."

I didn't ask if Shenanigans had recently passed the bar exam. Still, his ploy made sense. A lot of it.

$ $ $

We started experimenting with this watered-down version of an inside ploy. The key was to find a name people would recognize without actually knowing that individual. We usually tried to find an executive who was in a different city from the person whose organization we were targeting.

"Hi, operator, can you transfer me to Rick Ford in Accounting," I began one call. "He's in your Philadelphia office." Operators didn't transfer outside calls directly to executives, they patched us through to their assistants. Rather than being a hindrance, in this case it actually served our purposes better.

"Rick Ford's office," the assistant answered.

"Oh shoot," I said. "I got transferred to the wrong number. I think the operator on your switchboard is new. She seemed confused."

"I'm sorry. Who were you trying to reach?"

I gave her the name of the executive, Dan Curtin, whose organization we wanted.

"Sure, I'll switch you over."

Shen and I had realized that if we were transferred from an office we were pretending to work in, that phone number then showed on the internal dial display, making it seem as if we were actually calling from that person's office.

"Dan Curtin's office," his assistant answered.

"Hi, it's Rick in Accounting, down in the Philly office." It may have been splitting hairs, but I hadn't said what firm I was with. Shen and I figured if individuals didn't even ask us a token question to verify our identity, then that was on them.

"Oh, hi, Rick."

I listened to hear if she knew me, uh, Rick. To be safe, I added, "I've got a terrible cold. Forgive me if I cough or sneeze in your ear. My mother brought me up better than that."

"As long as I don't catch it over the phone." She laughed.

"Hey, I've got to list Dan on one of my docs, and I need to make sure I've got his exact current title."

She read it to me.

"Oh, and I need to list his direct reports, too."

I could hear the hesitation in her silence.

"Forgive me for asking," she said, "but you came in on your assistant's line. Why are you calling from her phone?"

"Oh my God, I picked up the wrong line again. I hope Dan is better at using the phone system than I am."

She snorted. "He's not. He can't even get his own voicemails. I have to do it for him."

"That makes me feel better. Anyway, I just need his directs and we're done."

She read Dan's reports and then answered every other question I had. After twenty minutes, there was nothing I didn't know about his organization.

I scratched the letter *Q* on a Post-it where I'd written her name, her phone number, and the name I'd given for myself. The *Q* stood for "Queen" (I used a *K* for "King" for male sources). The note would remind me to start with her whenever I called the firm next, which could be in a week, a month, or a year. She had serious mole potential. I wouldn't have to prove who I was the next time I called.

But I knew it was only a matter of time before someone called my bluff and asked for my full name. Merely saying I was Rick in Accounting or Bob in Tax certainly wasn't going to cut it every time. I'd have to decide whether to make up a phony last name to stay in the gray area or use the actual last name of the guy I was pretending to be. By 1999, most firms had begun to put the names of their employees into a computer database that could be viewed by others within the firm. If I gave a fake last name to an individual who was already suspicious of me, they'd just look it up and see that no such person existed. I'd be busted.

But I also knew the hard truth of what I was contemplating. Even with the elevated legal risk, I knew that once I started impersonating real people — and saw the lucrative results — I'd never stop.

CHAPTER FOURTEEN

Y2K

As we approached the turn of the millennium, there were two bugs going around that changed my life. The first was the computer bug Y2K, which was projected to wreak havoc on systems and networks across the globe. At the time, most computer programs represented four-digit years by using only the final two digits, making the year 2000 indistinguishable from the year 1900. Airlines, power grids, banks, and many other institutions and industries were panicked that the incorrect display of dates could cause a chain reaction of computer failures with catastrophic worldwide consequences.

I'd like to say I was the one who recognized the potential in using the computer bug to our advantage, but it was my old buddy Pax who was the genius. Though I lived in Santa Monica and he still lived in New York, we spoke on the phone regularly and remained competitive about our rusing techniques like we were fighting to be salesman of the month at my father's old dealership.

"I've got a wicked new ploy for the millennium," he bragged one morning. "It's totally nuclear."

"I hope it's better than your transfer agency one."

"I'm not sure I like your attitude," Pax said. "Why should I tell you?"

"How about because the last time I quit Leona, you got raised to $50 an hour," I shouted.

"You wouldn't even *have* this job if it weren't for me," he shouted back.

"Fuck you."

"Fuck you, too."

Silence bit into the line. But eventually, Pax laughed and I laughed back. Soon we were giggling like teenagers.

"The tech people are freaking out that their systems aren't going to work after January 1, right?" Pax said after he caught his breath. "So I say I'm in IT working on Y2K, and all anyone wants to know is whether we're going to make the deadline. I tell them we're working night and day, and that we have to input every single piece of information manually. I've never had people more willing to give up intel. They feel sorry for me!"

Pax was right. Y2K was a gold mine. There were daily articles in the papers as well as regular segments on the news about the impending disaster. Because of the way the ploy played off everyone's fear of losing money, we were able to obtain greater amounts of intelligence than ever before, which also enabled us to raise our rates. In 1999, I made more than $100,000 for the first time.

With the Y2K windfall, Gardia and I could afford to get married, something we'd dreamed of doing in Hawaii. We made it a destination wedding that October on the Big Island and hosted a number of outdoor adventures and lavish meals.

Even after an expensive wedding and honeymoon on Kauai, we still had money to sock away to buy a house. I should've been happy, but I was depressed about the state of my acting career, which was in its death throes. Now I was lucky to get auditions for B-grade shows such as *Renegade* and *Pacific Blue*, both of which I booked. Instead of these gigs leading to auditions for the top shows, they seemed to solidify me as a second- or third-tier TV actor. I was also beginning to lose my hair — a major no-no for a leading man. My agent suggested that I get a hair transplant, but I was in complete denial about the issue and its impact on my career.

Beyond the wrenching disappointment of my artist dreams slipping away lay the cold reality that all I was left with was the ruse. Yes, I was doing better than ever with it, but the situation had started to feel like whoring either way: take a bit part in a TV series I'd never want to watch just for the paycheck or continue to spin lies so at least I'd feel successful at something and be able to take my new wife out to a decent fucking dinner. As it happens, a few years earlier I'd done an independent film called *Bad Girls* that had to be retitled when a bigger-budget Hollywood Western starring Andie McDowell and Drew Barrymore as prostitutes on the run beat us to it. Our new title?

Whore 2.

It was enough to make a guy's hair fall out.

$ $ $

The other bug affecting me in late 1999 was related to my health: I called it my neck bug.

Most days, I was unable to turn my head without excruciating pain. I kept an old-fashioned (and old-person) neck brace handy and used it often, even though I was only thirty-five. I saw a chiropractor three times a week, occasionally more. I had massages, acupuncture, even an MRI. Nothing took the pain away. Out in public, I was constantly stretching my neck or attempting to crack it myself. Friends were concerned I'd developed some type of twitch. Why was my neck causing me so much discomfort?

I had no idea, but I was desperate for an answer. Doctors said it was because I'd played football and hockey. But I'd done those sports years earlier and had never developed any pain. I couldn't ever recall hurting my neck. Why had this pain come on so suddenly and severely? I bought the Louise Hay book *Heal Your Body*, in which she talks about neck pain being related to stubbornness and inflexibility. So I started doing yoga, but my neck didn't improve — though I did learn to do a handstand.

Meanwhile, Santa Monica was changing. When I'd moved there from New York in 1993 it was a sleepy little beach town, except in summer. But giant corporations such as Amazon and Yahoo! had started to build offices there as part of the tech movement that turned the area into Silicon Beach. More and more people now worked in the city, and many had moved there, as well. Gardia and I wanted to start a family, and we looked for a place we could afford away from the crowding and traffic jams. We looked at dozens of homes and found nothing we liked. It seemed that each home was either in a densely populated area or in the middle of nowhere. Once, we were looking at a home on an isolated hilltop in the Santa Monica Mountains when a bunch of guys on dirt bikes showed up for a motocross event next door. One thing was consistent, though: No matter where we searched, the prices were staggering.

One day, I saw a picture of an adorable Victorian home in the *Los Angeles Times* real estate section. The ad said *private and quiet*, which had become magical words to us. The home was in Malibu and had a slight ocean view. I'd recently learned to surf, and living close to the beach was a dream of mine, but the idea seemed so unrealistic that we hadn't bothered to look at any beach communities. Sure enough, the price — more than $800k — was far beyond our means. Still, it couldn't hurt to look.

Gardia and I drove up the Pacific Coast Highway as the sun set into the ocean. When we turned off the PCH and wound our way into the neighborhood, it looked like a slightly more rural version of the Pennsylvania farmland-turned-suburbs in which I'd grown up. The Victorian was painted yellow and had balconies and porches with white-picket railings perched on almost every face. It sat in the base of a small arroyo, with steep hillsides covered with flowers and scrub, creating a buffer on either side. We could barely see any other homes. With the car windows down, we heard nothing but crickets and the rhythmic crashing of waves. We both fell instantly in love with the home; Gardia because of its style, me because of its proximity to the surf.

But how could we afford such a paradise?

I began to work harder, devoting all my time to doing research. Gardia took care of everything else, freeing me to maximize my time on the phone. I took our savings and put them in risky stocks, a foolish thing to do. My father would have berated me for the move. I hoped the market would go up and that the house wouldn't sell before we could put in an offer. For the only time in my investing career the market went up exactly when I needed it to, giving us just enough for a down payment.

Fortunately for us, the house had been languishing on the market and the couple who owned it were under pressure to sell because they'd split up. We were able to purchase the house for far below the asking price, though the number still scared the crap out of me. I had only one good year of making any real money as a businessman, but lenders were giving money away at that time, and somehow they approved us.

We moved to Malibu in April 2000 after spending every dime we had on the down payment. We had to talk friends into helping us move since we couldn't afford to pay a moving company.

I planned to continue acting when we moved to Malibu, but I'd under-estimated the drive time to auditions, often ninety minutes each way. I calculated how much being away for half the day was costing me in terms of ruse income and cringed. I did land a role on two episodes of *NYPD Blue*, not realizing it would be the last TV job I would ever do. Shortly after, my agency dropped me. For the first time in more than a decade I had no representation. I made a few token attempts to get a new agent and kick-start my career, but no one was interested. It turned out I wasn't, either, for right as my acting career died something unexpected happened.

My neck pain went away. Practically overnight.

So did my chiropractor expenditures. Free from neck issues, I began to surf regularly. Going into the ocean every day was like being baptized anew.

I worked hard to accept that the end of my acting career needn't be filled with regret. Disappointment, perhaps, but not regret. I'd gone far further than most who entered the business. And I'd earned enough that when I reached retirement age at sixty-five I'd have a lifetime pension from the Screen Actors Guild. Not many actors could say that.

$ $ $

I turned my attention to growing my intelligence business.

In December, Peter McBee flew Gardia and me to New York and London — *first class* — to meet his team. He put us up in the finest hotels, took us to the best restaurants, even invited us to his company's Christmas party at the Ritz London, one of the most luxurious hotels in the world. The acting world might not be interested in what I had to offer, but Peter certainly was. He was the first executive recruiter to acknowledge the value of my intelligence work. With Leona, I felt like an expense, but with Peter I felt like a partner.

Now that I had a mortgage, I no longer cared about legal or moral implications. I figured if I got in and out of each call efficiently, the odds of any firm coming after me were slim. I also burnished a resentment toward my Penn classmates who had gotten MBAs from Wharton and other top-tier business schools and bragged about their millions of dollars in salaries and in some cases tens of millions in year-end bonuses. After how hard I'd tried to make it as an actor, I felt like I deserved a piece of that pie. Exclusively targeting executives making such ridiculous money felt like poetic justice.

Wall Street assistants were paid by the hour and left the second the clock struck five. After that, most executives answered their own phones. You'd think they'd be tougher to squeeze for information, but I found them to be far easier marks than their assistants.

"Jim Cassel," one executive answered. Wall Street guys didn't go in much for greetings or small talk when they answered the phone.

"Hey, Jim, it's Tom Chirico in Tax," I said, using the real name of the tax department head. "One of the partners from Price Waterhouse was in here this week. As you know, they do the audit for us. They've got tickets for the Knicks and the Rangers and have some openings for upcoming games. You guys in Institutional Sales have been killing it, so I figured you deserved first crack. You into it?"

"It's a suite, right? With booze and food?"

As if the free tickets weren't enough.

"Come on," I said. "It's a luxury suite."

"Hell, yeah! What games?"

"I'm not sure yet. I've got to put together a list first to send to them. Read me the roster of the people on your desk."

Jim told me the names of his team members.

"Anyone else? Don't be shy. The more names you give, the more tickets I can get."

"You want the traders, too?"

"Sure, why not? The more the merrier."

Jim read me the names of the traders, the sales traders, the research department, and the junior analysts. He would've given me the names of the janitorial staff had I asked.

"Perfect," I said. "I'll be in touch with dates."

I felt a twinge of guilt but reminded myself that the guy on the other end was raking in an unconscionable amount of money, as were most of the names he'd given me.

They could pay for their own damn tickets.

CHAPTER FIFTEEN

Hard Bark

In November 2000, my father underwent experimental heart surgery at the world-renowned Cleveland Clinic. I flew out and met my parents at the hospital so I could see my dad off into surgery, pushing his wheelchair until they would let me push no farther.

"You came all this way to see me," he said for the third or fourth time. I was gratified that he seemed touched, yet some part of me was hurt that he was so shocked I'd shown up for him. The tremors of my abandonment were still reverberating.

"Of course," I said. "You're my dad."

Wearing a standard-issue hospital gown, he looked older than his fifty-nine years. His whiskers were white, his hair pretty much gone. Now that he worked at home day-trading stocks, he no longer had to keep up his appearance. The elaborate comb-over hairstyle he'd had my mother do each morning for decades existed now only in my memory.

"It's just of all the kids, you're the last one I would've expected."

I nodded but didn't say anything, thinking he wished my sister or brother had come. My father thought of my sister as the kind one, my brother as the comedian. I wanted to do something sweet or say something funny, but showing up was as far as I could take it. My years paying my way through college and then supporting myself as an actor had made me tough, but they had also made me resentful toward him. My father used to say "there's some hard bark on this tree" when he would describe himself. It was a point of pride, a survivor's hard-earned self-reliance. Of all his children, it turned out that I was the one most like him. Same family tree, same hard bark.

After the orderlies took him off, my mother didn't want me to wait with her. As a registered nurse, she must have known that my lack of patience during the all-day surgery would drive her crazy. The only thing I could think to do was pray in my version of church: I went to the Rock & Roll Hall of Fame.

It was a weekday, so the museum was nearly empty, though a band was setting up in the main lobby. I spent the first hour or so listening to snippets from many of the hall's *500 Songs That Shaped Rock and Roll*. I'd pick one song from the screen then seconds later see something else I had to hear — the Kinks' "A Well Respected Man," Elvis Presley's "Suspicious Minds," Roxy Music's "Love Is the Drug" — and click over.

I easily could have spent the entire day listening to songs but decided to check out the rest of the museum. The small U2 exhibit was fine enough, but it was the John Lennon installation that got my attention. Billed as the largest collection of Lennon artifacts ever assembled, the exhibit traced the entirety of his life. I read his school report card. I studied his guitars, stage outfits, and handwritten lyrics. I saw the glasses, speckled with blood, that he'd been wearing when he was shot.

I walked through the memorabilia, no longer thinking of my father's potential death on an operating table but of Lennon's genius, and what a loss Lennon's murder had been. Weirdly, I heard ringing. I tried to ignore it, but it wouldn't stop. I followed the sound to a white phone sitting on a white table. There was a sign that said if the phone is ringing, Yoko Ono is on the line. I figured it was a recording from her, since most of the items on display had come from her estate.

I wasn't in the mood but picked it up anyway. "Hello?"

"Hi, this is Yoko Ono." It was a woman's voice with a thick Japanese accent. "What's your name?"

"Uh, Robert."

"Thanks for coming to see the exhibit. Are you enjoying it?"

"Yeah," I said, thinking that the quality of the recording wasn't very good. I was having trouble understanding her. Then the band I'd seen setting up earlier began to play in the main hall.

"What's that sound?" the voice asked.

I blinked. Wait a minute. She could *hear the music*? Holy shit. It was really Yoko. The most reviled girlfriend in rock history, though Courtney Love nearly dethroned her.

"It's, uh, it's a band downstairs!" I had to yell since the music was shaking the building. "I guess they're practicing for some event."

Just as quickly the band stopped. They were doing a sound check.

"Oh, that's better," Yoko said. "What do you do?"

"Well, I used to be an actor." What was I going to say? That I was a *corporate spy*? When I'd finally told my father the particulars of the ruse a few years earlier, he'd become worried. He pressured me to be honest on the phone, which was disingenuous at best coming from a car salesman. I explained that there was no way a firm would willingly give up the intelligence my clients wanted, that I had to lie to get it. Most of my friends believed I was an executive recruiter, which is what I told people whenever they asked. If I was at a party and had had a drink or two, I might say I did corporate intelligence. If I was then asked what that meant, I'd say, "I'd tell you but then I'd have to kill you." My father didn't think any of it was particularly funny.

"What kind of actor?" Yoko asked.

"The burned-out kind," I said without thinking, but as soon as the words were out of my mouth I knew they were true. I remembered how happy I'd been to star in the two Joyce Carol Oates plays, how proud I'd been to be part of the cast that won a Drama-Logue Award for *The Pink Triangle*. But those productions were ten years in my rearview.

"That happened to John, too."

"Excuse me?" I asked, astonished that she'd just casually implied that John Freakin' Lennon and I could have anything in common.

"That's why he wrote 'Watching the Wheels.' He'd lost his love for making music. Just like you have with acting."

I'd grown up listening to the *Double Fantasy* album and knew the lyrics by heart. Was Yoko telling me to let acting go the way John had done with music? Or was she telling me that I should hang in there until I had my version of a triple platinum album?

The band started playing again. Yoko said something I couldn't make out.

"I'm sorry," I said. "What was that?" I stuck my finger in my ear to better hear the career advice she seemed to be offering, perhaps the same advice she'd given John. "I'm sorry, Yoko, you have to speak up."

She mumbled something again.

"Yoko, I can't hear a word you're saying. Please speak up."

She seemed to get quieter as the music got louder.

"Yoko, speak up," I hollered, but it was no use. The band had made it impossible for us to have a conversation. So I hung up.

When I did, I heard gasps. I looked up and found myself surrounded by everyone in the museum that day.

"How could you hang up on Yoko Ono?" one woman asked.

Later, I was told people had come running when they heard the phone ringing. The staff had bolted out of their offices to hear our exchange. The museum had only been open for five years, and Yoko had been one of the ribbon cutters at the dedication. She was the one who'd insisted on the installation of the special white phone so that she could check in with visitors.

My phone call was only the second time she'd done so.

$$ \$ \, \$ \, \$ $$

Two hours later, I got a call that my father was coming out of surgery. At the ICU he was allowed one visitor, so my mother stepped out. There was an insane amount of equipment surrounding my unconscious father, most of it beeping or chirping. A nurse was moving from patient to patient. I walked to his bedside and stood there in shock. I'd been so happy to get the news that the surgery was a success I hadn't considered the toll it would take on him. I stared at the monitors and studied the constantly changing numbers. Were they good? Was lower better? Or higher? Unlike my nurse mother, who could have translated, I knew nothing of medicine. I only knew I was petrified to lose him.

"Are you Robert? The actor?" a nurse asked, suddenly beside me. She was young and attractive, in her early thirties. My mother, a chatty Cathy, had undoubtedly filled her in.

"Yeah," I said. She beamed up at me as if I were standing on the red carpet. I kept expecting her to introduce herself, but she didn't. She just kept smiling. Finally, she pointed at my father.

"He's gonna make it. He's been talking about you, about his kids."

This seemed unlikely, but as if on cue, my father started mumbling, and at a surprising volume considering his condition. "Robert, he's my oldest . . . Susan is my daughter . . . David's the baby."

The rest was incoherent. But it was about us. As close to death as he could get, and all he talked about was his children.

Maybe that bark was softer than it looked.

$$\$ \ \$ \ \$$

When I was young, my father didn't have much time for frivolousness. The one fun activity we engaged in together was Ping-Pong, which had held totemic value in his life from a young age. When they were teenagers in the 1950s, my dad and my uncle Jack had a table in the basement of their home in Philly. I doubt their father, JK, had bought it for them, though it's easy for me to imagine Bob and Jack begging him for the money during one of their periodic Sunday-afternoon get-togethers. I'm sure JK wouldn't have approved of his sons wasting time playing any game, let alone one as obscure as Ping-Pong. But this was the game Bob and Jack played together, for hours, while bad-mouthing their father, turning it into a family tradition when all other family traditions had been stolen from them.

That same table made its way to my mom and dad's first house. It served as their dining room table for years, until they were able to afford a real one. My mother would throw three or four tablecloths over the thing so that the green from the table's surface wouldn't show through — she didn't want guests to realize they were eating her home-cooked Christmas dinner on wedding china atop a raggedy Ping-Pong table. Later, while my mother was in labor with me, my father was down the hall in the lounge defeating every doctor at the hospital on the house Ping-Pong table.

When I was growing up, both my dad and my uncle Jack had tables in their basements. Since Jack lived two doors down and he and my dad spent so much time together, I played him nearly as much as I played my dad. Jack was a power hitter who used lots of spin, so beating him required patience. My father was a defensive player, which forced me to learn to attack. Jack had a dominant forehand, my dad a dominant backhand. Playing them regularly enabled me to incorporate the best from each of their games.

Because I was the oldest child, it was often just the three of us in the basement, so I got to listen as they told unadulterated stories from their lives. Indeed, the only time I ever learned anything about them was while playing Ping-Pong, which is unique in that conversations can go on while playing, or at least while warming up. I learned that at sixty-nine, my grandfather had a twenty-one-year-old girlfriend, and when he broke up with her she committed suicide by ramming her car (a loaner from his dealership!) into a brick wall. I often wanted to ask the men questions, but I was afraid to break the spell of their brotherly banter. It was like a tricky ruse call, where one wrong word meant getting hung up on, so for the most part I kept my mouth shut.

Whenever I got close to beating my father, he'd find a way to win. I must have lost to him dozens of times when I should've won. I'd already beaten my uncle by the time I was ten or eleven — as a power player, when Jack was on he was unbeatable, but when he was off I was able to take advantage. As a defensive player, my father wasn't going to give away a game. I had to beat him. When I finally did at age fourteen, it came as a shock to me. I felt such joy as I tore up the stairs to tell my mother that I'd beaten the "King of Pong."

Over the years I became a tournament-level player, and though he and I continued to play, eventually he couldn't beat me anymore even on his best days. That didn't stop him from trying. A friend organized a tournament at my wedding, and when I defeated my father in the semifinals he demanded an immediate rematch. After he lost again, he still wanted another shot. I think it's a fair assumption that he would have been fine delaying the ceremony if it meant potentially reclaiming the crown, no matter how many games it took. He just couldn't let it go. And on some level I didn't want him to. It would have meant the end of something meaningful between us. I admired and appreciated that he never wanted to put the paddle down. After all, I was as stubborn as he was.

In July 2002, I got a call from my uncle Jack. My father had gotten sick very suddenly, a serious infection that was attacking his sixty-two-year-old heart. I needed to fly back to Philly immediately. For two weeks, Jack and I visited my father in the hospital every day, hoping for a miracle, as the engine inside him kicked and sputtered. It was long enough for me to accept the inevitable, slowly and painfully.

At my final acting job, someone on set had handed me an *NYPD Blue* baseball cap as a parting gift. I was so over the business I never even wore it. Instead, I gave it to my father. And he wore the crap out of that hat. It seemed every picture I saw of him, he was wearing it. On the golf course. On the tennis court. At cocktail parties. Somehow, at the end of my career — and the end of his life — my father had become my biggest booster. It brought us closer than we'd ever been. We both understood what it was like to have a taste of the life we wanted — him working every day with his son at the dealership, me becoming a successful actor — only to have it slip away. In a sense, the hat became a representation of the letter I had always wanted to receive from him, a symbol of his acceptance of me, of my talents, of the choices I'd made. My uncle and I played Ping-Pong once during those last days, and he told me that he once had to tell my father to stop bragging to his friends about my TV jobs because they were sick of hearing about it. I hadn't known.

That Ping-Pong game is the only good memory I have of that time.

At the funeral home days after my father's death, we were all given a last chance to say good-bye. I brought my father's Ping-Pong paddle, on which I had inscribed KING OF PONG along the handle. It felt so light to me, as if the paddle, too, after so much vibrant life, had lost something vital. I had planned to put it in his casket, but at the end I couldn't do it. Instead, I asked my uncle to do the honors. I felt some shame that I lacked the courage to do it myself, but in a way there was no one more perfect, for it was originally their bond, their tradition before they had made it mine, too.

Jack nodded solemnly and took it to my father as if it were a sacred task. I watched him set the paddle down inside. And let it go.

CHAPTER SIXTEEN

The Compliance Ploy

Two months after my father died, in September 2002, my son, Davis, was born. Leona sent a baby blanket with his name embroidered on it and called to congratulate me. She told me she was dating a man she was going to marry. While her announcement didn't quite compare to the birth of my son, I couldn't have been happier that she'd found love so late in life.

I started a college fund for Davis that week. I wasn't going to put him through what I'd gone through to pay for college, working a full-time job yet still graduating with huge amounts of debt. I didn't want him to be unable to go out for pizza because he was broke. And I wanted him to be free to pursue a career as an artist (or anything he wanted) without having to worry about how he would pay his rent.

By this point the ruse was providing a powerful stream of revenue. From 2002 to 2008, my annual income increased rapidly—from $204,000 to $352,000 to $498,000 to $916,000 to well over $1 million to, eventually, nearly $2 million. Clients were so desperate for the non-public intelligence we provided that they kept offering more and more money.

With a college fund to feed, a mortgage to pay, and my dream of making a real living as an actor a thing of the past, it was a relief to be earning more money than I ever dreamed rusing would bring in. Of course, I needed something to worry about, and my mind latched on to the fate of my high school classmate Valerie Plame, the CIA agent who was involuntarily retired after operatives in the George W. Bush administration outed her as a CIA spy to get back at her husband in 2003. The way I saw it, two spies had graduated from the same Philly high school together, and when her story made headlines, it hit close to home.

Too close.

A major difference between her and me, of course, was that Valerie was patriotically spying for her country, whereas I was illegally stealing secrets to provide myself and my family a better lifestyle. If her career and personal life could be upended so thoroughly, what the hell would happen to me if I got caught? At a minimum there would be no more money. More likely, I'd go to jail for a significant portion of the rest of my life. Valerie did get the satisfaction of publishing a bestselling memoir, *Fair Game*, in 2007, but I was under deep cover.

The same year Valerie got exposed, 2003, LinkedIn was invented, though the employment-oriented service would not take off until after the crash of 2008. In 2006, LinkedIn had five million users. By 2009, fifty million. (Today, it's half a billion.) The developers of LinkedIn recognized that there was huge money to be made if corporations had a central source for locating talent, but before then hiring RK Research was (nearly) the only way to go. For global executive search firms such as Korn Ferry (the largest search firm in the world as well as a publicly traded company), Russell Reynolds Associates, Spencer Stuart, and many others, I *was* LinkedIn.

Once, I turned down a new client because we didn't have time to handle the project.

"Suppose I pay you double," he said.

I was confused. "Double what?"

"Your fee."

"Uh, wow, look, I'd like to but —"

"I'll FedEx you a check for the entire project in advance."

The next morning there was a check for $80,000 at my door.

I took the project.

There was such demand for top Wall Street talent that multiple clients often tasked us with extracting the exact same research, enabling me to make double or even triple for one job. It had never occurred to me that I could make this kind of money. My father wouldn't have been surprised.

He always said I would make millions. It just wasn't in the field I had been hoping for. In a way, it put me in the same league as the Wall Street executives I was helping shuffle around the board, even though they were making exponentially more.

Over the years, the hottest sectors to research were those that were booming usually because of political maneuvering. When I started for Leona in the late 1980s we researched defense industry titans like Lockheed and TRW because President Reagan had increased military spending.

In 2005, we started getting a ton of work in the financial derivatives space. I didn't even know what a derivative was, not that it mattered. All I needed were a few buzzwords to throw around to establish credibility and to ensure that I was researching the right area.

And the derivatives groups inside the Wall Street firms weren't hard to find.

They were the ones locked down so tight that getting information out of them was nearly impossible. Most infamous were the collateralized debt obligation (CDO) groups. Lenders were making loans of questionable quality to American homeowners, then Wall Street was packaging these loans into bonds, repackaging the bonds into CDOs, selling them to investors around the world, but often holding on to some of them for their own portfolios. They were also selling insurance on these CDOs, called credit default swaps (CDS). Names for the top people in CDS groups were the *second* most requested for me to research. Many of the names during these years ended up as main characters in Michael Lewis's bestselling 2010 book, *The Big Short: Inside the Doomsday Machine*. Lewis himself would've been on my research back in the early Leona days when he was an analyst at Salomon Brothers, an experience that inspired the book that made him famous, *Liar's Poker*. Not that we cared about junior analysts like him. They were the inevitable detritus obtained as we trawled for directors and managing directors, the big fish of Wall Street.

Greg Lippmann of Deutsche Bank, whom Lewis describes as "Patient Zero," the individual most responsible for recognizing the impending collapse of the subprime housing market, was on my research dozens of times. (Ryan Gosling's character in the *Big Short* movie, Jared Vennett, is based on Lippmann.) Morgan Stanley bond trader Howard Hubler, along with an eight-person team, made his firm $1 billion in 2006. My research has every one of those eight names. How much was it worth for Morgan Stanley's competitors to know those names?

A significant fraction of $1 billion.

But getting them was a major challenge. Many times when calling Lippmann, Hubler, and others in the CDO and CDS groups, the individual on the other end of the phone would laugh out loud at whatever ploy I was using and hang up without even bothering to tell me I wasn't who I said I was.

I began to worry that doing the job might no longer be possible. Already firms were using caller ID to identify outside calls. I could block caller ID, but then my number would come up as anonymous. Over and over, I was grilled. If I was a real person *inside* the firm, why was I calling from an anonymous number? For a while, I skirted the issue by getting transferred from an internal number to the area I desired. But firms caught on and eliminated that flaw in their system. I was increasingly stumped and frustrated.

Thank God for the intranet.

As the internet developed, so did company's internal directories, which they called their intranet. Increasingly, firms digitized their organizational charts and put them on their intranet. I discovered that as long as an individual had access to this internal treasure trove, which most employees did, they could tell me anything I wanted to know. Many of these firms had become enormous over the years as they snatched up smaller firms via leveraged buyouts or other M&A strategies. The beautiful thing was, as these firms grew, expanding until they had offices all over the country and the world, all it took was finding *one* person willing to access the intranet and tell me what I wanted to know. They could be anywhere. They often were.

This didn't solve the issue of my number showing up as an outside call. I needed to develop a ploy that would account for this. I needed a reason that an executive would be off-site and yet need critical information from the firm's intranet. Who would need such information? Why would they be off-site? Where would they be?

Leave it to the US government to solve all of my problems.

$ $ $

As the stock market rose and Wall Street, due to its sheer size, posed a bigger risk to the overall economy, there was a corresponding growth of financial institutions' compliance departments. Regulations had been put in place by an alphabet soup of governmental agencies — SEC, FDIC, FINRA — that firms were required to follow or suffer significant penalties, not to mention bad press. Compliance departments were housed within firms' legal groups under the auspices of their top-dog lawyer, the general counsel. I decided to try a new approach.

"Hey, it's Tom O'Brien in Compliance," I began when a male assistant answered my call. Even though I was now exclusively using real names, I still tried to find Irish ones. Most times I'd get some sort of pleasantry back. I hadn't asked for anything, so the person on the other end had no reason to be suspicious — yet.

"Hi, Tom, how's it going?"

"How good could it be? I'm off-site in Washington, meeting with the US regulators. When they say jump, I say how high." I manufactured a laugh.

If I got one back, I knew I was in good shape. But this time I got silence.

"How can I help you?" The assistant was all business.

"I'm filling out some compliance docs, and I need to list your boss on one. I just need his exact current title and we're done."

"Why don't you look it up on our system?" he said.

I could practically hear him sneering.

"Because I'm off-site, at the regulators' office."

"Which regulators?"

"Seems like all of them are here breathing down our necks. Good thing we only have to do this once every three years." I wanted to give the guy incentive to answer my questions, since he theoretically wouldn't have to hear from me again for years.

"He's the EVP of Fixed Income Trading," the assistant said, finally giving me the title. The guy was difficult, but he hadn't busted me or hung up, so I persevered.

"Perfect. That's what we had, but it never hurts to be sure in Compliance." I forced another laugh and still got nothing in return. "Oh, one last thing. I need to list his direct reports and we're finished."

"All of them?" The assistant acted as if the list was pages and pages long when, on average, most executives had between five and fifteen reports.

"Well, the seven or eight or so who report directly to him. For these, I don't need titles." I tried to make it easy for the assistant, who was becoming more truculent as the call went on.

"I'm not supposed to be giving this information over the phone," he said. "I looked you up, but as a Compliance person you should know that."

As we talked, I searched online for the name of the firm's global head of fixed income. It was highly likely the EVP whose teams I was hunting reported to that global head. I found the information just in time.

"Hey, I'm the one who wrote those rules. But when Olivier de Laurier says jump, I say how high." I knew I was repeating the same line I'd used earlier, but I was trying to sell him on the we're-in-this-together concept, that heads of Compliance, just like lowly assistants, gotta serve somebody, too.

"You work for Mr. de Laurier? I thought you said you were in Compliance."

"I am, but these docs are for Mr. de Laurier." I'd guessed right, so I pushed back. If I was from Compliance, the assistant had no choice but to help me. By knowing the name of the global head — the boss of the assistant's boss — I'd established credibility as a "trusted employee." I'd also put him in the difficult position of potentially getting his boss in trouble for not helping me.

"Can I email you the list?" The assistant still wasn't completely sure about me.

"Normally, I'd say yes, but anything I receive while I'm at the regulators I'm required by law to declare. We only want to give them what they've asked us for. Also, I'm inputting the list directly into their system. Let's just zip through this, and we'll be done."

"I'm not even sure it's up to date," he said, continuing to waffle. The call was like pulling teeth. He was doubting everything I said, but he continued to play ball.

"That's okay. The final doc comes to your boss for confirmation. He literally has to sign his name at the bottom."

The assistant read the list, though he hesitated after every other name. When he reached the end, I said, "All we need now are the titles and we're done."

"You said you didn't need titles."

"Whenever anyone is an SVP or higher, the form requires their title. Since your boss is an EVP, I'm assuming he has SVPs reporting to him." I paused. From the assistant's silence I knew I was right. After all, I was an expert in reporting structures. "Not having titles on a compliance document is like going out in the rain with no shoes on," I added with a chuckle.

The assistant gave me the titles, which included the heads of the CDO and CDS groups. *Booyah!* I suspected that as soon as we got off the phone he would call around and discover I wasn't with the company, let alone the compliance department. He was the type of person who normally would have shut me down right away. Yet he'd still given me everything I wanted. *Why?*

Because I was in Compliance.

As I was to learn, individuals working in Compliance were feared by others within the firm. This made even surly assistants hesitant to take a stand. No one wanted to be on the bad side of Compliance, the corporation's version of Orwell's Thought Police. This put me in a strategically powerful position. The flip side was that because almost all compliance officers were lawyers from top schools — Harvard, Columbia, Penn — they were exactly the types that could, and would, come after me. Before these super lawyers had moved to Wall Street to make the big money, most had worked in the public sector doing fraud enforcement for the SEC or the Federal Reserve or some other regulatory or legal entity. Now that I was actively *impersonating* them, they had more than enough incentive, both professional and personal, to bust my ass. They also had the know-how and resources to track me down. Departments with names like Insider Threat Protection, Surveillance Unit, and Financial Crimes Compliance scared the hell out of me. These groups — and many others — were designed to stop people like me from doing exactly what I was doing.

But it was a perpetually tempting gamble. During this time I went so far as to impersonate the CEOs and COOs of some of Wall Street's largest firms. Many of the men I pretended to be were regular talking heads on CNBC, Fox Business, and other news channels. Some were even on presidential commissions and advisory committees. I studied their inflections and the timbre of their voices. None of the men had accents, which was fortunate for me. Indeed, they all pretty much sounded (and looked) the same. Risky as it was, their elevated public status was why I chose them. If people believed I was this person, there was nothing they wouldn't tell me. Indeed, most were blown away that they had the CEO on the phone, like they'd been gifted a rare audience with the king. They fawned, they flattered, they gave it up. More times than I can remember they'd say, "I can't believe I'm actually talking to you." And I wanted to respond: *You're not.*

"Hey, one last thing," I said to the assistant. "I need the traders in the CDO and CDS groups."

I heard him groan, but even he knew it was too late to stop now. Just as I knew, doubts be damned, the same was true of me. Because the compliance ploy turned out to be my most successful ruse ever. I shared it with Pax and Shen, and soon all three of us used it exclusively. Indeed, the only thing that stopped the compliance ploy from working was the financial crisis of 2008, which demolished the economy. By the time the Great Recession was over, the American people had lost $9.8 trillion.

And this corporate spy saw it all coming.

CHAPTER SEVENTEEN

Out of the Lying Pan, Into the Fire

By 2008, with all the money we were making, Gardia and I started looking for a vacation home / investment property. Our plan was to rent out the beach house part time to cover the mortgage, property taxes, and expenses. Beyond that, I thought we might be able to turn a small profit. I'd always wanted a place right on the beach, but prices in Malibu were bonkers. We drove up the coast to look at homes in Oxnard and Ventura, but even in these less expensive beachfront communities the numbers were far beyond what we could afford. At the prices we were seeing, renting out the beach home for the *entire year* wouldn't even cover the mortgage — forget about the taxes and upkeep. Coming from a business family, I knew this was a huge red flag. And yet still the prices of homes went higher and higher — and not just at the beach. Our Victorian was already worth three times what we'd paid for it only eight years earlier. While we'd gotten a good deal, it hadn't been *that* good. Something was seriously screwy.

I felt like I was the only one who knew the country was about to go bust, though of course I wasn't. In *The Big Short*, Lewis introduced the key people who knew, and nearly all of them were on my research. So maybe it's fair to say that I was the only *actor* who suspected the global financial market was about to be destroyed.

Throughout the summer of 2008, clients kept hiring my firm to research the derivatives organizations of major firms, specifically targeting individuals handling CDOs, CDSs, and mortgage-backed securities. We must have done dozens of these projects. Even when the shit started to hit the fan with the collapse of giant mortgage lenders IndyMac and

Countrywide in July, we still had work. Then, on September 15, Lehman Brothers fell — the largest bankruptcy in US history — and the economy collapsed.

The flow of work stopped instantly, like a light switch had been flipped off. I went from having enough research assignments for Pax, Shen, and me to ruse full time to nothing. Over the next few months, I scraped to find whatever projects I could, but all commerce had ceased. Wall Street firms were going belly-up — or being sold before they did. The government bailed out behemoths such as Citigroup and General Motors, since they feared a depression if they let them fail, and for the first time ever the short-term interest rate was lowered to 0 percent. Companies were laying off people en masse. No one was hiring. The talking heads on CNBC were blathering away about what needed to be done to save the world economy before it was too late. One man hollered that it was *already* too late. It was a bloodbath.

My research for the years leading up to the crash had every name in every group at every firm responsible — directly or indirectly — for the gutting of the global economy that resulted in the worst financial crisis since the Great Depression. And I'd actively helped them get better jobs for even more ludicrous amounts of money so they could do even more damage. Whether these areas called themselves Global Structured Solutions or Structured Credit Products or FI Investor Client Management, they were the bloodsuckers who took and took and took until there was nothing more to take. Sometimes the group names were relatively straightforward, like Mortgage-Backed Trading, Securitized Trading, Proprietary Trading, or Distressed Trading, but as 2008 got closer the names became more and more like the type of gobbledygook language Pax used in his transfer agency ploy. There was Bespoke Trading and Exotics Trading and Collateralized Debt Obligation (CDO) Trading. As if those names weren't confusing enough, the groups then combined titles to create Exotics Bespoke Trading or Bespoke Correlation CDO Trading. The group names kept changing, too, as if they were trying to throw snooping regulators off their scent by altering the name of their hideout. Perhaps the complicated names were designed to keep outsiders confused about what the hell these assholes were up to. It certainly worked. Other than the few prescient oddballs profiled in *The Big Short*, no one saw the crash coming.

And not one of the hundreds of people listed on my research suffered a single consequence for ruining the world economy and causing extreme financial hardship for millions of people. Hubler, the guy who'd made Morgan Stanley $1 billion in 2006, also lost $9 billion for investors with the single worst trade in market history. But of course he wasn't punished for it. No one on Wall Street was. No one on my lists went to jail. No one was required to make restitution — or even just pay back their multimillion-dollar bonuses. If anyone ever wanted to go back and see who was actually responsible for the collapse, I may be the only one in the world with the complete roster.

But no one was truly blameless. Homeowners lied about how much they made. Lenders lied about their borrowers' credit. Wall Street firms lied about the quality of the mortgage-backed securities they sold. And the ratings agencies lied about the creditworthiness of these securities.

The truth? The entire financial crisis was the result of one giant ruse.

$ $ $

The housing market implosion wasn't the only nefarious skulduggery of the moment. It was just one destructive aspect of the dark side of the financial world. Bernie Madoff, who architected the biggest Ponzi scheme in American history, had been arrested by the FBI in December for operating an asset management firm that he admitted was "one big lie." In March 2009, he pleaded guilty to a raft of financial crimes that swindled investors out of an astonishing $65 billion. At the same time, Texas-born financier Allen Stanford was in February charged with committing billions in fraud as part of another Ponzi scheme. He surrendered to authorities in June and three years later was convicted and sentenced to 110 years in prison.

Meanwhile, flamboyant Malaysian businessman and fraudster Jho Low was laying the groundwork for the international 1MDB fund fracas that would shake out ten years later with indictments and settlements in multiple countries. As outlined in Tom Wright and Bradley Hope's 2018 book, *Billion Dollar Whale: The Man Who Fooled Wall Street, Hollywood, and the World*, the Low scandal involved Interpol, the Malaysian prime minister, Goldman Sachs, and celebrities such as Kim Kardashian and Leonardo DiCaprio. Low was even one of the primary financiers of — wait for it — *The Wolf of Wall Street*, the Oscar-nominated 2013 crime biopic about Jordan Belfort.

You can't make this shit up.

In January 2009, around the time the US government was bailing out Bank of America, I received a call from a small-time recruiter, Ted, looking for cheap research. Normally, I wouldn't even have returned his call, let alone done any work for him, but my situation was bleak. After all, there were no unemployment checks for business owners, and definitely no federal help for those running shady businesses (though one could be forgiven for suggesting that Bank of America, for example, more than fit that definition). I'd had no income since September. I had a significant mortgage and other bills. We had savings but were beginning to burn through them.

Ted was a throw-shit-up-and-see-what-sticks kind of recruiter, bombarding his clients with hundreds of candidates in the hope that one would be hired. He wasn't even a recruiter on retainer like every one of my past clients had been — top-tier search firms that received a third of their fee in advance. He only got paid if someone he introduced to a firm ended up being hired.

But Ted didn't want me to do new research for him. He wanted to buy my *old* research, since most of the people on my lists were now unemployed. His clients were third-tier firms, most of whom I'd never heard of. They were looking to snatch up top talent laid off from firms like Goldman Sachs or Morgan Stanley for a fraction of their worth.

I sold Ted some of my old work for a measly $800, but it was more than I'd made in months. More important, I got to know Ted, since he kept calling me for more information, which he wanted for next to nothing.

"Why don't I just give it to you?" I joked during one call. I wasn't used to dealing with cheapskate recruiters, but these were unprecedented times.

"I think you should. Better yet, why don't you use your own research and make a hell of a lot more than a couple of hundred bucks?"

"How so?" My ears pricked up at the possibility of making more money. I'd begun to wonder if I'd have to go back to selling cars. Not that anyone in America was buying those, either.

"Work with me," said Ted. "Call and recruit these guys yourself. I'll split fifty–fifty whatever the commission is. And I'll pay you a third of any commissions I get from names you had on the research I bought."

Given my circumstances, that sounded like a generous offer, so I took it. Joining up with Ted wasn't going to preclude me from doing research — not that there was any. It's not as if he had some fancy website like my other search clients and was going to throw my picture up on it. I could even use my real name on the phone, which I'd never done before. I started recruiting — "smiling and dialing" — the next morning.

Here's the thing about being a recruiter: It's harder than you'd think. I was shocked at how difficult and frustrating it was. Even with my major head start of having so many names in my database, just getting someone on the phone was a challenge. Those who still had jobs didn't want to talk to me because my client (in this case, Ted's client) was a fourth-tier Canadian bank looking to take advantage of the reckless-ness of American financial institutions and make inroads into the US market. Most candidates had never heard of the firm — not a good place to start a call when you're trying to convince someone to leave their employer.

The dilemma with calling individuals who were unemployed — and there were many — was that if you told them the name of the firm, they would often just contact it directly to offer their services. We could document that a hiree was "our" candidate and we were due a commission, but as Ted explained, that was an argument you didn't want to have with a client. As a non-retained search firm, we were at the bottom of the barrel. And there were many others like us, waiting in line to get a crack at supplying third- and fourth-tier firms with candidates. If we rocked the boat for one commission, we might not get the opportunity to recruit for that firm again.

This meant that when I did call people who'd been laid off, I couldn't tell them the name of the firm until the day of their interview. This made it difficult to get candidates interested. No matter how desperate people were, they wanted to know what firm they were meeting with. It took a lot of hand-holding to convince individuals, many of whom had held huge jobs at prestigious firms before the crash, that I was legitimate and not wasting their time, at least not intentionally.

I learned that my biggest selling point to get former top-level executives to meet with a bottom-feeding firm was that I lived in Malibu. I'd joke that I must be pretty good at what I did if I had a house near the beach. No one disagreed, though I never made an actual placement in the four months I worked for Ted. Granted, the recruiting process was usually quite long. People didn't make life-changing decisions overnight. Also, because of the crisis, firms were hesitant to hire. Some of the candidates I developed had five or six interviews, and I was shocked that the Canadian firm didn't snap up a single one.

Ted was constantly telling me I was "killing it," despite the fact that I hadn't made a dime. Apparently, he'd hired another recruiter to work on the same project, and the other guy had only had a handful of mediocre candidates while I had more than a dozen who were top-quality. I flashed back to my days working for Leona, when I first realized that our research was the secret weapon that enabled recruiters to excel. But the Canadian company was taking its time hiring, and there wasn't anything I could do about it, no matter how good my research was or how many recruiting calls I made. I was working ridiculously hard — and for free. If Ted's client changed its mind about adding anyone, they would simply cut us — and our candidates — loose.

"Not a fan of working for nothing," I complained to Ted during a call to schedule another round of candidate interviews. Setting these up was a time-consuming process, as I had to sync the candidates' schedules with those of the four or five executives with whom they needed to meet. I had to work around dentist appointments, kids' school events, and tee times. I preferred the old days when I simply obtained the names and got out. I wasn't suited for the patience and hand-holding that recruiting required.

"You gotta hang in there," Ted said. "You're going to get a placement any day."

I'd been telling Gardia the same thing. We had gone six months without income, and I estimated that our savings would last perhaps until

September, which was only a few months away. After that, all bets —
and mortgage payments — were off.

$ $ $

My old client, the Englishman Peter McBee, resurfaced in August 2009
with grandiose plans — as always. This time he wanted to hire me as a
recruiter and bring me "out of the basement" and into the world of high-
end executive search. Peter had been offered an opportunity to create
New York and London offices for one of the largest search firms in Asia,
Global Search, and wanted me to be his right-hand man. He told me the
firm would pay me $200,000 a year to recruit, plus commissions on
placements, as well as buy my research business.

He had me at $200k, which was what I needed to pay my bills. The guy
had arrived just in time, and I wasn't in a position to turn anything away.

The owner of Global Search was Jack MacDonald, an American based
in Hong Kong. Peter told me that Jack was flying to Los Angeles to
meet with me and my wife. I wasn't used to meeting clients. For years,
the only one I'd met was Peter, and that was because he'd forced the issue.
I liked being in my "basement" and feeling like I wasn't a part of the Wall
Street world.

But that was about to change — big time.

Gardia and I met Jack at the Beverly Hills Hotel. Despite my time
working in Hollywood, I'd somehow never been there, though it was one
of the premier spots for meetings among movie industry power players.
I had, of course, more than once imagined myself being interviewed by
the pool about the latest film I'd done. But here I was showing up for a
$400 dinner not to burnish my acting laurels but because I was desperate
for a Wall Street job to save my home.

When we arrived, we were escorted by the hotel staff to one of the
bungalows, where Jack was staying. Gardia, who'd grown up in LA, whispered that the bungalows cost thousands of dollars per night. Richard
Burton and Elizabeth Taylor had honeymooned in one, and Howard
Hughes at one point took over nine of them at once. The valet rang the
doorbell, and another staff member opened the door. Apparently, he was
the butler, for he ushered us into the living room and offered to make us

drinks. Gardia and I didn't want to seem demanding, so we asked for wine, even though the bungalow had an outrageously stocked bar.

As the butler handed us our drinks, a huge man descended a staircase I hadn't noticed. It turned out that Jack's bungalow had *two* floors.

"Welcome, Robert and Gardia," he boomed.

I'm a loud guy, something I've worked to control, but Jack's voice put me to shame. He sounded amplified — perhaps because he was six foot six and weighed more than 250 pounds. He wore what appeared to be a custom-made suit, as well as glasses that were too small for his enormous head. I estimated he was in his midforties, around our age.

"We're so glad to have you on our team," Jack said, shaking our hands. "At Global Search, we're like a family."

That sounded great to me. I'd been nervous about the meeting, since it seemed like an audition to me and the last years of my acting career hadn't gone well in that regard. But Jack acted as if my hiring was a done deal.

The butler brought us three glasses of champagne.

"To RK Research joining the Global Search family," Jack toasted.

Gardia gave me a look. I was the one joining the firm, not my company. Peter had said the acquisition of RK Research was something we'd discuss "down the road." But it appeared Jack considered that a done deal, as well.

He escorted us to the dining room, another room I hadn't noticed. The bungalow was that large. I'd never seen anything like it. Hotel waiters served us dinner. A sommelier asked Jack what wines he wanted for the evening. In my head, I was calculating how much this had to cost. Clearly, the Great Recession had not dented the pocketbook or spending habits of Jack MacDonald.

During dinner, he shared his plans for our future.

"Peter is going to run the Atlantic division, which will consist of our offices in London, New York, and Los Angeles."

I wanted to ask, *What Los Angeles office?* I knew Global Search didn't have one — but I kept my mouth shut, which is something I'd learned to do on the phone — and from reading David Mamet plays. *Never open your mouth until you know what the shot is.*

"You'll run the western half of the US and be Peter's number two. Because he's British, I'm going to have him spend more time in London than in New York, so I'll need you in New York a lot. Let me know what hotel you prefer. I'll put you up wherever you like. Of course, Gardia, you are welcome to join him."

"That's kind of you, but I have our son to take care of," Gardia said. "And someone has to mind the store while Robert is away."

Peter and Jack believed we had a business to sell, so Gardia and I did our best to promote that image. They knew we had no real office, but I was pretty sure they thought we had actual employees rather than outside contractors — and that we had more than two of them.

"Well, I'm not going to take no for an answer when Robert comes to our headquarters in Hong Kong. That's a trip I want you both to make. First class."

Gardia smiled the widest smile I'd seen in a long time, which brought me joy as well as a touch of shame, since I hadn't been pulling my weight as the breadwinner lately. "I'd love that," she said. "Thank you."

"Peter thinks the future of search is in corporate intelligence," said Jack. "RK Research is going to be our secret weapon. We're going to create a database of every piece of your intelligence and —" Jack stopped himself. "I'm talking too much shop. It's Saturday night, after all." He turned to Gardia. "Tell me about your career in the music business."

I listened as my wife told stories of working with rock bands and for Madonna at Maverick Records. She told Jack about how she'd stepped on the Queen of Pop's toes once at a music event — on her first day at the job, no less — and he laughed hysterically as she imitated the screams. I marveled as course after course of gourmet food was served, especially since Gardia and I had stopped going out to dinner. For months we'd been worried about surviving, going over every budget item for ways we could save money, though the cuts we made would never amount to enough to cover the shortfall in our mortgage. And here was this boisterous corporate titan, come out of nowhere to offer us an instant reprieve. It was baffling and nerve racking as much as it was a relief.

I wasn't keen about the new career path in front of me, but what choice did I have? I had to support my wife and son. I had to hold on to our house. I had no other decent options.

I knew what my father would say.

So I had to do what I had to do.

$ $ $

The following month, I was drifting down over Manhattan while sipping a Tanqueray and tonic in Virgin business class. Stepping out into the early-fall crispness at Kennedy airport, I saw that a driver awaited me, ROBERT KERBECK sign in hand. As he drove me to the W Hotel in Midtown, I felt a mix of apprehension and depression. If I'd been arriving for a press junket for my latest film, I would have been over the moon. Instead, I was beginning work in a job that seemed one rung above car salesman. I quickly dropped my stuff in the room so I could make it over to the Global Search office before five o'clock. Peter wanted to have an introductory meeting of his new team then take everyone to an expensive dinner.

The office was located in a skyscraper around the corner from Rockefeller Center and Radio City Music Hall. I took the elevator to the eleventh floor and strode as purposefully as I could into the office, which was larger than I'd expected. I'd been told Global Search had a token presence in New York, yet the office was spacious and ornate, with tapestries on the walls protected behind glass. They looked antique to my untrained eye — as well as valuable.

"Hi, Robert, I'm Sheryl," the receptionist said in a thick New York accent. I was a bit surprised she identified me so quickly since Peter told me he'd made a number of new hires.

"I saw your picture," she added, somewhat sheepishly, by way of explanation.

"I'm sorry? What picture?"

"They told me not to say anything, but I think it's amazing," she said, blinking up at me as if there were bright lights in her eyes. "I love *Star Trek*. I can't believe you were on that show!"

Less than a minute into my new career as an executive recruiter and the remains of my acting career were already getting in the way. There were three types of *Star Trek* collectible cards: common, uncommon, and rare. Paramount Pictures had made one that featured my *Deep Space Nine* character, Borad, a Cardassian warrior. It was classified as rare, but somehow someone in this office had secured one. At times I'd thought it cool, but now it was mostly embarrassing. I'd played lead roles in plays at some of the most respected regional theaters in the country, and yet I'd become most well known for playing an alien on a *Star Trek* spin-off.

"What was it like? What was your favorite thing?"

I wanted to say that it was how much I got paid, since getting in and out of the Cardassian makeup took hours. Working on *Deep Space Nine* was the most overtime I'd ever received, which thanks to the Screen Actors Guild added up fast. But I got the sense from Sheryl's Disneyland-wide eyes that she was a genuine Trekkie. I didn't want to be cavalier about it. I wanted to get off on the right foot with everyone. This was my first true corporate job. So I scrambled to come up with a cool — but short — anecdote.

"Probably when I sat in the makeup chair next to Commander Riker."

I thought she was going to swoon right out of her ergonomic desk chair. "Oh my God, you worked with Riker! He was my favorite on *Next Generation*. I didn't know he was on *Deep Space Nine*, too. What was he doing there?"

Before I was forced to explain the entire plot of my episode, Peter rushed in to rescue me. He was wearing a handsome gray suit, bright white shirt, and gleaming purple tie.

"Ahh, it's the Brad Pitt of the search world!"

Of all the actors in the world, how had Peter chosen the one that represented the greatest what-if moment of my professional life? Peter had no way of knowing I'd gone down to the wire for the Pitt role in *Thelma & Louise*. And it wasn't like I even *resembled* Brad beyond falling under the same broad tall-handsome-actor rubric. So why, minutes into my new job, a job I didn't even want and saw as the miserable consolation prize to my dashed dream, was I being brutally reminded of how close I'd come to launching a major film career? It felt like a dark omen.

"Come on," Peter said. "Let me give you the tour of Global Search. We're not going to be here long. We'll outgrow this space before you know it. You'll see."

Peter wasn't a good-looking man, but he was fit and charismatic. He enthusiastically showed me the conference room and an adjoining waiting room for candidates and clients. He took me into the bullpen, a series of desks in the middle of the space where people were working jammed in next to one another. I hadn't considered the possibility of not having my own office. It wasn't an ego issue, it was that I was loud on the phone. I'd worked alone in the privacy of bedrooms and basements and surf shacks for years. How was I going to handle being so close to others? I wouldn't mind them hearing me recruiting, but I was still going to need to do research on occasion. What would happen if they heard me? I didn't want anyone to steal my techniques — or turn me in.

This wasn't a small concern. Gardia and I were still in discussions to sell our business to Global Search. I didn't want them to know *exactly* what we did until the ink was dry, though I was sure Peter knew the lengths we often went in order to obtain the intelligence we did. Maintaining the mystery of RK Research worked to our advantage and made a bigger payout much more likely.

Peter introduced me to his new team, which he referred to as the Magnificent Search Seven. Besides Peter and myself, there were three other men and two women. Martin was a Canadian kid from Toronto with a perennial five-o'clock shadow that made him appear older than his twenty-five years. He was in charge of our database and social media, which was how we were going to differentiate ourselves from the much larger US search firms. Martin would code all of the intelligence from RK Research so it was searchable by any detail. He'd also mine social media for trends, a tactic that was practically brand new at the time. Myspace and Facebook were fighting for supremacy with hundreds of millions of users apiece, and YouTube and Twitter, each a few years old, showed accelerating engagement. Martin said no search firm was utilizing trending, though I wasn't sure how he would know that.

After Martin loaded my research into the Global Search system, Lori Berman would take over. She was a whiz with spreadsheets and word processing applications. She put together giant PowerPoint documents that we called decks since they ended up being around fifty pages — the size of a deck of cards. They were filled with slides of graphs and charts tailored to each particular client, and at the end there were multiple samples of my corporate intelligence.

The other three people were recruiters like myself, though of course none of them also did research. Phil was a tall guy from the Bronx responsible for handling the East. Donny was a wiry former NFL wide receiver living in Kansas City, so he was in charge of the Midwest. Beata was based in London and would handle the calling of European candidates. All three were in their mid- to late thirties.

We signed the employment contracts placed at our workstations. I didn't study mine in depth since I had no choice but to take the job. Peter then led us to the conference room.

I realized I'd never sat around a conference table in my life. When I'd graduated from Penn during the height of the Reagan years, it seemed everyone wanted to work on Wall Street except for me. At the same time, I could have made millions working for my father in the car business, and eventually been my own boss, but I'd turned that down, too. Despite every effort to live a different kind of life, the ruse had led me here. Somehow I'd circled back to having the kind of life I never wanted — and, as I was about to find out, working with people I despised.

CHAPTER EIGHTEEN

The Brad Pitt of the Search World

As recruiters, Phil, Donny, Beata, and I were expected to call candidates on behalf of our clients — except we had no clients. First, we needed to win business. Since we were a small firm, Peter wanted all of us in New York to attend pitch meetings to make our firm appear larger than it was, which enabled me to get to know the others.

Donny was a sweetheart but a bit slow. As a former football player he could follow a play if you drew it up for him, but left on his own, well, he'd run in circles. Phil was constantly calling people "pikers," a term I hadn't heard before. I googled it and discovered that a piker was a small-time, trashy person not to be trusted, which defined Phil's character perfectly. Beata was from the former East Germany and embodied characteristics of those who'd grown up in a communist state. She was instantly jealous of anyone's success, as if she was going to be left out of the team's rewards.

Most of the clients we were pitching were international conglomerates with offices around the globe. Though we had loosely defined territories, we were a small group. Whatever projects we won would be handled by all of us. After all, it didn't really matter where a recruiter lived. But Beata struggled with that concept. At our introductory dinner, held at an insanely expensive Greek restaurant near Columbus Circle, she freaked out when she learned I could speak German.

"He's not going to be calling Germany, that's my territory," she said as a flaming cheese appetizer called saganaki was fried tableside.

Far from tamping down the tension, Peter seemed to encourage it. "Perhaps his German is better than yours. He went to an Ivy League school."

Beata scowled at me and said something in German that I didn't understand.

"See, he has no idea what I said."

"Most Germans speak English," Peter said with a chortle. He waved over the waiter and ordered another two bottles of the wine. "Plus, who wouldn't want to speak with the Brad Pitt of the search world?"

Peter hadn't once called me by my name, which was causing tension. The others at the firm had spent their lives as recruiters. Now they were competing with someone who'd been on *Melrose Place*. The drama at the table wasn't dissimilar to the plotted tension of the TV episodes I'd starred in. Peter had thrown some young recruiters together (okay, we weren't that young), and he was willing to let us go at one another for the big money. Any minute now, someone was going to get thrown in the pool.

"What's the word for *piker* in German?" Phil asked me.

I looked toward Beata to win favor by deferring to her, but I also had no idea. She ignored me.

"Come on, Borad," Phil continued, using the name of my *Star Trek* character. "You're supposed to be the genius here."

I had no idea why Phil thought this. I had less recruiting experience than any of them. "I don't know, maybe —"

"Dummkopf," Beata said, glaring at me.

Donny sat there smiling, the only one in our group somewhat sober. The rest of us were drunk on the high-quality booze. As the carousel of passive-aggressive comments and hostility-laced bonhomie spun around the table, I mostly just bit my tongue, taking swigs of wine instead of biting back. By the end of the night, I was as drunk as I'd been in years.

I was already halfway to becoming a hardworking, hard-drinking Wall Street douchebag.

$ $ $

The next morning, I could barely get out of bed. I had to get to a pitch meeting with Harold Sorrington, a major executive at Bank of the World, but when I saw my bloodshot eyes in the bathroom mirror I realized I needed Visine if I didn't want to scare the hell out of our potential client. In suit and tie, I hustled to find a drugstore and made it to the office just in time to climb into a limo with the rest of the team.

"Brad Pitt's looking a bit peaked this morning," Peter started in at me as the limo pulled away from the curb. "Must be the jet lag from La La Land."

Everyone laughed at Peter's joke, including Martin and Lori, who'd joined us for the excursion. I was discovering that Peter was more than our boss. He was the star of the show. We were his laugh track.

The limo dropped us at the gleaming Midtown skyscraper in which the Bank of the World offices were situated. After clearing security, we marched single-file to the elevators, Peter leading his troops. When we arrived on the forty-second floor we were met by a twentysomething Black woman, the first person of color I'd seen in the building.

"Welcome to the Bank of the World executive headquarters," she said with a British accent. "I'm Emmanuelle Mensah, assistant to Harold Sorrington, chief executive officer for the North American Private Bank."

Peter glided over to the young woman. "What a beautiful name. I bet Americans ruin it with all sorts of terrible nicknames."

"They do." Emmanuelle smiled and rolled her eyes. Peter didn't get into offices like this one without the ability to win over assistants, who were the gatekeepers for executives like Sorrington.

Peter had told us that Sorrington was in charge of the Private Bank in Europe before his recent promotion to the North American CEO role. With the stock market on the ropes because of the economic crisis, there was only one place to go to make money: the people who had so much of it that a global recession wouldn't affect them. The Private Bank handled the investments of the world's richest people — as they put it, "serving the needs of high net worth and ultra high net worth individuals and families." The minimum threshold for clients was $25 million — and that was cash. Mansions and yachts didn't count.

Part of Peter's strategy to survive the Great Recession was to align Global Search with a firm that had no chance of going under. Unlike many of the investment banks that folded (Lehman Brothers) or were acquired before they did (Bear Stearns), Bank of the World was also an asset management firm, with billions under their control.

Emmanuelle led the way to Sorrington's office while Peter chatted her up.

"You should hear some of the names I've been called. The CEO of Lehman called me Petey, like I was his pet parakeet. No wonder they went under."

I thought Peter was playing the British card a bit hard, but when we walked into Sorrington's massive office I discovered why. Sorrington was sitting not at his desk but in a giant leather chair in the middle of the room, sipping tea. There was one other large chair and two small tables covered with old books, as though this was a reading lounge in an exclusive social club and not the office of a major Wall Street executive. It seemed like a movie set to me, as well as the height of pretension.

"Ahh, Peter," Sorrington exclaimed like he was an Oxford don. "I've been wanting to meet you for a long time. You've done quite well for yourself here in America."

"Nothing like you, Harold." Peter gestured to the windows that surrounded us. I tried not to look since the view was spectacularly distracting. This was my first meeting with a Wall Street CEO, and I wanted to stay focused on the task at hand.

"The bank needed someone with a British accent. Apparently, Americans write bigger checks when they hear one."

Sorrington and Peter laughed, so I joined in. I figured since it was the Harold Sorrington show now, he, too, would need a supportive audience. I often used this sort of fake laugh in my rusing calls. It was another small kind of lie, designed to manufacture camaraderie and bolster a mark's ego.

Sorrington scowled at me, as if noticing my presence for the first time. "Are you British?"

I silently shook my head at Sorrington, trying to undo the damage.

"This is the Brad Pitt of the search world," Peter said. Before, it had seemed like some sort of compliment. This time it was a put-down. "He played a Cardassian on *Star Trek*."

"What does he do for you?"

"He's supposed to stand there and look pretty."

Sorrington laughed, and the team joined in. I turned red, not with shame but with anger. I was a grown man with a career and a family, not some kid just out of business school. But I was going broke, so I swallowed my pride and stood there and smiled like an idiot.

Somehow my faux pas, and Peter's response to it, seemed to bond the men. The CEO invited Peter to sit in the other chair, and they began to discuss Sorrington's need for private bankers, investment advisers, and wealth strategists. Though I'd researched these areas in the past, I had no idea what they did. Fortunately, Sorrington explained each role in detail, as Peter sat sipping the tea Emmanuelle brought him. The rest of us continued to stand, scribbling down every word like reporters on deadline.

Apparently, private bankers did no banking. They were salespeople. Their job was to find super-rich people and get them to write enormous checks. Sorrington said that though the bank's minimum was $25 million, the average assets under management, or AUM, was closer to $250 million per client. Wealth strategists came up with a financial plan specific to each client that was then implemented by the investment advisers, who decided where to place massive amounts of cash to ensure that ultra-high-net-worth individuals stayed that way. The bank was looking to hire in all three areas and in multiple offices around the world. It sounded like they were looking to hire dozens, if not hundreds, of people, many with seven-figure salaries, which meant tens of millions in fees for us. Sorrington asked Peter if Global Search had the bandwidth to handle such an enormous — and valuable — request.

"Of course, Harold," Peter said, pushing their relationship into new territory. "This is a fraction of our team." Peter gestured toward the windows as if Global Search recruiters were everywhere, when the only employee not at the meeting was our receptionist.

"Wonderful. I'll get you set up for meetings with our various team leaders. They can give you the head count allocations we need to fill. Oh, there is one other thing." Sorrington paused as though he was embarrassed by what he was about to say. He looked away from Peter and up at me. "My grandson is a big *Star Trek* fan. Any chance I could get an autographed picture of you?"

CHAPTER NINETEEN

Locked In

Because we'd won the Bank of the World account, Peter wanted me to get an office in Malibu. He said I would need to expand my ruse team to handle all of the research for the private banking project. He wanted intelligence on the top fifty wealth management firms globally, which would make it the largest project I'd ever done. More than that, he wanted to know the size of each banker's book of business so that we could recruit away the biggest of the big leaguers. I couldn't even estimate how long an assignment like that would take, but in terms of fees for RK Research, the price tag would be enormous.

Since I was going to be busy recruiting, I wasn't going to have time to do research myself anymore. Shen and Pax were excellent researchers, but this project was too big for them to handle by themselves. Also, both had downsides. Shenanigans had a habit of screwing up at critical moments — obtaining intelligence on the wrong area at an important target, or mislabeling the firm name on a document. Often he went AWOL and wouldn't return emails for days. He was a musician, after all.

Pax had been doing the job as long as I had and was burned out. He liked the money when it had been easy to make, but he'd come to hate rusing. He'd always objected to it morally, but when the money was pouring in he'd looked the other way. Now that every dollar was a struggle, he'd turned bitter, resentful of kowtowing to Wall Street types. Also, his wife kept getting promoted at her telemarketing firm, they'd just had a baby, and he was moving into a Mr. Mom role. Even if he did agree to working more hours, his attitude would be contentious. I was getting enough of that from my Global Search co-workers, who were jealous of the special attention I'd received from Harold Sorrington.

Relying on a fuck-up and a grouch to complete the most important research project of my career wasn't an option. I needed an office, a real one. And actual employees, not independent contractors. RK Research was going to have to go legit — sort of.

By spring of 2010, I had located a suitable space and was prepared to commit to it. Peter flew in at the end of March to check out what I'd found, though I suspected he really just wanted an excuse to see where I lived and worked.

I picked him up at LAX and drove him into mid-Malibu to visit the office building. Because of the crashed economy, the entire space was empty. I had my choice of six or seven office suites ranging from two to four rooms each.

"These are too small," Peter said to Dahlia, the woman who owned the building. I imagined in the past she hired someone to show suites like this to potential tenants, but everyone was cutting corners to survive. "You've got to think bigger, Brad."

Dahlia eyed me since she knew me as Robert, but I sensed she would've rented to me even if I was using the name El Chapo and running drugs out of her offices. Times were that tough.

"We do have one larger vacant space," Dahlia said. "It was used by the biggest realtor in Malibu."

"Where did they go?" I asked.

"Bankrupt."

Sometimes the severity of the crash surprised even me. I was still in shock that a thriving business like mine had almost gone under, not because of mismanagement or because I had personal problems with gambling and strippers, but because of issues far beyond my control. There had to be a silver lining somewhere in the catastrophe that had forced me to take a job I didn't want. I swore to myself I was going to find it.

Dahlia took us to the building's nicest suite, which had a dolphin fountain in its entryway. She opened the door, and we entered a reception area that had a desk for a receptionist and a waiting room for guests.

Farther inside, there was a bullpen-type area with cubicles, and along the far wall were four or five offices for executives. There was also a conference room and a kitchen.

It was far beyond what I needed.

RK Research would have to hire at least ten people just to make the office not seem ridiculously large. The space could easily hold twenty workers or more. At the moment, the firm consisted of only me and Gardia. Oh, and our part-time assistant, Angie, who was a student at nearby Pepperdine University. Shen lived half an hour away, but he'd worked from home for years. Pax lived on the other side of the country.

"Welcome to the Global Search Los Angeles office," Peter boomed.

"It's too big," I said.

Peter leered at me. "You'll outgrow this space in a year. You'll have the entire building by then."

The funny thing was, I believed him. Peter was the best client I'd ever had, as well as one of the few I'd actually met. He'd come along with the Global Search offer at a time that I was desperate and saved me. Why wouldn't I trust him?

Dahlia's eyes brightened at the potential for renting her biggest suite since Gardia and I had been nickel-and-diming her to cut the rent on the smallest space she had.

"I'll leave you two to the negotiations." Peter walked outside to check his email and make some calls. By doing so, he made two things clear: First, he wanted me to take the space. From the beginning he'd talked about bringing me out of the basement, not knowing that I plied my rusing trade from an old toolshed. Second, Global Search was not paying for the office.

I felt like he was testing me to see if I was willing to go big time, putting my own capital on the line. Dahlia seemed as desperate to rent the office as I'd been to get the Global Search job. Malibu, despite its allure, was not a hub for corporations or businesses. The office was too big for the needs of most of the firms in town. Because of that, she offered me a tempting deal on a one-year lease. It was a precarious moment.

Ultimately, I took it, despite the cost being more than Gardia and I felt we could handle. I wagered that if I stepped up, Global Search would eventually do the same: buy my business for a few million, take over the lease payment on the office, and leave me sitting flush for the first time in years.

$$$

After the signing, I took Peter to my home in Malibu so he could see my current office. I was nervous. I'd met fewer than a handful of my clients; I'd taken none to my home. The peek into my personal life suggested a level of intimacy we hadn't yet established. But Peter was doing so much for me and my family, shouldn't I trust him enough to show him my home?

His eyes widened as we pulled into the driveway of my ocean-view Victorian. Peter lived in a tony area of Connecticut. I'm sure his house was quite nice. But it wasn't Malibu. I took him to the shed I used as my office since that was what he wanted to see first. He practically fell over laughing when he saw the BIG DADDY'S SURF SHOP sign hanging outside. I opened the door to my workplace, the modest space where I'd generated millions of dollars with nothing but a telephone and a legal pad, and his jaw dropped. A tool bench served as my desk. The floors were bare plywood, as were the walls. There were no curtains. There was no insulation. In winter, I wore a beanie and used a space heater to stay warm. In summer, the black-tar roof tiles turned the shed into an oven. Emerging after a day of work, I often felt (and looked) like I'd done a six-hour hot yoga class.

"All of this," he said, gesturing at my lovely home and scenic property, "from *this*."

I nodded and smiled.

He shook his head in amazement and mumbled, almost to himself, "All of this from a *shack*."

I imagined Peter thinking how much harder his life was than mine. He had to wake every day before the crack of dawn, throw on a suit and tie, drive to the train station, ride into Manhattan, and hump a subway to the Global Search office. His workday hadn't started and he'd already been up for two hours. He then had to repeat the exercise on the way home. I, on the other hand, rolled out of bed and threw on whatever I wanted —

usually board shorts if it wasn't too cold — grabbed a coffee, and walked the *ten feet* from my kitchen door to the shed. I was at work less than fifteen minutes after I'd gotten up, which came in handy when I had to call different time zones around the world. I'd wake up at 3:00 A.M., pop into the shed to call Germany or the UK for a couple of hours, then head back to bed. I didn't mind. I billed time and a half for international calling.

But then I assessed the look on Peter's face and realized I'd been totally wrong. He was disgusted, if not outright *offended*, by the simple environment in which I worked. The truth was, sometimes I was disgusted by it, too.

Gardia came over to escort Peter to her office in the basement of our home so he would know we weren't complete savages. Inside, there were two proper desks: one for Gardia and one for our assistant, Angie. The windows had curtains. There was carpeting on the floor. There were file cabinets. Unimpressed, Peter looked but didn't go inside. Instead he turned and took in the setting.

"I want to breathe this air," he said, and filled his lungs with the breeze that came off Zuma Beach less than half a mile away.

Peter was only in town for the day, so there was no time for a fancy meal. Instead, we sat at a table on the flagstone patio noshing on the snacks and iced tea Gardia had prepared. Peter munched away while checking emails and making calls, but every few minutes he would walk to the edge of our grass and peer out at the ocean, then return to his chair. He must have done it a dozen times.

Finally, it was time to take him to the airport. It amazed me that he'd flown all the way to LA for a few hours, but I was to learn this was not uncommon for him. My eight-year-old son, Davis, asked to come along with us. He was excited to visit my new office on the way home, and even threw on his suit and tie. Oh, and a top hat. My little guy had style. He sometimes spoke of coming to work for me when he was "old enough." I humored him because it was cute, but I knew that would never happen, and I feared he'd hate me when he found out what I really did for a living.

When we dropped off Peter, he seemed pleased with the day's events. We'd taken a big step. I had deep concerns, not least of which was the rent I'd now be paying, but the proud look on his face was the one I imagined my father wearing had I stuck around. In the moment, that was good enough for me.

$ $ $

I drove Davis and me back up the PCH to the new office building. It was after 7:00 P.M., so the parking lot was empty. My son oohed and ahhed at the dolphin fountain, and once inside he wanted to know which office would be his. I walked into the largest office, the one designed for the CEO, and shut the door. My son stared in at me through the glass, a happy look on his face. I'm not sure why, but I locked the door. I guess I was checking to make sure it worked. When I went to unlock it, the door wouldn't open. The handle turned, but nothing happened.

"What's wrong, Dad?"

"I think the door's broken." I pulled out my cell phone, but I had no reception. "Hey, Davis, poke your head outside, see if anyone is around. Tell them I'm locked in the office."

He looked nervous, but he went outside and came back a few minutes later.

"I didn't see anybody. What are we going to do?"

I had no idea. The offices were empty. The windows didn't open. I briefly contemplated going full John McClane and crawling out through the ceiling panels but settled for kicking the door a couple of times. It wouldn't budge.

My son was scared now, no doubt imagining that the two of us were stuck here for the night. Even if I'd wanted to chance my eight-year-old venturing the streets of Malibu to find help, there were no other buildings within walking distance. I tried calling and texting Gardia, but nothing went through. On a whim, I decided to text a surfer friend, Chip, who worked at a nearby car wash.

Help! Stuck in building on PCH.

After a couple of tries from all corners of the room, the text went through. I almost jumped up and down.

Where? What building?

But I couldn't respond to his text. Nothing else I sent went through. Fortunately, my buddy was smarter than the average surfer. He tracked down Gardia to get the address, which I didn't know anyway, and came to my rescue, toolbox in hand. Surfers may not be bright, but they're handy. Chip used a crowbar to break the door open. Davis hugged him.

"Thank you," I said. "Thought I was going to spend the night in there."

"What the hell are you doing here anyway?"

I explained that this was going to be my new office, that I was expanding my business. Though getting locked inside alone on the first day seemed a bad omen.

"You're going to be hiring a lot of people," Chip said as he glanced around the large, empty space.

"Tell me about it."

I wasn't looking forward to it — any of it. I'd have to set up a payroll service, computers, insurance, phones, furniture, kitchen supplies, office supplies, and God knows what else. The list Gardia had made seemed endless. But all of that would just require money and time. The real challenge would be to find people both willing and able to run the ruse.

"What about hiring me?" Chip asked.

I looked at Chip and blinked. I doubted he'd finished high school. He also wasn't an actor. I thought of the qualifications required to get hired by Bank of the World, a firm worth hundreds of billions of dollars. While my father would have been impressed by Chip's "moxie" and hired him to sell cars, I wondered what Harold Sorrington would think of me hiring a guy who washed cars as my first employee.

"Welcome aboard," I said like I was inviting Chip onto the *Titanic*.

$$$

While he lacked nearly every skill required to be a good researcher, Chip was fearless about getting on the phone. Whenever he was busted and shut down, which was often, he didn't let it dent his confidence. He had the gift of gab, the most important quality for a ruser, but he lacked the ability to understand the information being obtained or to write it down in a coherent way. When Chip would write up the information, he frequently couldn't remember how the names connected to each other in the organizational structure. He was unsure what the titles were and often forgot to ask key questions, so his intelligence had gaping holes. Research intel could have no holes.

Fortunately, Chip was a hell of a handyman. He set up the desks Gardia ordered from IKEA, hung the giant flat-screen TV in the conference room, and helped install our computers and phone systems. He had a great disposition, which was invaluable during those stressful early days. I decided to focus on Chip's positives and used them as justification to keep him around.

Gardia and I placed ads in *Backstage*, where long ago Leona had found Deirdre. We listed the jobs in other places, too, since I wasn't sure actors would be willing to make the long drive out to Malibu. Once I'd lined up enough people who wanted to give rusing a shot, I flew Pax out from New York. I hadn't told anyone what they were going to be asked to do. In telephone interviews, I'd been purposely vague.

"We're looking for employees with a take-no-prisoners attitude."

"We want workers who aren't afraid to roll up their sleeves and get their hands dirty."

"We want researchers who will get the information we need by any means necessary — within reason, of course."

I was attempting to prep candidates without scaring them away.

To help us with the administrative side of the business, Gardia hired an old friend, Suze. She was an actress but had made her living as an executive assistant for many years. We also promoted Angie to full time.

On the day of the first in-person interviews, I drove Pax from my place to work. It was good to have him close so we could catch up properly, but in reality, I couldn't have afforded to pay for a hotel room. Gardia and I were racking up huge expenses to open the office, and it was draining our savings. Dahlia, the owner of my building, had pitched in, billing me for the repair to my crowbarred office door. The lease I signed hadn't gone into effect until the following day, so by returning that night with Davis to check out the space I'd technically been trespassing.

In the car, Pax explained his plan to tell our candidates the truth about what we did and then get them on the phone as soon as possible.

"If they're gonna run," he said, "might as well be right away."

I was with him on this. Peter needed research desperately for Bank of the World, but I'd been too busy to ruse. Already I was working fifteen-hour days. Each morning I had dozens of emails waiting for me since Peter started firing them off from the treadmill at 5:00 A.M. East Coast time.

When we arrived at the office, I could tell that Pax was shocked and impressed by my digs. I'm sure he expected a smaller version of Leona's plain office in New York all those years ago. Instead, he stared out my windows at the rolling grandeur of the Pacific Ocean. He didn't have long to admire the view, though, since young people were already lining up along the dolphin fountain. Because of the economic crisis, a slew of college grads were unable to find employment.

I left Pax to his process. I had to have a series of long phone meetings to discuss job specs with various executives from Bank of the World's Los Angeles office, its Western Region headquarters.

By lunchtime, I was already exhausted. The executives I dealt with loved to have conference calls that went on and on without anything being accomplished. It was baffling — is this what these guys got paid millions of dollars a year to do? Global Search was no better. Our company-wide conference call every Monday was the biggest waste of time ever. My attitude may have been influenced by the fact that the call took place at 6:00 P.M. Hong Kong time, which was 3:00 A.M. for me. I'd set my alarm, stumble to the shed in the dark, get on the call, say nothing, hear next to nothing, and go back to bed.

Pax, on the other hand, wasn't wasting a second. He plowed through his interviews. Most people lasted less than five minutes. If there'd been a revolving door on our office, it might not have stopped turning. I sat in on a couple of interviews, though I could tell Pax was worried I was going to cramp his kamikaze style when the opposite was true. I needed researchers on the phone *that day*. Also, I was paying Pax by the hour. The sooner he had people hired and trained, the sooner I could send him home and get him off my payroll, which had already ballooned higher than I'd ever considered possible. I rationalized my growing expenses with the knowledge that there *was* work waiting — it would pay off the moment I had people who could do it. Money would come in from Global Search for the research, and then we'd get paid for all the placements I'd make from that research. I just had to hang in until then.

Pax's interview style was unlike any I'd ever seen — or would see again. He didn't introduce himself or offer any kind of greeting. He didn't care about the candidate's name, let alone their résumé.

"Are you willing to do whatever it takes?" he asked one pale young man with curly red hair.

"Um, sure." Like most of the people lined up outside, he looked as if he was in his early twenties and had just graduated from college. He smiled awkwardly.

"Beg, borrow, or steal?" Pax continued, drill-sergeant serious.

"Uh, steal?" the guy asked.

"Next!" Pax hollered out the door. He'd kept it ajar to keep the process moving.

"Wait." The redhead's face now matched the color of his hair. "I've got no problem with lying or anything. I just want it to be worth it."

Pax glanced over at me. This was an objection we could work with.

$ $ $

We hired three people that day, including the redheaded kid whose name, we finally learned, was Ocean. I now had ten employees, if I counted myself and Gardia. I'd gone from working in my shed shirtless in sandals to signing checks in my office in a suit and tie to pay for the delivery of purified water. At home, tap had been just fine.

I wasn't keen on the new dress code, even though I was the one who instituted it. I figured if I was going to spend money like a real Wall Street firm, then we ought to look the part. Suddenly Sorrington's ludicrous reading chairs and Jack MacDonald's two-story bungalow made more sense. I assumed at some point we'd have clients who'd want to visit the West Coast office of Global Search — though the placard on the door still said RK RESEARCH. Global Search could call my office whatever they wanted in their PowerPoint decks and on their website, but I wasn't putting their logo on my door until they were paying the rent.

Joining Ocean on the research team were Randy and Strider. Pax and I discussed hiring one more researcher than we needed since it was guaranteed that at least one of them would flame out. I prayed it wasn't all of them, which was a distinct possibility. I didn't spend much time getting to know the new recruits, though I did learn that Randy was a helicopter pilot. Pax figured anyone brave enough to fly a chopper could handle the pressure of lying on the phone. I wasn't so sure.

He gathered the newbies around a phone in the bullpen for what amounted to Liar's Boot Camp. I left my door open so I could eavesdrop. Pax wanted everyone in the suite to hear them when they got on the phone to make it as embarrassing as possible if they didn't get the desired intel. Ocean went first and stumbled his way through a call. He chatted about the weather, though it seemed unlikely that he knew what it was like that day in Manhattan. He only got some basic information before he was shut down, but right away he had a style. He was playing the nice guy. As I learned with Andi and Deirdre many years earlier, preying on the kindness of strangers was a valid ploy. We just needed to give Ocean an Irish name to use instead of his choice: No one wants to help a Herman.

Randy went next. He did a lot of hemming and hawing then fell into silence. I wasn't sure if he'd been put on hold, but then he walked by my office door, never to return. Our pilot had crashed and burned.

Strider was last. I was worried, as we desperately needed him to work out. I wasn't confident about his chances. He was the quietest of the bunch — not a good sign for someone who needed to be gabbing on the phone all day. But with receiver in hand, Strider transformed. He put his call on speakerphone as if showing everyone, *This is how it's done.* No matter what the person on the other end said to dissuade him, Strider persevered. He asked for names, and when he got a hesitant response he *demanded* the information. Strider played the higher-up executive, the one no one wanted to cross, using his rank in the hierarchy as a cudgel. Most people would rather cave than chance making an enemy at the top of the corporate food chain. It was a ploy after my own heart.

The day continued like that, with Ocean and Strider in rotation making practice calls, learning by getting on the phone but also by listening to each other's successes and failures. I had to admit it was starting to look promising. Eventually, I got up to close the door, since I had massive amounts of work to do. As I did, I gave Pax a salute. He'd saved my ass — and most likely my home.

CHAPTER TWENTY

Coffee's for Closers

With my research team in place, it was time to become a full-fledged, honest-to-God recruiter. I'd been wanting to give up the ruse for more than a decade, and now it was happening. I was going legit! But before I could smile and dial, I had to meet with the local Bank of the World team leaders for whom I would be finding executives. This included Harold Sorrington's number two, Jasmin Shirazi. I'd already spoken with her and most of her key team leaders via multiple, long-winded conference calls during which they droned on about the importance of office culture, yet I'd never met any of them in person.

A week after I'd opened my office — and the day Pax flew home to New York — I drove to Bank of the World's elegant offices in Beverly Hills. Like Leona's apartment when I first started my rusing career, everything was white and spotless. Perhaps that was the reason for the $25 million client minimum: They needed that kind of cash for the army of janitors required to keep the place as pristine as it was.

A man in his midtwenties was waiting for me in the lobby. "Mr. Kerbeck, would you like coffee, tea, or water? We have cappuccino, lattes, espresso. We have hot tea, green tea, or iced tea, and for bottled water we have sparkling or flat." After a beat, he added, "Unless you'd like tap."

The final offer was uttered with disdain, as though the mere mention of such an unsophisticated option made him physically uncomfortable. I imagined my father asking for it anyway, just to mess with the guy, and briefly considered doing the same. I asked for sparkling water, and he showed me to a waiting room with white couches, white chairs, and large, white Apple computers for visitors' use. No sooner had I sat down than a woman around my age walked in and handed me a bottle of Badoit, my favorite.

"Thank you," I said and stood.

"Jasmin Shirazi. Nice to meet you." I hadn't expected to be served by the head of the Western Region, so I was glad I'd jumped up. I couldn't imagine Harold Sorrington serving me no matter how many autographed pictures I gave his grandkids. "I've heard a lot about you," she went on. "You're Global Search's secret weapon."

I playfully put my finger up to my mouth — *shhh* — and looked around the room surreptitiously. She smiled at me warmly. I was glad someone finally recognized what I brought to the table. My interactions with my fellow recruiters (and Sorrington) had reminded me that researchers were often treated, and paid, like second-class citizens when the truth was, that without us, recruiters would have no idea who to call.

Jasmin escorted me to her office. Though it was expensively furnished, it had a homey, lived-in feel. Pictures of her three small children adorned her desk and walls, and she'd mounted their artwork, as well. She caught me admiring one of the crayon drawings. It was an effective reminder of why I was doing this silly corporate dance.

"Do you have kids?" she asked.

"My son turned eight in September."

"What a wonderful age. Mine are eleven, ten, and eight. What's his name?"

"Davis."

"That's an unusual name. Is he named after someone?"

"My grandmother's maiden name was Davis."

"You must have been close."

"We were. She lived to be ninety-three, so she got to meet Davis before she died."

Jasmin's hand went to her heart. "That's so special."

She pointed for me to sit in one of the chairs that faced her desk. Instead of sitting behind it, she took the chair next to me. I was grateful and a bit thrown by her friendliness.

"Family is important to me, as well. As you can tell." She gestured toward the artwork and photos on the wall. "These drove Harold

Sorrington crazy when he visited after his promotion. He wants me to have reproductions of Hockney and Rothko on the walls, not stick figures and sunrises. He wants us to become the number one private bank in the world, and to add a hundred new bankers. He also wants me to move up to San Francisco."

She didn't look happy about any of it.

I knew about the first part of Sorrington's plan since Global Search was going to be the recruiting firm for every one of those hires. High-end search firms like ours generally received payment equivalent to one-third of the first-year salary and bonus of the individual they placed. Because of the volume of hires Bank of the World had engaged us to find and the ongoing economic crisis, Global Search had agreed to a reduced rate of 25 percent. Even so, it was a huge potential payout. If the average salary on those one hundred hires was half a million dollars, which was a conservative estimate, Global Search stood to earn around $12.5 million in recruiting fees. It would likely be far more. My contract stipulated that half would go to Global Search and half would be divided among the recruiters based on the number of hires they'd handled. If things went as well as Peter predicted, I would make more than I ever had — in the ballpark of $1.5 to $2 million just on the Bank of the World assignment. And that wasn't counting what I'd make from the research, which I billed separately since RK Research was still an independent company. That could add another mil.

"Why does he want you to move?" I asked.

"There's more wealth in the Bay Area. He wants our Western Region to be based there."

Over the years, I was regularly asked to research firms in New York, San Francisco, Chicago, Dallas, Houston, Boston, and Charlotte — but rarely Los Angeles. Outside of the film, TV, and music businesses, there wasn't much corporate activity there.

Jasmin shrugged at her dilemma. I'd done my due diligence and knew she'd been with Bank of the World for close to twenty years. The connections she'd made had placed her on the boards of key charitable and philanthropic organizations around the city. She was a leader in the wealthy Iranian American community that made up a third of the population of Beverly Hills. She didn't want to leave everyone she knew and all she'd worked for, let alone uproot her children. I could relate. One of the reasons I'd quit acting was to be more present to raise my son.

"Sounds like a tough situation."

"Ah, well, such is life in the corporate fast lane," she said with a rueful smile.

I nodded in sympathetic agreement even though I didn't know a damn thing about it.

$ $ $

An hour later, my notepad filled with details on the hires Jasmin wanted to make, I called Peter. He'd wanted a report the moment I left the meeting.

"She's out," he said.

"What? Who?"

"Shirazi. Sorrington wants her gone. You and I are flying to San Francisco the day after tomorrow to interview candidates to replace her."

"Why? She seemed nice."

"Sorrington doesn't want nice. He wants killers. He wants rock stars. You gotta start thinking bigger, Brad."

An hour after meeting Jasmin and already I was conspiring against her. It made me sick, especially since I would be talking to her frequently in the coming days even as I was interviewing people to take her job. I thought being a recruiter meant getting people better jobs, that at the end of the day I'd feel good about my efforts. But now I was scheming in a way that felt far more nefarious than calling to get a list of names under false pretenses. Also, for the first time I knew the person I was going to harm. I remembered my father begging me to get out of the rusing game because it was dishonest, which bothered him more than its illegality. But what could be worse than presenting myself one way directly to someone's face while actively working to wreck their career at the same time? It was a new kind of lie, a fraud of a different character. Something curdled in me.

Peter wanted research ASAP on the top private banking candidates in the Bay Area, so I hustled back to my office to redirect my team from researching to fill roles on Jasmin's team to finding an individual to replace her. Unlike LA, where we were struggling to find enough firms to research, San Francisco and Silicon Valley had a plethora of wealth management targets. We spent the next forty-eight hours banging out Peter's emergency request, obtaining an array of valuable organizational charts and the cell numbers of most of the key individuals. Even I got on the phone so we could hit all the firms Peter wanted.

Once we had the intelligence, I started calling on the wealth management executives. Peter didn't want me to provide details on the role, since we couldn't risk Jasmin finding out about our efforts to replace her. I certainly couldn't mention Bank of the World. Predictably, every executive I spoke with wanted to know the name of the firm and the title of the open position. I understood, but I couldn't divulge the information. Each executive then told me they weren't interested, that they were happy where they were.

Yet by the end of my calls all of them agreed to meet. Why?

Because they were impressed I'd reached them on their cell number.

$ $ $

In San Francisco, Peter and I reserved the library room at our small but upscale boutique hotel. Executives came in to meet with us, one an hour. We'd scheduled it that way to ensure that our candidates didn't run into one another, which could start the gossip flowing. The world of wealth management leaders was an exceedingly small one.

Most of the executives we interviewed were white men in their mid- to late fifties. It seemed each one had the same spray of gray hair at the temples and a similar designer suit and tie. The interviews were strange to me. They seemed almost pointless. I knew nothing about the wealth management business so had no idea what questions would differentiate a good candidate from a bad one. I suspected that Peter didn't know any more than I did, though he pretended otherwise. He'd have made a pretty good actor.

The candidate who most impressed me was a woman named Stacey Warburton, who'd wanted to meet us for lunch instead of coming to the hotel. We had no problem with that. One perk of traveling to different cities was the restaurants we were able to try. The restaurant she chose, the Barnacle Inn, was located on the water near an abandoned wharf. Far from an epicurean hot spot, it was as run-down as the pier. It looked like the kind of place where fishermen would bring in their fresh catch and clean it right at your table. Stacey was in a back booth with her face buried in a menu as if she were Nicole Kidman trying to make sure she wasn't recognized.

"Hi, Stacey," I said as I approached. "I'm —"

Peter shushed me even though the restaurant was nearly empty. He slid onto the bench opposite her. I sat down next to him. She raised her head, gave us a brief smile, and then scanned the restaurant to see if we'd been followed. It was very cloak and dagger.

"I can't take any chances," she said. Maybe she'd caught me rolling my eyes. "If I'm seen with you, it could impact my current position."

"We completely understand," Peter said. "This is a brilliant choice to meet."

"I bet the fish is good," I said.

Both of them looked at me like I was a doofus.

"Trust me, we are quite sensitive to your situation," Peter said. "What happens in the, uh . . ."

"Barnacle Inn," I reminded him.

". . . stays in the Barnacle Inn. You have my word." For what that was worth.

"And as a gesture of good faith," Peter continued, "I want you to know who our client is: Bank of the World. They're looking for someone to run their entire Western Region."

"Thank you. I'm excited to learn about the position. But first . . ." Again, she glanced around the restaurant. There wasn't a server in sight, let alone anyone who gave a crap that some unknown corporate executive was meeting with a search firm.

"Does Jasmin Shirazi know she's being replaced?" Stacey asked me.

"She should," Peter said before I could respond. "And if she doesn't, it's her own fault. Bank of the World is lagging because of her. She should be up here in the Bay Area every week. Instead, she's focused on her kids' recitals and concerts. Not that there's anything wrong with that."

Yet clearly there was — at least in the mind of the man who had asked Peter to replace her, Harold Sorrington. Peter eyed me like I'd failed him in some way. It took me a second to realize he didn't know whether Stacey had kids and was worried he'd just put her off. I hadn't asked her about this in my initial call, a rookie mistake.

"I don't have children," Stacey said. "In case you were wondering. No time."

She took on a wistful look, as though she still hoped to squeeze one or two in somewhere along the way.

"Well, the issue isn't her children, of course," Peter said. "There are myriad reasons why Harold wants to replace her."

"I've met her, you know," Stacey said. "She has an excellent reputation."

"It's a shame," I started, then thought better of what I was about to say. "What is?"

I looked toward Peter for permission to talk, but he glared at me as if I'd disappointed him once already and needed to keep my mouth shut.

"Come on," Stacey prodded. "What happens in the Barnacle Inn . . ." She smiled warmly at me.

"It's just, I met Jasmin, too, and she's wonderful. It would be a shame for Bank of the World to lose her." As I spoke, I felt a burst of compassion for Jasmin. "Why couldn't she work under you and stay in charge of LA?"

"I wouldn't have a problem with that," Stacey said. "It would actually make it easier for me to be successful. Bank of the World has little presence in a number of West Coast cities: Seattle, Portland, Phoenix. I could focus on building up those locations rather than finding a replacement for her in LA. You think she'd agree to it?"

What the hell did I know about whether Jasmin would accept what was essentially a demotion? I'd met her one time. Or whether Harold Sorrington would even consider it? But like I'd done all those years on the phone, I kept on bullshitting.

"She might. I don't think she likes traveling. I know she doesn't want to move."

Stacey nodded like this was important intelligence as well as a positive development for her consideration of the role. I was pleased with my handling of the conversation. In the interviews at the hotel, Peter had taken the lead. This time I had. I was proud of myself for coming up with the idea to keep Jasmin around. Should Stacey get the job offer, perhaps I could convince Jasmin to stay. This way, Bank of the World would be strong in San Francisco *and* Los Angeles. It seemed like a classic win-win.

After we finished eating, we said our good-byes and promised to be in touch. Stacey asked if we would give her a five-minute head start before leaving. Once she'd departed, Peter pulled out his phone and set the timer. I expected him to praise my outside-the-box thinking.

"Get over there," he ordered, pointing for me to move to the other side of the booth. A stern and intense look took over his face. "I'm going to say this only once: *Don't ever cost me money again.*" He may as well have been Alec Baldwin in *Glengarry Glen Ross.*

"Huh?"

"You cost me — and Global Search — a million-dollar commission."

"Wait, I got Stacey interested because of my idea of keeping Jasmin."

"You think I care who gets the job? I want two commissions: one for replacing Jasmin as head of the West Coast and another for replacing her as head of LA. Now if Stacey gets hired — and I can tell Sorrington will like her — you cost me that second one with your big mouth."

I sat stunned, annoyed, chagrined. But he had a point. I was still thinking like a paid-by-the-hour researcher, and a human being with a shred of common decency, not a recruiter. The timer went off on his phone, Buddhist temple chimes. Peter got up and walked out without another word.

We were silent on the ride back to the hotel. I considered asking him to stop at a Starbucks since I was going to need caffeine to make it through the rest of the interviews, but then I remembered.

Coffee's for closers.

CHAPTER TWENTY-ONE

Flirting for Dollars

After our long day of interviews finally ended, Peter had to hustle to the airport to make his flight to New York. I wasn't in the same hurry, so before my flight home to LA I planned to hit a fine local restaurant — this time one with less sea shanty decor.

"You're coming with me," Peter said as he packed his briefcase. We'd already checked out of our rooms and left our bags with the bellman.

"What? Where?"

"Back to New York. We're meeting with Sorrington tomorrow to discuss the candidates. I'll let you be the one to present your little plan to keep Jasmin around."

My son had a school play the following day that I was loath to miss, but I knew how Peter felt about demonstrations of commitment so I kept my mouth shut. I was sad, though. Working from home and setting my own hours had meant I'd never once missed a special event in Davis's life.

"I don't have a ticket or anything," I said.

"I had the office take care of it."

We took a taxi to the airport, barely making the flight. We were the last ones to take our seats in business class. I was glad to see Peter hadn't demoted me to coach, though my seat wasn't next to his. It was probably for the best. He hadn't said much since lunch.

My seatmate was a woman my age who already had two empty airplane-size bottles of vodka on her tray table. "Captain said it's gonna be a bumpy flight," she said and raised her glass as if to toast me. "Might as well enjoy it." As the male flight attendant took my suit jacket, she told him: "Get this guy a drink."

"It's too late," he said. "We're about to take off."

She glared at him until, to my surprise, he asked me what I wanted.

"Gin and tonic," I said. "Thanks."

"Make it a double," my seatmate said. "And bring me another, too."

He scurried to the galley area. I was used to flying coach; the power structure in business class was clearly much different.

"We seatmates have to look out for each other," she said. "I'm Jane."

"Robert," I said. "Thanks."

The attendant brought the drinks as the plane began to taxi. I worried I was going to have to chug mine, but he simply asked us to put up our tray tables.

"I'm platinum status," Jane said. "So I don't get pushed around. What about you? What's your status?"

She eyed my wedding ring. I couldn't help myself and eyed hers, as well. She smiled.

"I don't have any status. Airline-wise, anyway. I've just started flying business class. I'm with a new company."

"Oh, what company?"

"You've probably never heard of it. It's a recruiting firm based out of Asia. Global Search."

"You're right. I haven't. What industry?"

"Mainly Wall Street."

"My husband works on Wall Street." She rolled her eyes, then looked at me as if I were supposed to understand what that meant. "I'll introduce you. He could use a good headhunter." She chuckled like she'd made an especially funny joke and took a big swig of her drink to celebrate, then reached forward to her purse and pulled out a business card. "Email me and I'll put you in touch. You can help him. He certainly needs it."

"Sure, thanks."

I wasn't sure what I could do for the guy. People didn't realize that most headhunters worked for companies, not individuals. I'd be able to assist someone only if they happened to be working in the wealth management space at a very senior level. What were the odds her husband qualified? Her card was interesting, though. She was head of fundraising for an organization I'd never heard of. And her name, Jane Monahan, seemed familiar.

Once the plane was at cruising altitude, I grabbed my laptop from the overhead bin and glanced at Peter. He was seated behind me on the opposite side clacking away on his computer, no doubt sending emails to the other recruiters telling them how much I'd cost them. Though I was standing right in front of him, he ignored me.

Annoyed, I sat back down and tried to make myself productive. Even if I was failing as a recruiter, I could make sure that my team was delivering high-quality research, which was, after all, my specialty. I reviewed every piece of intelligence we generated before it was sent to clients. I'd make notes and corrections on my researchers' work, sometimes asking them to go back for more information or better clarity. It was this level of quality control that had made RK Research the preeminent intelligence firm in the business.

When it had been just Pax and Shen, I'd review four to eight documents a day. But now when I checked my emails there were documents from Ocean and Strider, as well. Reviewing their work took hours. I also had dozens of emails from the Global Search recruiters. I had to read every one or risk being unaware of some critical piece of information and looking like a fool somewhere down the road.

Before I started in, on a whim I angled my computer away and googled Jane Monahan. She had her own Wikipedia page. It turned out the reason her name seemed familiar was because it had been on my research for years. At least, her *last* name had been. Her husband, Ken Monahan, was the fucking CEO of Stadt Bank, one of the largest financial institutions in the world. I startled, elbowing my drink off our shared center table and sending it straight into the lap of the woman married to the biggest white whale I could ever hope to harpoon.

"Oh my God, I'm so sorry." I had the presence of mind to slam my laptop closed before she could see that I'd googled her, then quickly began to dab at the side of her chair with my linen napkin. Before I could catch myself, I was dabbing her lap, too. I stopped and looked up sheepishly.

"It's okay." She wagged her fingers like she wanted me to continue.

I thought about it but instead offered her my napkin, which she reluctantly took to soak up the spots I'd missed.

"I hope I didn't stain your outfit."

"Please, that was the highlight of my day." Under her breath, but loud enough for me to hear, she muttered, "Maybe my year."

Jesus. It was like the opening dialogue of a porn movie. I worked to cast out any impure thoughts as the flight attendant came by with a replacement drink and a new napkin. I took the latter but passed on the former. I needed to stay sharp and let Peter know who I was sitting next to. He'd have theories on how I could work the situation to obtain business for Global Search. Though Stadt Bank was based in Germany, I'd heard the firm was attempting to make inroads into the North American market. To accomplish this, they'd recently hired their first non-German CEO: Ken Monahan.

I emailed Peter, and almost immediately he deluged me with a series of emails heavy on the ALL CAPS and exclamation points:

WTF???!!!!!!!!!!!!!!!!!!!

OMG!!! $$$$$$$$$$$$$

GO GET HER BRAD!!!

So much for the silent treatment. Now Peter couldn't stop. I received what seemed like fifty emails in less than fifteen minutes.

"Is that your wife?" Jane nodded at my computer as it blew up with dings and dongs.

"Uh, no."

"Girlfriend?" She leaned close to nudge me in the ribs, a classic of adulterer's semaphore. I wasn't ready to take the bait.

"My boss."

"Tell him you're sitting next to the wife of the CEO of Stadt Bank and that if he wants to get a meeting with my husband he needs to leave you alone."

I smiled genuinely. "You're funny."

"I'm not joking. Write it."

Her flirty demeanor disappeared. She glared at me aggressively, though her eyes were slightly unfocused. I hadn't been counting her drinks but estimated she'd had three, all of them doubles. She wasn't a big woman, either. Maybe five foot six, 120 pounds, give or take. I'd made it halfway through one double before knocking it over. I couldn't imagine having three in such rapid succession.

I decided to keep my mouth shut and follow orders, something I wished I'd done in the Stacey Warburton meeting. I typed an email to Peter explaining the situation.

"Let me see it." Jane took the opportunity to lean on me, though it was more like she *rubbed* on me. The vodka on her breath swept across me intensely enough to kick up a little buzz. I contemplated what her marriage must be like if she was this forward with a complete stranger. But I needed to support my family and keep my home, which meant winning business for Global Search. What were we always asking potential ruse recruits? *By any means necessary?* Allowing a little casual molestation might just have to be part of the ploy.

"Tell him you're mine," she slurred after reading it. "At least, for the flight." She giggled and pushed herself off me to reach for her drink, fondling my biceps as she did. As interested as she appeared to be in me, the alcohol was clearly her priority.

I emailed the cease-and-desist to Peter, who'd likely see it as a great sign. I knew he'd eagerly encourage me to give Jane whatever the hell she wanted: an ear to listen, a shoulder to cry on, entry into the mile-high club.

She definitely wanted to talk. At first it was all about her charitable work, but it quickly degenerated into a rant against her husband. He was never around. He ignored her. He'd gotten fat. He cheated on her with expensive prostitutes, a common affliction among the CEO class. She came off as both pissed and resigned.

The attendant arrived with dinner, which gave me a brief respite, but once the dishes were taken away Jane leaned in again, as if she wanted to make out. I did my best to keep some distance without offending her.

"How the hell did you end up on Wall Street?" she asked. "You don't seem like the type."

I couldn't very well tell her the truth. I doubted Ken Monahan would want to hire me because I'd guest-starred in two episodes of *Melrose Place.* "It's a long story," I said.

I feared she was going to ask me to tell it since our flight still had a couple of hours to go. Instead, she leaned back in her chair and passed out, complete with snores so loud the folks in coach probably heard them.

I considered emailing Peter to give him a status report, but I didn't dare risk waking her. I glanced back, and this time he was staring right at me, as if he'd been waiting for me to turn around. He waved his hands in a *what's going on* kind of motion. I tilted my head and simulated sleeping. Peter gave me a wide smile and two thumbs-up, as if Jane had passed out after an incredible bout of lovemaking. The whole thing felt pretty gross.

When the plane landed in New York, Jane was still asleep. Drool had cascaded down one of her cheeks. If I'd actually known her, I would have suggested she go to AA. Many of my actor friends had been in the program. Some still lived in New York. I was positive that if I called one they would come running to take her to a meeting — or straight to detox.

I shook her awake.

"Hey, we're here," I said neutrally. "So nice to meet you. I'll email you about meeting your husband."

I had my bag ready in case she suggested we go someplace and I needed to make a quick exit, but she looked at me as if I were a stranger. I realized it was possible that she didn't remember a thing. Which disturbed me. Not because I was confronted with a potential blackout drinker deserving of help and compassion, but because she might not remember that she'd agreed to set up a meeting for me with her bastard of a husband.

And with that thought, I moved yet another step closer to unrepentant Wall Street douchebag status.

$ $ $

The next morning, Peter had all the recruiters standing around his office as he regaled them with the epic tale of my seduction of Jane Monahan. The elegant British accent did nothing to undercut the childish frat-house nature of the embellishment.

"You're such a piker," Phil said, punching me in the shoulder. Donny gave me a high five as if I'd scored a touchdown, while Beata shot me a dirty look.

"Really, she was the one doing the seducing," I said, trying to tamp down Peter's portrayal of me as someone who would do anything to get a client.

"God, you're such an egomaniac," Beata said, her upper body shaking in disgust. "You think every woman wants you because you were on TV."

Ugh. The day had barely begun and the tension was already unbearable.

"Please," Peter said, "this is incredible news. If Brad can get us a meeting with Stadt Bank, we can leverage our work with Bank of the World to our advantage. We all stand to benefit."

"Him more than the rest of us," Beata sneered like I'd just cut the bread line.

The Global Search contract specified that if Peter or Jack brought in clients, the recruiters split the commissions for the most part equally. But there was an entirely different pay structure when a recruiter brought in new business. Essentially, that client was theirs, and they would decide which recruiters got to work on the account. I hadn't paid much attention to that clause because I didn't know anyone on Wall Street. Hell, I'd hardly met any of my clients during more than twenty years of rusing. How was I going to win the business of a major financial institution?

"Let's not worry about that now," Peter said. "First we need to see whether Brad has staying power or if Jane Monahan was a one-night stand. You better email her right away and find out."

All the innuendo had me wanting to punch a hole in something. Or someone. "I was going to wait a couple of days," I said.

"Why? So you don't seem desperate?" said Phil, exchanging a look with Beata. "We're sitting around here with our thumbs up our asses because of you."

"What are you talking about?"

"All the research your team is doing is for positions on the West Coast, which means only you get to call those people."

"It was Sorrington's idea to focus on the West Coast, not mine. That's where Bank of the World is weakest." I looked at Peter to confirm this, since he was the one who'd given me Sorrington's instructions, but he said nothing. I couldn't tell if he was uncomfortable with conflict or trying to stoke it. "What does it matter anyway?" I added. "The commissions go into a pool and get divided up."

"*If* we're around to collect," said Donny. "Executive search is like the NFL. If you get cut you don't get paid, no matter how big your contract was."

"So you handling all the placements makes *you* indispensable," Phil said, "and *we* get fired by Jack MacDonald."

"Brad isn't indispensable," Peter said derisively. He'd finally chosen to speak up just so he could take a turn jabbing me.

"I'm not," I said matter-of-factly. At that point, I would have said anything to keep the peace. My neck had started to hurt for the first time since I'd quit acting.

"It's more like he's incompetent," Peter added. I squinted at him, my fists starting to tighten. "He told Stacey Warburton that if she gets hired she should keep Jasmin around as head of LA."

"You cost us a fucking placement?" Phil asked.

"Are you stupid?" Beata piled on.

Before I could answer, Peter said, "No, just very green. If Warburton gets hired, and if she keeps Jasmin around — both big ifs at the moment — there will be consequences for the loss of that commission."

"How is he going to pay us back a million-dollar commission?" Phil whined.

"Well, if he wins business from Stadt Bank, there will be much more revenue coming in than that. I imagine Brad would be happy to put any commissions he receives from them into the Global Search pool."

Fuck. Hadn't seen that coming. Of course, it was all still hypothetical, but rough calculations would put my loss at potentially close to eight figures if I actually did reel in Stadt Bank. But what could I do? If I rejected his suggestion, I'd be spurning not just Peter but the entire recruiting team. Then I might be the one getting cut.

"Sure, of course," I said, as though I had been about to make the same offer. "You know what they say. There's no *I* in team."

Peter smiled and exhaled deeply. "This is why I love Brad so much. He's not just a pretty face. He's a pretty person, too."

"He's still a piker," Phil said as he punched my shoulder again. This time it actually seemed affectionate. Donny gave me his standard high five. Beata pocketed her sneer.

"I want you three," Peter said, pointing at them, "to get the research from Kerbeck's team and start calling people on the West Coast. Focus on Portland for now."

He looked at me to gauge my reaction. That was supposed to be my territory. If I were to call someone in Germany, Beata would be shouting, *Nein!* But it was barely 10:00 A.M. and I was already spiritually depleted by all the bullshit. So I shrugged like, *Whatever it takes, Coach.*

The three of them hustled out of the office. Beata turned back at the door. "What's he going to do?" she said, wagging her finger at me.

"Brad is coming with me to Sorrington's office. I'm going to let him present his idea about Jasmin. I'll see you three later for lunch."

Beata grinned as if I'd be gone by then.

CHAPTER TWENTY-TWO

The Whore of Wall Street

This time Sorrington gave me a chair. He never brought up the *Star Trek* autograph I'd supplied for his grandkid, as if he were too significant to offer a thank-you. Maybe the chair *was* the thank-you.

"How was San Francisco?" Sorrington asked.

"We met over thirty candidates in one day," Peter said, doubling the number of interviews we'd conducted. "Everyone wants to work with you and Bank of the World."

Sorrington smiled. "Great to hear. Have you found my Mick Jagger?"

Peter nodded and looked toward me. "Since Robert is handling the West Coast, I'll let him brief you."

"I thought his name was Brad." Sorrington looked at me sternly, then cackled. Peter joined in, as if Sorrington having "gotten" me was the funniest thing ever.

"I think I've got something better," I said. "How about a Gwen Stefani?"

"What firm is she with?"

Was Sorrington pulling my leg again? "She's a pop star."

Sorrington looked confused.

"A Chrissie Hynde then?"

"Who?"

"The lead singer for the Pretenders?"

"Look, Brad, tell me who the rock stars are and how much they're going to cost me."

"We met with a lot of candidates, but there was only one rock star. Stacey Warburton."

"I've heard of Stacey, but isn't she a tad green? I don't think she's got any gray hair yet. We like our private bankers with some seasoning. Makes it easier when they're talking to our ancient client base."

"You want green. Stacey is the same age as the techies running Silicon Valley. That's the money you're after. Hiring Stacey will increase your assets under management, and it might also save you money."

"That would be a first."

"Stacey is a powerhouse in the Bay Area, which is what you want. But she doesn't know the LA market."

"So?" Sorrington said. "We'll find someone who does."

"That's the thing. She said the best person to run LA is already a Bank of the World employee there."

"We'll promote them then. Who is it?"

"Actually, you're going to have to *de*mote them."

Sorrington looked at me like I was crazy, then glared at Peter. "Please tell me Brad's plan isn't for Jasmin Shirazi to stay. She is deadwood and must be removed."

"I told him it was stupid," Peter chirped. "And that you would hate it."

"Maybe it's stupid," I said, "but it's honest. Why would we give up a commission if we didn't think this was the best solution for Bank of the World — and the best move for your future, as well?"

Sorrington eyed me with hostility at my reference to the recent articles that had him in line to take over the entire bank. I was stepping on the third rail of the recruiting business: worrying about someone's future. Peter had told me we only concerned ourselves with filling currently open positions — the ones we were getting paid for.

"Look," I continued. "Jasmin knows LA like no one. By leaving her in charge, you remain strong there. But you give the rest of the region to Stacey. She's the one who will build Portland, Seattle, Vegas, Phoenix. Jasmin will have nothing to do with anything but Los Angeles."

"And Stacey wants Jasmin?" Sorrington asked in disbelief.

"She does. Like you, she wants to build assets under management, but the best places to do that aren't in the LA area. Keeping Jasmin enables her to maintain what you have. Who knows? Maybe the demotion will inspire Jasmin to push harder to increase her assets."

"I doubt that," said Peter. "Lifers rarely get religion this late in the game."

"I must say I've never had a recruiting firm pass up a commission," Sorrington said. "I guess it couldn't hurt to give Brad's plan a try. We can always fire Jasmin if she proves difficult or starts dossing about." He turned back to me. "How do you know she'll accept the demotion?"

"I don't," I said.

"Will Stacey take the job without Jasmin staying on?"

"I'm not sure."

"It appears you have some convincing to do." Sorrington stood, indicating our meeting was over. He gave me a look of bewilderment, then glanced at Peter. "Turns out Brad Pitt isn't as dumb as he looks."

Both men snickered. I turned red but offered a chuckle.

"Oh, Peter, I nearly forgot," Sorrington said. "Do you think Global Search could help us with some hiring in our European offices?" Sorrington was still acting as interim chief for Europe until a replacement was named, which meant he had the wherewithal to hire us on multiple continents.

"I'd be honored," said Peter.

I glared hard at my boss, wanting to see some recognition that my idea had worked — and brought us more business to boot. But Peter was too busy half bowing to catch my eye. Before I patted myself on the back too hard — or forced Peter to do the same — I reminded myself that I still needed to convince Jasmin. Here I was an executive recruiter, supposed to get people better jobs, and my first official responsibility was to demote someone. It seemed more likely that Jasmin would just tell me to shove my plan and quit first.

Fortunately, as an actor I knew more about rejection than just about anybody.

$$$

At lunch with the other recruiters at an upscale café overlooking Rockefeller Plaza, Peter took credit for the European business Sorrington had granted us.

"I had to do some damage control after he heard Robert's plan," Peter said, "but once I told him we were sacrificing a commission I had him eating out of my hand." He glanced at me to see if I was going to call him on his bullshit. I just stabbed at my Waldorf salad.

I wanted to shout that I was the one who had won us those placements — and with an idea that everyone at the table had shit on. I might have, too, if Beata, to my shock, hadn't put her hand on my shoulder and smiled at me. The gesture told me she knew what had actually happened in the meeting, that Peter was lying. She couldn't praise me openly because she knew he had to take credit.

"Did you write your love letter to Jane Monahan yet?" Beata asked, removing her hand before the others noticed.

I shook my head. I'd tried a few times, but I was struggling to find the right tone that would get me the meeting with her husband without signaling openness to an affair.

"Such a dummkopf," she said, but the insult seemed tinged with gratitude since she'd be in charge of the European recruiting I'd just won from Sorrington. "I'll help you. You need a woman's touch."

"He needs *Jane Monahan's* touch," Phil said. "I'd send her a one-liner. *Meet me at the W Hotel at 3.* Don't need more than that."

"I don't think Robert is going to cheat," Peter said, "no matter how much it's worth to us. I've met his wife. She's beautiful. And I can tell how much he loves her."

I was surprised by Peter's words. I thought he'd want me to take one for the team and give Jane what she wanted so he could get what *he* wanted.

"He doesn't have to," Peter continued. "He just needs to make it *seem* as if he might. After lunch, I want you to work on that email. It must convey a tone of wanton desperation."

"I'm not going to lie to the woman," I said. "I'm happily married. I'm certainly not desperate."

"I disagree." He paused until everyone stopped eating. "You are *financially* desperate."

The sounds around me — the chatter, the traffic, the clanging of utensils — seemed to go quiet. I started to protest, but Peter cut me off.

"Please, I've been to your house in Malibu. I can imagine what your mortgage payment is. That's why you took this job. You needed it.

Desperately. Otherwise, I'm sure you would've been happy to stay in your basement forever."

He waited for me to respond but knew I wasn't going to.

"So, the note will reflect the urgency of your situation. You'll tell her you may lose your house, perhaps your family, if you don't excel in your new job, and to do that you need to win business. Then grovel, if necessary."

And I'd thought the acting business could be humiliating.

I was about to stand up for myself when Beata interceded on my behalf. "Isn't Jane going to invite him to her room then?"

"*His* room," Peter said. "She won't chance anything being tied to her. Not because she cares about her marriage. It's her charitable foundations she wants to protect."

Evidently, Peter had also done some research on Jane. He wanted to win Stadt Bank as a client as much as I did.

"Fine, *his* room," Beata said. "But if we don't want to force Robert to do something he doesn't want to do . . . ?"

I could feel my face go bright red as the conversation moved from my money troubles to my new life as a sex worker.

"Jane Monahan doesn't want to sleep with a loser," said Peter, "which is what Robert will be if he loses this job. And if that *were* to happen, Robert wouldn't be returning to New York any time soon. So it's in Jane's interest to get him a meeting with her husband, though she'll not give that up right away. She'll start with someone lower in the organization. That way, she still has a bargaining chip and can see how Robert performs."

Peter gestured like he'd concluded a TED Talk on a scientific problem that could be proved conclusively, not a harebrained scheme that might actually work. The team tittered, oohing and ahhing at his genius.

"She's gotta give a little," said Donny, "to get a little." He held up his hand with his thumb and index finger an inch apart to indicate the size of my penis.

"And if there's anyone on our team capable of performing," Peter said condescendingly, "it's our very own Brad Pitt."

$ $ $

After lunch, the Global Search team hustled back to the office. Phil and Donny took their seats in the bullpen and started making recruiting calls. Peter disappeared into his office and closed his door. Beata suggested we work on the Jane Monahan letter in the conference room so we'd have the privacy necessary "to be creative." She closed the door, though everyone could see us through the glass.

"Nice lunch," Beata said. "Stimulating conversation."

I sat in one of the chairs and opened my laptop. "Can we focus on the email? I have calls to make, and I have to check in on my research team."

"I'm focusing, I'm focusing."

Beata stood over me and stared down over my shoulder at my screen. I realized that while the others could see what we were doing, they couldn't hear us. Beata was in a surprisingly warm mood, though I wasn't sure why her attitude toward me had changed so quickly. She'd gone from hating me to liking me to *really* liking me, as if by winning the European placements I'd somehow won her, too.

"'Dear Jane,'" I said, reading aloud. "'It was wonderful to meet you on the flight from San Francisco to New York.'"

"You're awfully stiff," she started to critique immediately. "Why don't you put your flight number in there, too, Rain Man? 'So nice to meet you on flight 928 out of San Francisco heading to LaGuardia at 4:23 P.M. Your presence in seat 1A really made the trip worthwhile.'"

I took a breath and started over. "'Dear Jane, I enjoyed meeting you on our flight. What a small world that your husband and I work in the same industry —'"

"Save the husband. Focus on her. And it isn't that much of a coincidence that you both have a connection to Wall Street. Who else can afford business class?"

"How's this? 'I enjoyed meeting you and learning about all your charitable work.'"

"Oh, that's good, since you want to be one of her charities."

I cringed at the zinger. Beata giggled and leaned down as if to read my computer screen.

"By the way, I'd appreciate it," she purred into my ear, "if you could get your team to start researching Europe as soon as possible. If there's *anything* I can do to help expedite the process, let me know."

"Let's get this done first, shall we?"

"I just don't want the ball dropped," she said, sounding worried.

I wasn't sure what she meant and turned to look at her. She was very close.

"Global Search can already barely handle all the Bank of the World work," she said in a whisper. "Imagine if you won Stadt Bank as a client. It's almost like you'd need to be part of a bigger firm to service them properly."

Service them properly? Come on.

She went on, her expression serious. "I bet one of the huge search firms would die to have Stadt Bank as a client. Which means they'd die to have you. And since Stadt Bank is a German company and I'm German, it makes sense to partner with me."

Partner with her? She'd loathed me until an hour ago. And now she wanted me to abandon Peter after only a few months? This office was getting more Machiavellian by the minute.

Beata glanced out the conference room windows as if making sure we weren't being spied on. "How about adding this to the letter?" she said loudly while facing the door. "I'd like to learn more about your charities and have the opportunity to be of assistance to your husband as he builds his team here in the States. If I can be of service, any service at all, please let me know.'"

"I'm not gonna say that. I'll sound like a gigolo."

"You'd be a rich gigolo. You win Stadt Bank, you can write your ticket. If you get a meeting with them, you should research Bank of Switzerland and put that into your pitch deck since Stadt Bank is trying to replicate what they did in the US."

It wasn't a bad idea. Beata was proving herself to be shrewd in her machinations. Of course, I had already exploited that tactic on many occasions. While most of RK Research's clients used our intelligence merely to recruit, more proactive firms hired us whenever they were trying to win business. Our organizational charts enabled them to get up to speed fast in industries or territories where they had no prior knowledge or experience.

"You might even be able to negotiate a larger commission percentage," Beata said, continuing to fantasize about the millions I was going to make — for the two of us. "Think about it. Right now, half of everything we make goes to Hong Kong. Then Peter takes a cut. After that, they take expenses out. Then, finally, we get paid. Why bother with all the middlemen?"

I hadn't concerned myself much with percentages. I just knew my base salary was enough to pay my bills. But, much as it pained me, Beata was right. If I wanted to make a career out of being a recruiter, winning a client was the key. I'd have control of Stadt Bank the way Peter did with Sorrington and Bank of the World. To secure that position, however, I needed a personal connection. Jane Monahan was all I had. Maybe that was enough.

"Okay, but I am not saying the 'any service at all' part."

"Fine. You don't want to seem too easy. But you do need to seem desperate. Say, 'As I mentioned, I'm new in the search business. A meeting with your husband would do a lot for me. I'd be extremely grateful. I'll owe you one.'"

I typed away like I was taking dictation. Beata paced behind me.

"For the finish, say something like, 'I look forward to reconnecting very soon.'"

I wanted to puke. *Be of service. Owe you one. Reconnect.* I wondered what Gardia would think. Actually, the fact that I wouldn't want her to see the email I was drafting was enough to tell me I already knew it was a kind of betrayal. Basically, the subtext of my email to Jane was: Get me a meeting with your husband, and I'll be your side piece. The question was, what happened if Jane did her part? I told myself I was just stringing her along to get what I wanted, what my family *needed*. Right?

Finally, we went to Peter's office and showed him the letter. He approved of the text and the subtext.

"It's gonna be like that scene in *Thelma & Louise*," he said with a leer.

I hadn't seen the movie in years and so wasn't sure what he was referring to.

"Come on, Brad, you were in the movie. Don't you remember?" He tittered. "Too much weed, huh?"

"You sleep with one of the women," Beata said. "Rock her world, rob her blind, and then leave. Send that email, bad boy."

I fired it off, the taste of ash in my mouth.

Peter had gotten a breakdown on the European placements from Sorrington and filled us in. It turned out Global Search had been handed a huge number of roles to fill in a variety of European cities.

"I'm going to need help," Beata said.

"What about taking Donny?" Peter said. We weren't doing much recruiting yet in the Midwest, which was Donny's territory, so if anyone had time to assist it was him.

"Does he speak any languages?"

"I doubt it. Why? Doesn't everyone in Europe speak English these days?"

"In England, Peter, but not in Madrid and a lot of other places. Besides, knowing a candidate's language is a way to build trust and win them over. That's why I want Robert to come."

As much as I wanted to travel around Europe all-expenses-paid, I worried that being alone with Beata could be problematic. There had been a lot of talk about my wife and my sex life, yet she'd never once mentioned her husband. She hadn't had the slightest interest in me until money was involved. As for many on Wall Street, it appeared to be an aphrodisiac for her.

"I've got a lot on my plate with the West Coast," I said. "Plus all the research."

"What languages do you speak again?" Peter asked me.

"Some Spanish, but mainly German. I haven't used it since college. I don't remember much, if anything."

"Say something Deutschey," Peter said.

I attempted to sound like the worst German-language speaker ever. "Uh, *was ist los?*"

My phone dinged. It was Jane Monahan responding to my email in record time. I read the note, then read it out loud when I realized it would get me out of a European trip with Beata.

"It's from Jane," I said. "'Hi Robert, so lovely to meet you! Happy to help! Email my husband's COO, John Liu. I'll tell him all about you! Lunch? Cocktails? ☺'"

I didn't mention that she used a battery of exclamation points, and gave me a smiley face.

"Looks like somebody's going to be busy." Peter came out from behind his desk, and for a moment I thought the Brit was about to give me a fist bump or a high five, but he merely slapped me on the back in a well-done-ol'-chap way. "You're staying in New York."

Beata shrugged in disappointment. Peter stared her down.

"The only way you're going to take Brad from me — or from Global Search — is over my dead body."

I tried not to look shocked or to look at Beata but failed on both counts. Had Peter been listening to us in the conference room? Was there a hidden audio device in there? Or was he just a devious step ahead of her? After all, it's what he would do in her position. I couldn't handle any more cloak-and-dagger stuff. The backstabbing was reminding me — and my neck — of why I'd quit acting.

And Beata? She just backed quietly out of the room.

CHAPTER TWENTY-THREE

The Dropping-the-Grapefruit Ploy

Within an hour, John Liu, the chief operating officer of one of the largest financial institutions in the world, emailed me to set up a meeting for the very next morning. Jane had delivered.

"I bet she did," Peter said when I gave him the news. "The fact he emailed you so quickly means one of two things: Either Stadt Bank is desperate for a search firm with new ideas, or Jane Monahan is the boss in her family. Let's hope it's both." He seemed giddy.

I understood Peter's excitement, though what I felt was more like panic. Because the Monahan name had been familiar when I met Jane on the plane, I'd had my team in Malibu search our past work for her husband's name. We didn't have an expensive database like the one Martin designed for Global Search. Our records were spread out over countless printed files and hard drives, so it took awhile. When I received the old research, I noticed that John Liu's name was on most of the documents related to Ken Monahan. This made sense, since anyone chosen to be COO has usually worked with the CEO in some previous capacity and been picked for their willingness and ability to handle the dirty work. So Liu was Ken Monahan's consiglieri. Though I doubted I was the first man Jane had tried to cheat with, I was surely the only one stupid enough to go to her husband's office looking for work. For all I knew, Liu was only having me in to threaten me never to contact Jane again — or end up swimming with Luca Brasi.

I also knew that — unlike Bank of the World — Stadt Bank had minimal presence in the US wealth management space. They weren't looking to expand; they needed to build from *scratch*. If Global Search was hired, we'd be placing hundreds of executives. And unlike the Sorrington meetings, which Peter ran, I'd be in charge of this one.

"Don't be nervous, Brad," Peter said, taking in my reaction. "It's like acting."

"What do you know about it?" I snapped.

Enough already with the Brad Pitt bullshit. I'd just completely on my own — okay, with a little luck — won a meeting with a huge international firm. Was it possible that a failed actor could sit in a room with the second most powerful person at a Wall Street bank and win tens of millions of dollars in recruiting fees without ever having made a single placement? Evidently, the answer was yes. But no matter how fed up I was with Peter, I couldn't go to the meeting without him. Even if I wanted to quit Global Search (which I did) and I won the Stadt Bank business (which I might), I would still have to execute those placements. I couldn't handle it alone.

"Well, you're the expert," he said. "Didn't mean to step on your toes."

Peter seemed genuinely chagrined. I felt like the balance of power had shifted in our relationship. I was no longer the flunky newbie, I was a potential equal — if not in experience, at least in terms of winning business.

"I was just thinking your Brad Pitt good looks are your secret weapon," he continued. "Most executives aren't good looking. Look at Sorrington. Hell, look at me. They don't expect you to be smart. But you are. You'll wow them with your corporate intelligence. You'll make them want to be you, but they can't be. The closest they can get is to hire you. Which they will."

Peter's belief in me took me by surprise. But his words also made me sad, and not just because each time Pitt's name came up it reminded me how close I'd come to a successful acting career. I felt sorry for Peter, and by some strange extension the people who worked on Wall Street. Were they all as unhappy as Peter seemed to be? Did they regret spending their entire lives working only for money? Was the reason for the greed and corruption endemic to Wall Street some underlying resentment or overcompensation for dreadful insecurities? Was the most honest definition of the American Dream: *I didn't get to be what I wanted to be, so I'm going to make everybody pay?* And now, because I hadn't "made it" as an actor, was I going to do the same? Was I going to pretend to help Jasmin grow her team while scheming to get her fired? Was I going to cheat on my wife for . . . money? So someone would point to me and say, approvingly, *He's loaded.*

Working as a recruiter had already made me depressed. A few days earlier, a photographer had come to the Global Search office to take everyone's picture for the website and for promotional materials. In many of the images I had a hangdog look. In a few, it seemed like I might cry.

"Thanks for the vote of confidence," I said to Peter.

"You deserve it," he said with a small smile. "And don't forget to book that lunch with Jane. Better yet, do cocktails."

$ $ $

I emailed Jane to thank her for facilitating the meeting and said I'd let her know how it went. I didn't mention lunch, and certainly not drinks. There was no way I could have a meal with her. I imagined her drunk and propositioning me. I'd turn her down, of course, or try to take her to AA. It was one thing to lie over the phone to get corporate intelligence; it was something else entirely to pretend, face-to-face, to care about another human being for financial benefit. Holding Jane off long enough to win over John Liu on my own merits was as far as I was willing to take things for this particular ruse.

To accomplish that I needed to pull some high-quality research for the deck. I didn't have time to reach out to my team for help. This was an emergency. They were all swamped with work, anyway. They also weren't as good as I was. I wanted the intelligence I dropped in front of Liu to be pristine and perfect.

I recalled Beata's advice to research Stadt Bank's biggest rival, the Bank of Switzerland, which had developed a strong presence in the US wealth management space. But where was I going to make my rusing calls from? I needed to use my fake Skype account so calls couldn't be traced back to me, but that required a strong Wi-Fi connection, which the Global Search office had. I couldn't have anyone overhear me on the phone, though, lest they steal my techniques — or testify against me in federal court.

Recently, Ocean had dialed directly from one of the phones in my Malibu office without blocking the number — a rookie mistake, and a potentially catastrophic one. Within days, a letter arrived from the Swiss investment bank he'd called warning us that because RK Research was breaking a zillion national (and international) laws we were now in some deep shit. The name of the firm was, of course, familiar to me, but so was the name signed at the bottom. It was the same lawyer, then deputy head of the Swiss bank's US legal department, who'd faxed me a similar letter years earlier when I'd stupidly given out Leona's fax number — except now this man was the head of the legal department *globally* and was based at the firm's headquarters in Zurich. The timing of his threats could not have been worse, since I now needed to call *another* Swiss investment bank. While I knew the head of Legal at one firm wasn't calling the head of Legal at another to warn them, it was highly likely he'd alerted the Swiss authorities, who would certainly inform other Swiss financial institutions of our, ahem, activities.

Ocean's call had likely been recorded, too, since that was standard operating procedure for all calls to Wall Street switchboards and most internal desks. I didn't want a young kid to go down because of me, even if I was paying him far more than Leona had ever paid me. But also, unlike her, I hadn't insulated myself from the ruse. I'd sat in on Ocean's training and offered many tips and tutorials along the way. If Ocean was arrested, he'd have no reason not to crack and implicate me as the ringleader I most certainly was. My only prayer was that the Swiss authorities were as lax as their country's infamously loose banking regulations. I was positive that if this legal executive worked at a French or German or — God forbid — American bank I'd already be sitting in a federal jail cell facing serious questions from stern-faced investigators and years of potential prison time. I'd always warned Gardia that the knock on the door may one day come, and when it did not to answer any questions, just immediately call an attorney.

I had no choice, though. If I wanted to get out of the ruse business I had to make it as a recruiter, which meant I had to win the Stadt Bank account. If I did that and Interpol or the FBI came a-knockin', perhaps I could come clean and talk my way out of it, say I'd found religion and would never do it again.

I looked around the Global Search office, and when no one was watching I grabbed my laptop and slipped into the room for candidates waiting to be interviewed, which had a solid door. Already it was past five in New York, which meant I was limited in my options. I did a bit of online research and found the name of the head of corporate communications, Sebastian Offner, who was based in Zurich, where everyone was already long gone for the night. I dialed the Bank of Switzerland's New York office but got an automated response that they'd shut down the switchboard at four thirty. This meant their other offices on the East Coast would be closed, too. Racing the geographic clock, I called the Chicago office, where folks had often been friendly. I got an automated response that the switchboard closed at five, though it was only four thirty there. Midwesterners liked to shut things down early.

My last chance was the Bank of Switzerland's San Francisco office, the only one they had on the West Coast. This meant I had one shot at the information I desperately needed before I met with Liu in the morning.

"*Guten tag*," I said when the receptionist answered. Since German was the only language I was actually proficient in, I'd learned to do a half-decent German accent, though it often bordered on a bad imitation of Arnold Schwarzenegger's Austrian one. "Zis is Sebastian Offner from za Zurich office. Vat iz your name?"

"This is Catherine."

"Zo nice to meet you. Forgive my accent. It is difficult, ja?"

"I can understand you perfectly."

"You are too kind. Ve are updating our records for za US, and I need to list za head for za San Francisco team on my documents."

"Don't you have access to that on our system?" I could tell that Catherine was trying not to be rude but that she wasn't buying my request. Perhaps it was the accent, since I hadn't used it in a while.

"I am off-site in Brussels meeting zis veek vith za European Union regulators, so I cannot access za system."

"Isn't it awfully late there?"

"Ja, but when za regulators say jump, ve say how high." I gave a big laugh.

Catherine didn't respond in kind, not a good sign. I could hear her typing. She was looking me up.

"The head of our office is Chris Sorenson."

She'd undoubtedly found Sebastian's name in the system and felt it was safe to give out that one piece of information.

"*Sehr gut.* Whoops, I am speaking German again. One last zing, I need to list Chris's reports and ve are finished."

"Forgive me, I know this is going to sound strange. But how do I know you are who you say you are?"

"You zink I could pretend zis accent?"

That made her laugh for the first time.

"I could tell you my office number if you like zo you could look me up on za system."

"Thank you. I want to be sure I'm not giving out anything I shouldn't."

I read her the phone number I'd found for Sebastian online. Most firms list the direct numbers for their corporate communications team members right on their websites.

"Well, all right," she said, still hesitant. "It just doesn't make sense that the European Union needs the San Francisco team."

"Ve have za US regulators here zis veek, too. Ve are, how you say in English, killing all za birds vith one stone."

My mangling of the saying seemed to appease Catherine. She read me the names of everyone on Chris's team. I then asked her for the charts on the firm's other US locations since those offices were closed. I could tell she wasn't quite buying my story, but what were the odds that someone was calling her and *pretending to have a German accent?* It would be ridiculous. Which was another psychological ploy, however counterintuitive, that reliably paid off: The more outlandish the ruse, the more believable one becomes.

Once I'd obtained all the names, titles, and phone numbers, I asked for the intelligence I most wanted: the size of each banker's book of business.

"Ve need to list za names in za order of za size of za book of business."
I wondered if I was pushing it with the request — and using *za* too
often.

"Wait, why would you need all that?"

"Za European Union regulators need zat."

"But why would the US have to give all of that information?"

I chuckled. "Why do you zink ve are opening more offices in za States?
Your regulators are not so strict like za European Union is. I can hardly
turns my neck from za stress. It is midnight here and still I am
working."

"They sound awful," she said sympathetically, which to me was the
sound of the final click before the safe door swings open. "Let me go
grab the production charts."

$ $ $

I spent the rest of the evening working late with Global Search's techies:
Martin, who ran the firm's database, and Lori, who created the
PowerPoint decks we would present to John Liu in the morning. The
showstopper of the pitch was going to be my corporate intelligence on
the Bank of Switzerland. Any search firm could walk in the door and *say*
they knew all the top people in a given space. My intelligence would
prove we had the ability to determine anything — and everything — our
clients wanted to know.

I decided to have Lori put the old research I'd done that had Liu's
name on it at the end of the deck. That way, he could see that RK
Research had essentially tracked his career. We had his entire résumé,
but, more important, we had every colleague he'd ever worked for or
with, including his current boss, Ken Monahan. I imagined Liu being
impressed with that kind of nitty-gritty, in-depth intelligence and hoped
it would ultimately win us the Stadt Bank account.

Martin filled out the first half of the deck with the data he'd mined
from social media, still a relatively new technique in 2010. He'd created
bright charts and graphs that detailed Stadt Bank's brand recognition in
the US, which was low. For the percentage that did know the firm, he
had included slides that delineated their perception of its reputation. I

wondered how those numbers might change if they knew the firm was thinking of hiring a recruiter whose track record included more failed TV pilots than job placements.

The following morning, Peter and I took a car down to the Stadt Bank office in Lower Manhattan. I'd only been to the Wall Street district twice in my life, as it wasn't exactly a hot spot for auditions. But as I checked the perspiration stains on my dress shirt, it occurred to me that the meeting with John Liu was essentially an audition — as big, in its way, as any I'd done.

We checked in with security, handing over our IDs.

"You're on the list," the guard said, pointing at me. "But he's not."

Peter looked at me. "Did you email him I was coming?"

I hadn't. The process of winning a meeting was so new to me I'd forgotten to take care of the simplest of details.

"Oh shit," I said. "I completely spaced it. I'm sorry. Let me call up there."

"Perhaps it's best if you go on your own," Peter said, retreating into phony British polite speak. He wanted to chew me out, if not claw my face off, but he was in the lobby of a Wall Street building with hundreds of witnesses streaming past. "That seems to be what you want to do anyway."

"I don't. I promise. I just screwed up."

"Well, hurry up and fix it, Brad."

It took a few stressful minutes, but soon enough Peter and I were on our way to the sixtieth floor. I'd had to pull from the ruse handbook and lie to Liu's assistant, which was second nature at that point and greased the wheels just enough to save my ass.

We exited the elevator into a huge open space with thirty-foot floor-to-ceiling windows. Rows of computers lined the room. Hundreds of traders sat in front of them studying their screens. Though Stadt Bank had no presence in the US wealth management space, they were quite active in the equity and fixed income markets. I took in the dramatic views of the Brooklyn Bridge and the Statue of Liberty. Tourists paid money for views like this, and for a quick second I considered myself lucky.

A woman in her midfifties scurried over. "I'm John's assistant. Come with me," she said with a slight scowl.

As we followed behind her I said, "Bet you don't get tired of the view," trying to win her over just a little.

She gave me a polite nod but kept moving. If anything, she walked faster, as if trying to avoid any further attempt to bond.

"Here you go." She escorted us into a large see-through conference room with a table that could seat thirty people, which effectively underlined the disparity of power since it was just Peter and me representing a recruitment firm that was pretending to be a bigger fish than it was. "John will be right in."

"Thank you, Diane," Peter said. "Sorry for the confusion downstairs. I'll make sure John knows it wasn't your fault."

She seemed surprised he knew her name but appeared grateful for his acknowledgment that the mix-up may have made her look bad. "I appreciate that."

After she left, Peter said, "I heard the guard use her name. You're supposed to be the master spy."

Pitching in this environment was going to be a new experience for me, completely different from the atmosphere in my toolshed. If I won this account, I would be making more money than I ever had before — really, more money than I ever thought I *could* — and the stress was soaking me in sweat under my shirt.

Liu entered, moving as quickly as his assistant, and shook my hand. I hoped he didn't notice my flop sweat.

"You must be Peter McBee," he said as he shook hands with my boss. "Unlike Robert, I've actually heard of you."

That quickly he'd belittled us both.

"Don't take that the wrong way," he added after a pregnant pause. "Ken *is* looking for new talent. We just didn't expect it to come from his wife." He chortled and sat at the head of the table, interlacing his fingers as if he were Michael Corleone waiting for us to beg his favor.

"Robert certainly qualifies," Peter said. "Though we hired him less as a recruiter and more because of his intelligence capabilities."

"Jane didn't mention the intelligence part."

I ignored the obvious dig and opened my briefcase on the table. Peter gave me a dirty look since I'd purchased the thing on sale at Staples. I pulled out a printout of the PowerPoint deck, my first ever, and handed it to Liu. He paged through it as though he'd seen a million of them.

Until he got to my corporate intelligence.

The flapping of the pages stopped, and he began to read the profile of Stadt Bank's biggest competitor, the Bank of Switzerland. I had the names, titles, and cell numbers of everyone they could possibly want to recruit. More than that, *I had their books of business.*

Liu glanced up as if reevaluating me. Peter and I exchanged a look: The deck had done its job. This was what Peter had envisioned when he hired me. My corporate intelligence was our difference maker.

"Impressive," Liu said. "Actionable, too."

He returned to the deck to continue reading. Or maybe he was trying to memorize the data so he could get it for free.

"This is good stuff." He shook his head like he couldn't believe it. "Jane said you're working with Bank of the World. Wouldn't that be a conflict since we're both hiring in the wealth management space?"

Search firms usually had to agree to be exclusive with their clients, at least in the specific space in which they were hired to recruit, but sometimes there was wiggle room. I counted on Peter to find it.

"We are exclusive in private banking," Peter said, "but that's the ultra-high-net-worth space. Stadt Bank is looking to make inroads into the high-net-worth space. The candidates are completely different."

This was only somewhat true, but it was good enough for Liu to go back to reading. Finally, he got to the part of the deck where I'd included old research documents with his name.

"What's this," he asked, scrutinizing the information.

"We've been tracking you over the years," I said, peacock proud.

The documents started in the mid-'90s, when I first began to keep electronic files.

"This is wrong," Liu said.

At first, I thought he was voicing a moral objection to the concept of competitive intelligence.

"I didn't work with this guy," he continued, pointing at a name on the research. "Or this guy."

He began to flip through the pages in time to the rapid-fire beating of my heart. When he came to the end, he said, "A lot of this stuff is off." Obviously, he couldn't question the names listed for the Bank of Switzerland research, but by including his old groups I'd inadvertently enabled him to check my work. I couldn't believe that it was wrong, but certainly Liu would know who had been on his teams.

I was devastated.

"What else you got?" he said, leaning back in his chair again.

But that was it. That was all we had. My CI was supposed to be the secret weapon that won us his business. Instead, it had caused the whole enterprise to blow up in my face.

$ $ $

On the way down in the elevator, I realized I'd left the deck behind. I had other copies, but I didn't want him to get my intelligence for free no matter how crappy he thought it was. The Bank of Switzerland intel listed inside was worth insane amounts of money — to all of us. Using that research, Stadt Bank could secure hundreds of millions of dollars from poaching the candidates who handled the most assets, targets I had just supplied them. For Global Search, getting Stadt Bank as a client was worth tens of millions in recruiting fees. My personal haul would come from two streams, recruiting and research, which would amount to millions in additional income. For my new career in recruiting, it would have been the equivalent of landing the Brad Pitt part in *Thelma & Louise* — a step that would catapult me to entirely new levels of success. Except, once again, I'd fallen just short.

"I'll go back for it," I said.

Peter shook his head.

I thought it was because my research had been exposed as flawed, something that hadn't happened in all my years of rusing. Which is not to say we obtained every financial group organizational chart or that our intelligence was always 100 percent accurate, though I'd believed it close. But John Liu had insisted that my work was substandard.

"He doesn't even want the deck," I said, recalling the disgusted look Liu had given us when we left. We were like two Lincoln-Mercury car salesmen being told the quality of American cars was a disgrace.

"Oh, he wanted it," Peter said. "The reason you forgot to pick it up was because he slipped it onto his chair when he got up. Basically, he palmed it so he could keep it."

"Why didn't you say anything? That research was worth a lot of money."

Peter didn't respond. The elevator doors opened onto the building's gleaming marble lobby. We trudged across it, exited through the revolving door, and found our Town Car waiting. I slumped into the backseat and pouted. At least I could blow off lunch with Jane Monahan without feeling any guilt.

After a few minutes of painful silence, I finally asked, "Why did he want our deck so much if my work sucks?"

"Your work doesn't suck."

Peter sounded as if he was exhausted from having to explain things to me. I thought he might be furious and demand some of his money back for all the research I'd done for him over the years. Instead, he seemed to be supporting me in his tepid British way. He glared at me, then at the driver.

"You don't get it, do you?"

"What?"

"John Liu lied to you."

"Huh? What do you mean? About what?"

"Your research wasn't wrong. He was saying that to fuck with you."

"What? Why?"

"Because he can. Because he was putting you in your place. Because he was pissed he had to meet with you. Because he was pissed he may actually have to *hire* you."

"Really?"

"Yes, really. Because of the quality of your work, he now has to show that deck to Ken Monahan. That means they have to consider hiring us. You did well, Brad."

I chuckled, feeling better about myself — though I was perturbed by how clearly Peter had understood everything that happened in the room.

It's like we'd invented a variation of good cop / bad cop called smart cop / dumb cop. It reminded me of the very first performance I did at the Actors Studio, a scene from Arthur Miller's Tony Award–winning drama *All My Sons*. My acting teacher had taught me to choose an older, experienced actor as my scene partner since legends of the entertainment business could be in attendance and I would be insanely nervous. The heavyweight, in this case longtime character actor Bill Moor, would anchor me. Indeed, right before we were about to perform, I had to pee. I raced down the stairs from the theater to the restroom and found myself at a urinal next to Al Pacino. There was no way I could urinate beside Tony Fucking Montana and ran back up the stairs bladder unemptied, anxiety amplified.

Sure enough, when I walked onstage carrying a breakfast tray, I promptly dropped it. Poor Bill Moor spent the entire scene covering for me by cleaning off his grapefruit. At the end of what I considered to be a career-ending debacle (before my career had even begun), those in attendance — including Mr. Pacino — raved at how fresh and original the scene had seemed. Many commented that my choice to drop the tray was brilliant.

Sometimes you work the ploy. Sometimes the ploy works you.

CHAPTER TWENTY-FOUR

Spy vs. Spy

Back in the Global Search office, I emailed Jane that the meeting had gone well. I told her that I hoped we might have the opportunity to be of service to her husband. I didn't mention performing any kind of service for her, just said that I was heading home to California in a few hours. She replied with a sad-face emoji.

I didn't tell Peter that I'd moved up my flight to avoid him pressuring me into hooking up with Jane. Because I'd asked the office manager to make the change, and she knew who signed her checks, of course she told him.

"Leaving so soon?" he asked after calling me into his office for an impromptu meeting.

"I've got to handle that Jasmin demotion."

"You could've handled Jane first, then left."

I summoned the courage to tell Peter that I wasn't going to meet with her. It wasn't right to use her or lead her on, though I'd already done both. "Listen —"

"Tut, tut. I don't want to hear it. Maybe you're right." Peter suddenly appeared to agree with me. "If you gave Jane what she wanted, you'd have nothing left to offer."

I nodded like it was my strategy, as well.

"I don't want you to get lonely on your flight," Peter said, "so I booked a buddy to go with you." I had no idea who he could be referring to and eyed him quizzically.

"Jack MacDonald wants to make sure we're getting all of your research onto the Global Search database, so we're sending Martin with you to train your team on how to do it."

As if he'd been hiding outside the office door listening for his cue, Global Search's tech guru burst into the room.

"I'm excited to meet the RK Research team and see how you do things."

Peter gave him a dirty look, as if Martin had somehow said the wrong thing.

"You want to *help* him do things," Peter said, doing some kind of damage control. "Starting with getting the research we've paid for — handsomely, I might add — into our database."

RK Research was still an independent company contracting with Global Search. While I was being paid for the research, I was also paying my researchers. We were a distinct entity. No one ever mentioned that we'd have to log our work into *their* system. It seemed presumptuous.

"Eventually," Peter said, continuing, "you're going to need to log everything you've ever done into the system so it's searchable by any detail. Won't that be exciting?"

I nodded hesitantly. When I signed up with Global Search, Jack stated that he wanted to buy my company. Gardia and I had had a call with him to provide our income history so he could come up with an offer. But we hadn't heard back. Now Peter was talking about putting research that Global Search hadn't paid for into their system for free, and while old research wasn't as valuable, it wasn't worthless, either. Many times, clients had bought older intelligence from me so they could track who was at a firm at a certain time and where they went after that.

I wanted to ask Peter if an offer to buy my business was forthcoming, but I couldn't with Martin in the room. I wasn't sure if Peter had any say in the matter anyway. Though he was running the New York and London offices, he was, like me, still just an employee. To my knowledge, he didn't have any partnership equity in Global Search, so asking him would've been pointless. I needed to reach out to Jack MacDonald to get the matter resolved. Gardia and I were anticipating an offer in the millions — likely low millions, but still a great deal of money. Until then, there was no way in hell I was giving away my research for free.

$ $ $

The next morning, Martin met me at the RK Research office in Malibu. His mouth was agape at the dolphin statue — and the view of the Pacific behind it. He couldn't believe I got to work in this place.

"I mean, you can go surfing after work," he said, shaking his head.

"Before work is better," I said. "The wind comes up in the afternoon."

"You surf?"

"You can't live in Malibu and not." This wasn't far from the truth. Sometimes it seemed like the whole town stopped whenever there was a big swell. Not that I had surfed recently. Since I'd joined Global Search I'd stopped working out. There just wasn't time.

"Could you take me? I'd love to learn."

He looked relatively fit. He was certainly young enough. "Can you swim?"

He nodded like it was a stupid question.

"Can you handle cold?" I asked, then remembered Martin was Canadian. Of course he could handle cold. "Okay, tomorrow morning."

It couldn't hurt to win Martin over. I figured if I bonded with him over some tasty waves perhaps he could push Jack MacDonald to make me an offer, since he was the only member of Peter's team Jack had personally hired.

Once inside the office, I introduced Martin to Angie and Suze, who together ran the administrative side of the business. They took the Word documents from our researchers and turned them into great-looking PowerPoints, each one starting off with my picture and bio. They'd also be the ones Martin would train to enter our research into the Global Search database. Angie was Martin's age, in her midtwenties. Suze was two decades older and had a thing for younger men, a fact whose relevance will be revealed momentarily.

"Can I meet your researchers?" Martin asked.

"Sure, why not." I took Martin into the bullpen area and introduced him to Chip, Strider, and Ocean. "Guys, this is Martin. He runs tech for Global Search."

They exchanged pleasantries and got to know each other as I headed into my office. I had emails to return, recruiting calls to make, and the demotion of Jasmin Shirazi to schedule. I got ahold of her assistant and set a meeting for the following day. I was beginning to call candidates when Suze walked into my office and shut the door.

"Why is he listening to them?" She gestured toward Martin, who had his laptop open but was leaning toward the researchers, blatantly eavesdropping as they made ruse calls.

"Our job is pretty compelling," I said drily.

"He seems awfully interested in what they do. And he had no interest in these." Suze indicated her surgically enhanced breasts.

"What are you saying, that he's gay? Who cares?"

"Robert. I was an actor, too, remember? This guy is full of shit and not good at hiding it. I'm surprised you don't see it." I'd forgotten about Suze's big-screen past, which consisted of playing scantily clad women who died gruesome deaths in obscure horror films — often before the opening credits had finished. "He's here to steal your techniques."

I jumped out of my ergonomic desk chair because I instantly knew she was right. For years, I'd protected the ploys Pax and I developed. The only individuals we'd shared them with were my three new researchers. But now Martin was here listening to them work, *with intent*. Someone had put him up to it, and I was annoyed that I'd been blind to the con.

"He's a dead man." I started toward the door.

"Wait, sit down!" I did so reluctantly, annoyed with Suze now, too. "You can't let him know you know. Not yet. You have to figure out who's pulling his strings first."

"I already know. It's Peter." But then Martin was Jack's hire, so maybe not. "Or maybe Jack."

"Exactly. You have to find out which."

I felt sick to my stomach and like I wanted to go full Gandolfini and heave a desk chair at Martin's sternum. It was like my office had suddenly become contaminated. The feeling reminded me of walking into my New York apartment after it'd been robbed.

"Call the team in here," I said. "Tell them we have a new rush project."

"But all the research we're doing is for Global Search. Peter will hear about it and realize it was an excuse to get Martin away from the researchers."

"This is my office. Those are my researchers. I can do research for whomever I like. Global Search was supposed to buy my business, and they haven't. So let Peter — and Jack — think I'm starting to take work from old clients."

If people were playing games with me, I was going to start playing, too.

Suze corralled the researchers into my office, closed the door, and explained the situation. I told them to move from the bullpen into the empty offices and to keep the doors closed. If Martin came in while they were on the phone, they were to terminate the call. Then they were to chat with him pleasantly until Suze or Angie came in to pull him away with some question about how to enter information into the database, which was ostensibly the reason he was there. The last thing I told them was to make sure Martin knew that the "emergency" research project wasn't for Global Search.

While I was glad we'd caught Martin before he got many details — thanks to Suze — I felt like there needed to be some consequences for spying.

After all, I was the only one allowed to get away with that.

$$\$ \$ \$$$

The next morning at six, Martin met me at my house.

"Wow, you *live* here," he said when he saw my ocean view.

"I do, but it's expensive." I opened the garage and went through my old wet suits looking for one that would fit him. I made sure to give him one with a lot of holes. Revenge is a dish best served Pacific Ocean cold. "That's why I'm doing two jobs right now: running my research team and recruiting. I need both to survive."

"I bet." He grinned at me.

I loaded up my Audi Q5 with surfboards, towels, and two wet suits. "Hop in. I'm taking you to my secret spot. I can trust you, right? You won't tell anyone?"

The surf spot was in front of the beach house I'd rented when times were good. It seemed like a lifetime ago now. The owner of the property even felt sorry for me. He knew I rarely got to surf anymore, so he continued to let me drive down his private path to surf the spot as long as it was just me parking on his gated road. He didn't want anyone to disturb his new tenant, Gore Verbinski, the director of the *Pirates of the Caribbean* movies.

"No way, man," Martin said as he climbed into my SUV. "I won't say a word."

"You better not."

I held his gaze with an omertà-level seriousness, then finally chuckled as if it were all a big goof. Martin chuckled back in relief, but he was off balance now.

We drove to the Encinal area of Malibu, which is my favorite part, especially in the winter when the beaches are as deserted as the houses. Most of the properties are second or third homes — God forbid those homeowners spend any time in Malibu when the weather dipped below seventy-two degrees.

One of the central misconceptions of Malibu and the thirteen thousand people who live there is that everyone is rich and famous, when really for the most part it's only those who live on the ocean side of the Pacific Coast Highway. The rest is populated by middle- and low-income teachers, firefighters, sheriffs, and blue-collar workers — there's even an RV park. My Victorian is on the land side of the PCH, and just when it seemed I'd have enough money to cross over, the crash eliminated the possibility.

I put in the code for the private gate and drove down the steep path to the beach. Martin gasped when I parked right at the sand. There were no other cars or people, just the ocean, unridden waves, and empty beach-front mansions.

We put on our wet suits and sunscreen. While the water was ice cold, the sun was shining. I had considered withholding the sunscreen and letting the pasty Canadian get a sunburn, but I wasn't that cruel. I didn't want to give him skin cancer, I just wanted to teach him a lesson I'd cribbed from *Risky Business*: In times of economic uncertainty, never ever fuck with another man's livelihood.

"Okay," I said after we were geared up. "Let's charge it."

Martin was sweating in the black wet suit, the white sunscreen running down his face into his beard, making it seem as if he'd turned gray before my eyes.

"Aren't you going to give me a lesson first?"

I squinted at him. The biggest issue with beginning surfers wasn't getting up on the board and riding the wave, it was having the conditioning to be able to paddle out to where the wave broke and then the power and strength to catch the damn thing. Malibu has a few select spots where waves roll slowly enough that newbies can catch them. My secret spot was not one of them.

"Okay, let me see your pop-up," I said, acquiescing.

"What?"

I lowered myself until my chest was on my board. "Pretend I'm going for a wave." I paddled the air with short choppy strokes that differed from a swimmer's. "My neck is slightly craned. I'm looking down the line where I want to go. I'm stroking as fast as I can. I can feel the wave under me, but I don't stop paddling yet. I take an extra two strokes to make sure I've caught the wave, and then as I'm sliding down the face I pop up."

I whipped my legs up under me, landing square on the board in a deep knee bend. The fingers of my left hand pointed straight out over the nose of my board. I held my right arm at a ninety-degree angle.

"You try it," I said.

Martin made himself prone on his board, moving like the wet suit was a spacesuit. He tried to pop up and pull his legs underneath him, but he only got one foot on the board and tumbled into the sand. When he got up, a large chunk of the beach had attached itself to the sunscreen in his beard.

"Pretty good for a first try," I said.

Martin looked at me skeptically.

"It's a lot easier on the water," I added. "You'll see."

We walked to the water's edge, and I scanned the horizon searching for signs of a set. The best time to paddle out was immediately *after* a big set when there was a lull. This time, however, I wanted to send Martin straight into a set as it built. When I finally saw the waves coming, I shouted, "Go! Paddle!"

Martin flopped onto his board and started windmilling his arms like a cartoon character. He generated a decent amount of speed, but it was no match for the white water that crashed into him, knocking him off his board. I followed, pushing my board underneath the waves in a technique known as duck-diving. I watched him and tried not to laugh.

His eyes were wide, almost in panic. I could tell the cold water had shocked him. The wet suit took a moment to work, since a layer of water needed to get trapped inside and warmed by body heat. It didn't take long, but that first minute was painful. I could tell Martin was rethinking the whole thing and decided to give him some incentive to keep trying.

"What kind of Canadian is afraid of the cold?" I shouted.

Set waves kept rolling through. Martin got back on his board and paddled like a maniac, then got knocked off again. He began hyperventilating as if he might drown, but I wasn't going to let him off that easy. Besides, he was attached to his board with a leash and the water was barely over his head.

"I don't think I can make it out to the break," he gasped. "The surf's too strong."

"You want me to push you? I do it all the time with my eight-year-old."

In New York, Martin had bragged about how many fights he'd been in while playing ice hockey as a kid. Right now the goon looked like I could push him under with two fingers. He nodded, too winded to speak.

I got close to him and waited for the set to end. When the lull came, I gave him a giant shove. "Paddle. Paddle hard."

Martin was so afraid of getting caught in the impact zone again that he paddled frantically well beyond the break. I let him go. If I was lucky, he'd get run over by a container ship.

"Get over here," I yelled. "You're too far outside to catch any waves."

I knew he wasn't catching shit, but I wasn't going to tell him that. He paddled to where I sat in the lineup. I could tell he was exhausted. He was shivering, too. The wet suit was in bad shape — I counted close to a dozen holes.

"You okay?" I asked, beginning to feel a bit bad for the snooper.

"A little chilly." His lips were a light purple.

"I thought hockey players were tough."

He nodded like they were.

I saw another set on the horizon, bigger than the previous one. "Follow me." I paddled closer to the beach. I could tell Martin wanted to stay in the relative safety of the middle of the ocean, but he did as I instructed. When the first wave came through I took off on it, letting him see my surfing prowess. After the set finished, I paddled back and sat up on my board.

"Why didn't you go for any of those waves?"

Though I knew the answer.

Fear.

Martin didn't respond, he just stared at the next set rolling in, bigger than the last. The rising tide was helping to increase the size of the waves. It wasn't a day for an intermediate, let alone a beginner.

"I want you to paddle for this one," I hollered.

Martin shook his head. His eyes were big.

"Don't make me tell everyone you chickened out."

Reluctantly, he began to paddle.

"Stroke," I shouted, "stroke."

To my surprise, Martin got some board speed going. As the wave rose up behind him, he began to drop down the face. He might have made it, too, if he'd remembered my lesson and taken two last strokes before popping up. Instead, he stopped paddling and lost momentum. With Martin caught on the lip, the wave came down and drove him underwater. His board went flying and then disappeared. It took me a moment to realize that his leash had snapped. After a few seconds, I spotted the board hurtling by itself toward the beach.

So much for there being no chance of him drowning.

Martin popped to the surface whipping his head to find the board so he could climb on and catch his breath.

"Your leash snapped," I said. "The board's gone."

Martin thrashed around, using up too much energy. I was a certified rescue diver and had seen it before. Instead of relaxing and letting the buoyancy of the wet suit help to float them, inexperienced ocean-goers flailed to exhaustion.

Then they drowned.

I hadn't planned it this way but figured I may as well take advantage of the situation now that Martin was completely at my mercy.

"Want my board?" I asked. "I can swim in."

He nodded. "That'd be great. I don't know if I can swim that far."

"I have one question first. Who put you up to it?"

Martin looked genuinely confused. "What?"

"Who told you to try to learn what my researchers do? Peter or Jack?"

Martin's face took on a different kind of fear. "Did you set my leash so it would break?"

"This isn't Spy vs. Spy," I said, though maybe it was. All it would take now was a murder and I could sell the film rights. I made my face go hard. "You flew out here to steal my secrets. I want to know who put you up to it."

Martin lunged to grab my board, but I easily paddled away. The effort seemed to take something out of him because he sank below the surface momentarily. When he came up, he hollered, "Help! Help!"

I'd often worried that if anything happened to me while surfing my secret spot — if a white shark took a bite out of me, for example — there wouldn't be anyone to hear my cries. At the moment, I was glad for that. "Help! Help!" I joined in to show him that no one was coming, sounding a lot like Jack Nicholson in *The Shining*. I could've just as easily been shouting *"Here's Johnny!"* All of the stress working for Peter and Jack and the toll of the 2008 crash had taken me to the edge.

"You're crazy," he said and took a deep breath. He looked around again, panicked.

"Do you want to drown, motherfucker?"

He turned back to me. He did not want to drown.

"You're charging Global Search too much money. That's why they sent me."

I stared at him in enraged disbelief. That was ridiculous.

"I'm charging the same rate I've always charged. If they want a discount, they should buy my business." Something struck me. "Wait a second, who the fuck is 'they'?"

A look of resignation came over Martin's face. I imagined it was similar to the expression of those about to drown. "Peter and Jack," he said.

"*Both* of them?"

I plunged my head into the water in fury. Those duplicitous assholes. They were going to steal my trade secrets and then not only drop RK

Research but probably, sooner rather than later, cast me off, as well. Jack and Peter had turned on me despite my honest attempts to win business for them and make their firm successful — even as I pushed up against moral boundaries I'd never wanted to go near. In return, they'd made false promises and engaged in trickery.

I came back up, unstrapped my leash, and threw it to Martin. "Put that on and paddle in. I'll swim."

Not that I had room to judge. I'd peddled in false promises and trickery as a car salesman. And I'd handed out both regularly on the phone for twenty years. This time, however, I wasn't the rus*er*, I was the rus*ee* — the victim, the dupe, the sucker. As evidenced by my consideration of whether to actually let Martin drown, clearly I could dish it out but couldn't take it. It was an eye-opening experience. It was also, as I was learning, just another day in corporate America.

CHAPTER TWENTY-FIVE

The Traitor's Reveal

The encounter with Martin had been sobering, but it was also energizing. After sending him off with the ratty wet suit and a warning never to set foot in LA again, I returned home with a shift in strategy. I knew there was no way Global Search would fire me, not after I'd scored a meeting with the COO of Stadt Bank, a firm worth billions of dollars. Even Sorrington at Bank of the World appeared to have taken a liking to me. Not to mention I'd done nothing to deserve getting canned — Peter and Jack were the ones caught scheming. So I resolved to focus my efforts on recruiting in Southern California. I could build a local clientele that would enable me to travel less and avoid the backstabbing of Global Search, then eventually start my own firm. I already had the fancy office in a prestigious zip code.

But before I could hire anyone, I had to demote someone first.

That afternoon, Jasmin Shirazi greeted me warmly in her office, though I suspected she knew something was up. When I scheduled the meeting with her assistant, I'd said I wanted to discuss Bank of the World's future in the LA market. I'm sure Jasmin knew it was actually her future we'd be discussing.

"I heard you're close to winning Stadt Bank," Jasmin said. "Congratulations." When she noticed the surprised look on my face, she added, "You're not the only one who's good at spying."

I raised my eyebrows. "I guess not."

Clearly she hadn't gotten to where she was by being clueless about the people with whom she interacted. I wasn't sure if that news was problematic for Global Search. Perhaps Bank of the World wouldn't like the idea that we were working in a similar space with Stadt Bank. Then again, having multiple major firms interested in our services made us look like rock stars.

"How are you liking it?" she asked. "The recruiting?"

"I haven't done much of it yet, to be honest. It's been a lot of getting our ducks in a row."

This was a backhanded way of saying we couldn't recruit for the western US until we replaced the head of that region, which was her.

"If I can give you a bit of advice?" She looked to me for approval, and I nodded. "Sometimes we think the people we work with are like family. Don't buy into it. And don't trust anybody. Ever." She certainly pulled me up short with that. Did she know why I was there, or only suspect?

My father had once given me the corollary to Jasmin's advice. The only people you *could* trust were your own blood.

"And I thought acting was competitive," I replied in an effort to ease the tension, but I heard my teeth grind.

Jasmin laughed. "Let's talk about why you're here."

I plastered on a fake smile and reverted to the car salesman I'd once been. "I'm here to offer you a new role," I said, "one uniquely matched to your special talents."

Jasmin grimaced, and then shot me a cut-the-crap look.

"You're right," I said, catching myself. I took a deep breath. "I'm here to ask you to accept a demotion."

She smiled and nodded her head in respect. "I would handle the LA market?"

"Yes."

"No responsibilities for any other offices? Phoenix? Vegas?"

"No."

"Salary?"

"It will remain the same."

"You mean my base will. I won't be eligible to earn bonuses since I won't be running anything."

"You'll have the opportunity to receive bonuses for any increase in assets in the LA market."

Jasmin scoffed.

"I already have the LA market cornered, so there'd be only incremental growth, which means a minimal bonus at best. My bonus last year was as much as my base. Why would I accept such a radical pay cut? Not to mention a public humiliation in the organization."

Her body shuddered momentarily. It was the first time I could see how hurt she was. I understood now why Stacey Warburton and Harold Sorrington had looked at me like I was insane when I suggested my demotion idea.

"I remember back in my acting days when I booked my first series regular role in a pilot," I said, recalling one of my own demotion experiences. "I was over the moon. The script wasn't very good, but I didn't care. If the pilot got picked up I'd get to work every day on a TV series. Right before I was going to fly to Atlanta for the shoot, my agent called to say that the lead actor had requested his buddy play my part. The producers loved me, but they had no choice. They had to make their star happy. They offered me a smaller role, which wasn't a series regular. I was devastated but I took it, despite the fact that everyone on set knew I'd been hired for the bigger part. The actor who got my role complimented me on my lack of ego, but it wasn't that. I wanted to work. I wanted to hone my craft in front of the camera. I wasn't going to do that sitting at home griping about my misfortune, however justified."

Jasmin looked at me appreciatively. *Go on*, her eyes seemed to say.

"There's another reason I took that job," I added. "My sister lived in Atlanta. She had a new baby, and I wanted to meet my niece. The acting job gave me that opportunity."

"You're saying I should stay?"

"I know how important your kids are to you." I gestured around her office. Jasmin hadn't just hung up her children's artworks. She'd *framed* them. "If you stay, you get to spend more time with them, avoid possibly uprooting them. And you're still the top person in LA. You keep your clients. You stay on your charitable boards. But I can't tell you what to do. We both know you shouldn't trust me."

She laughed, so I did, too.

"Who's my replacement?" she asked.

I'd assumed she might know, but apparently our secretive lunch meeting with Stacey Warburton was still a secret. "I can't say."

"Come on, you can trust me." She smiled wide.

I didn't know why, but I did trust her. "She's from the Bay Area. Stacey Warburton."

"I know who she is. Was it her idea to demote me?"

"No, but she loved the idea because she respects you so much."

Jasmin shot me a look like I was veering into car salesman mode again.

I raised my hands in defense. "Honestly, she said having you in LA would make her job easier. She could focus on the cities where Bank of the World is weak."

Jasmin flinched at the implicit criticism. "Was it Sorrington's idea then?"

"No."

"Of course not. He'd prefer to see me gone."

"That's not true. He's totally on board with the idea."

"Because he knows I'm the best in LA. And now he'd get me at a steep discount."

I nodded. There was no arguing that point.

"I'll have to discuss this with my husband. In the meantime, send me a list of all the potential candidates for our offices in the West."

I was confused. Didn't she understand the ability to hire had just been stripped from her?

"Uh, Stacey will be handling those."

"I'm clear on that. But once Stacey accepts the role, she'll have to sit out on garden leave for ninety days. I'll handle the initial screening so she can hit the ground running once she joins."

Most corporations insisted on a sitting-out period whenever an executive left the company, and they had it written into their employment contracts. Euphemistically known as "garden leave" or "being on the beach," the practice ensured that a trusted leader wasn't at one firm one day, then at a major competitor the next. It gave companies time to circle the wagons and prevent the departing executive from poaching clients or taking other employees with them. I was impressed that Jasmin was willing to take on the extra burden in the interim.

"Plus, it'll be fun to work with you," she added.

I nodded in agreement. Of all the people I'd met since I left my toolshed, Jasmin was the kindest — and had the most integrity. All in all, the situation seemed to be playing out smoothly, and I was pleased with the way I'd handled it. If Stacey took the job, Jasmin seemed open to staying, and both would then be predisposed to working with me since I'd brokered a solution in good faith that worked for everyone. Which represented not only recruiting bonuses through Global Search but also groundwork for my establishing more of a presence in the recruiting space on my own.

Jasmin and I shook hands, and I headed for the door.

"Wait," she said. "If it wasn't Sorrington's or Stacey's idea to demote me, whose was it?"

I turned back, and though inside I was cringing I kept my face impassive.

"Mine," I said.

Years earlier I'd seen Dame Judi Dench perform in a production of Brecht's *Mother Courage and Her Children*. In a key scene, her character was standing with one of her sons as the covered body of a dead traitor was brought onstage. If she showed any recognition of the traitor, she and her son would be killed. When the sheet was pulled off the body, the traitor was revealed to be her other son. I'd never seen anyone, before or since, show — and not show — such overpowering shock and devastation as Dench did in that moment.

Until I saw the look on Jasmin Shirazi's face.

$ $ $

I spent the remainder of the fall of 2010 trying not to return to New York. I couldn't take the backstabbing that awaited me. Surely Martin had told everyone that I attempted to drown him in the Malibu surf. Not surprisingly, Peter and Jack hadn't mentioned a word about their spy getting caught. I attempted to rationalize my decreased travel schedule by explaining to Peter that there was too much research to be done and I needed to be on-site in Malibu to manage it. Of course, he wasn't fooled, but he didn't balk, either. Our conversations were as cordial as ever and as phony as a ruse call.

I reached out to John Liu a couple of times to follow up, but he never responded. Without a lunch (or something else) with Jane on my calendar, it appeared I was in a holding pattern with Stadt Bank.

I kept busy by setting up interviews with hundreds of candidates in LA and other major West Coast cities for Bank of the World positions. My job was to reduce that list to two dozen or so names, then set up meetings for those individuals with Jasmin. She'd agreed to give the demotion a chance to work, though I was positive she was meeting with other firms. She would've been a fool not to. But high-status jobs like hers, even with the demotion, didn't come around every day. I figured she'd stick around until she had a good idea what working with Stacey Warburton was going to be like.

It was tedious work, but at least it represented some small kind of momentum. Then, in mid-December, Global Search received the news that while Stacey had accepted the role at Bank of the World, her old firm would not relent on the six months of garden leave her contract required. This meant we wouldn't be able to hire anyone in the West until Stacey actively came on board — almost halfway through 2011 — since she wasn't going to take a job where she didn't get to choose her new team members. And because the recruiter doesn't earn a commission until after the individual has started, I wouldn't even be paid for Stacey's placement until June.

It wasn't surprising, then, that I was not looking forward to flying to New York for the Global Search Christmas party. I had no year-end bonus to look forward to. I'd be working my ass off for the first half of 2011 setting up interviews for Jasmin when she had no authority to hire anyone. And for all I knew, Stacey Warburton would hate every person Jasmin liked, forcing me to start over.

I was feeling less secure about my position now, too, since Phil, Donny, and Beata were making placements for Bank of the World all over the East, the Midwest, and Europe. My hands were tied from a recruiting standpoint, but I felt that not showing for the year-end gathering would not be a good look.

The thing that kept me going — and my bills paid — was doing the research that Peter and the recruiting team needed, which Global Search still paid for separately. But the number of research requests had mysteriously begun to decline. I had the urge to ask Peter what the deal was, but something told me I wouldn't like the answer.

CHAPTER TWENTY-SIX

A Good Ol' Christmas Fucking

Usually, flying into New York for a few days held a kind of magic for me. The sense of possibility and promise I'd felt during my time there as a young actor was immediately accessible the moment I stepped back into the scene. But walking up the Jetway into the JFK terminal this time felt more like climbing the stairs to the gallows. I knew my value, but I couldn't ignore the evidence signaling a bad outcome. The icy-cold air that raked my face as I stood at the curb outside only heightened my sense of dread.

The next day, on the morning of the Global Search Christmas party, no one spoke to me except Peter, who barely acknowledged me. We were all hanging around in the conference room waiting for Jack MacDonald, who'd flown in from Hong Kong the day before, to give a speech on the year that was. It was the first time I'd seen him since the dinner he hosted at the Beverly Hills Hotel to woo me to join Global Search. Based on the way he glared at me now, the honeymoon phase was long over.

"Welcome to the 2010 Global Search year-end summation," Jack said as if he were addressing hundreds of people instead of the eight of us — Peter, myself, Phil, Donny, Beata, Martin, Lori, and Sheryl the receptionist — gathered around the table. "Thank you to those who came from such far distances."

He nodded toward Beata, who'd flown from Europe, while failing to acknowledge the twenty-five hundred miles I'd traveled to get there.

"This year has been an unprecedented disaster, I'm not going to lie," he said. "But after a wildfire destroys a forest, new opportunities for growth can be found. As I found Peter McBee. And as he found all of you. Together, you are the wildflowers that will bloom in 2011 to take the search world by storm. I can't wait to see what you do in the new year. I am looking forward to writing big checks."

The implication being that there would be no bonus checks *this* year, certainly not for me. Stacey Warburton was the only placement I'd made, but we would not see a fee from it for several months. I could see by the expressions on faces of the others that they were crestfallen — and pissed.

"Wait," Phil said. "I made three placements. My commissions on those are definitely more than my base, so I'm entitled to a bonus."

Jack nodded toward Peter, who got up from the table to join Jack at the end.

"You're right," said Peter. "But we've had a lot of expenses as we've geared up all of the searches for Bank of the World. The largest one is sitting right there." He pointed at me.

Everyone's head swiveled in my direction.

"But I'm not getting any bonus," I said.

"Of course not. You haven't made any placements. I'm talking about all of your research charges." Peter twitched his shoulders as if the idea gave him a chill.

I was stunned. Jack and Peter were using *me* to justify why they weren't paying bonuses. The two of them glared at me like I'd caused the Great Recession, too.

"That's a separate issue," I said.

"One we will discuss in private," said Jack.

Part of me wanted to get it out in the open, though I knew there was nothing I could say that would help matters. The recruiters didn't care that I'd opened an office at my own expense. They didn't give a shit that Jack had reneged on his offer to buy my business. They didn't want to hear how I'd taken an $8-an-hour job and turned it into a thriving enterprise.

They just wanted their fucking Christmas bonus.

$ $ $

A little later in Jack's office he let me have it.

"I could choke a horse with your bills." He gestured toward a huge stack of papers on his desk as though they were invoices from RK Research.

"Peter has been paying those for years and never complained once." I pointed at Peter, who sat next to me in one of Jack's burgundy velour chairs.

"Perhaps I should have," Peter said.

"But you didn't. You know why? Because you were making money, tons of it, from my work."

The conversation was reminding me of my days with Leona when my research was undervalued — and I was underpaid. I was not going backward.

"These are different times, this is a different situation," Jack said. "You're part of a firm now. Don't you value that?"

From his tone, I sensed the threat.

"I do. That's why when Peter said to get an office, I did. An office you still list as one of your own yet haven't paid a dime for. If that's not being a team player, I don't know what is."

Jack nodded, ceding the point, but I was just warming up.

"You were supposed to make me an offer," I said, "but you haven't. My research is highly sought after. It enables everything else that happens here. Don't you value *that*?"

He stared at me for a moment, then his face softened. "We don't have the money," he said. "The economy hasn't recovered yet. Sometimes it seems like it's getting worse."

Jack lowered his head like he was praying for a miracle, or about to break down. I felt a twinge of sympathy but then remembered that he was staying in a two-story bungalow at the Beverly Hills Hotel when we met.

"I'm doing everything I can to contribute value," I said. "Besides the research and the recruiting, I've been trying to win new business. I've even got a meeting today with Stanford Mutual."

I'd been saving that intelligence precisely because I thought it would bail me out of a situation like the one I was in. After the Martin fiasco,

Suze and Angie were adamant that I market RK Research not just as part of Global Search but also as a separate entity, since technically that was what it was. We sent out Global Search decks that focused on our recruiting abilities, but we *also* sent out RK Research decks that consisted of nothing but my corporate intelligence. In many cases, we sent both to the same bank, though obviously not to the same individual.

Stanford Mutual had responded to the RK Research deck. I figured I could use my firm's intelligence capabilities to win Global Search recruiting business just as Peter's Bank of the World placements had brought me research assignments. We were supposed to be a team, after all.

But Peter and Jack appeared nonplussed. They exchanged a look I couldn't decipher.

"You should go then," said Jack.

I waited for him to add *and don't come back.*

Instead, Peter said, "Take Martin with you."

I shot Peter a murderous look, and he quickly corrected course. "No, take Lori," he said, "she'll be better suited."

It was an odd suggestion, but I'd had enough of the two of them already and just wanted to get out of there, so I didn't bother to challenge it. When I approached Lori at her desk and told her she was coming with me to Stanford Mutual, she thought I was kidding. She was part of the office staff, used to putting together presentation decks, not glad-handing to win business. She'd never been to a pitch meeting. After I assured her it wasn't a joke and that we had to leave ASAP, she looked as if she might throw up.

"I'll ruin it," she said. "I won't know what to say."

I knew Peter wanted her there as his eyes and ears. He had to be sure that if I won business with Stanford Mutual, I couldn't take the account for my own.

"You'll be fine," I said. "I'll do all the talking."

"So why do you need me?"

"Because you'll be the smartest person in the room," I said, giving her my best Brad Pitt smile.

She beamed back at me.

$ $ $

Lori and I sat in the hallway outside of the office of Stanford Mutual's head of human resources for nearly an hour. I wasn't sure why we were even meeting with HR since I'd originally emailed the COO of the investment bank. Despite the name, the human resources department didn't do much hiring on Wall Street, campus recruiting excepted. It was filled mainly with bureaucrats who managed benefits packages, handled problems and issues with current employees, and administered severance packages. New hiring was done by those on the front lines, usually the COOs of particular groups or divisions, and nearly always with the help of a search firm.

Lori was fidgeting in her chair like we were outside the principal's office and mangling the printout of the PowerPoint deck she'd thrown together for the meeting.

"Gimme that," I said, before the thing became unpresentable. Her decks were normally fifty pages or more, but this one was short. It had an opening page with the Global Search logo and office locations, but after that it consisted entirely of the research I'd done on the Bank of Switzerland. I figured if John Liu was blown away by that work, Stanford Mutual would be, too.

Finally, a short, chubby, balding man in his early forties came out of his office.

"Come in," he said brusquely.

Unlike Sorrington's faux reading room or Liu's crisp, high-tech conference room, this guy's office was furnished with a beat-up desk and a couple of cheap plastic chairs for visitors and cluttered with piles of papers.

"How can I help you?" he said without offering us a seat.

I handed him the deck, which he sat behind his desk to read. Lori and I sat, too.

"No, no, no," he said, rising from his chair after reading the Global Search cover page. "I'm not meeting with any headhunters."

"What? Why?" I said.

He looked at me as if I were stupid — and should be going. Lori was already standing to leave.

"Stanford Mutual has a new firm-wide mandate to do all recruiting internally," he said. "We've already hired dozens of your laid-off colleagues. We're creating an entirely new division called Sourcing that will fall under the umbrella of HR. Basically, we're cutting out the middleman, which means we no longer need headhunters like you."

For a moment, I thought he was going to add *thank God*.

I hadn't heard anything in the news about their strategy, probably because Stanford Mutual wanted to make sure they could pull it off before they bragged about it. In the past, I'd heard of other huge banks trying not to use search firms, but to my knowledge none had ever made it work. Before the crash, search firms had been thriving and were bigger than ever; led by Korn Ferry, Heidrick & Struggles, Russell Reynolds, and Spencer Stuart, the industry's global revenue topped $10.5 billion in 2008. Now Stanford Mutual was attempting to dump the entire industry. Obviously, with the global economic crisis they had serious incentives to cut costs. More important, they now had access to large pools of talented, recently unemployed recruiters, a group I did not want to find myself part of.

"So why did your COO ask us to come in and meet with you?" I asked.

"I have no idea," he said, "but you need to leave."

And I thought Harold Sorrington had been obnoxious. This dick hadn't even introduced himself. He'd also made us wait an insultingly long time, something neither Sorrington nor Liu had done.

Lori scurried out of the office. I followed, but when I got to the doorway I turned back.

"You're rude." Though I wanted to use words with sharper edges. "Your COO believed our intelligence could be of value, but you didn't even bother to look at it. That makes you incompetent, as well."

He looked flabbergasted at being spoken to this way. I was gauging whether he was going to jump his desk or call for security.

Instead, he said, "Intelligence?"

It hit me then that the RK Research deck the COO had responded to had no information identifying me as a Global Search employee. The deck I'd handed Dickhead consisted entirely of my research, but was branded with the Global Search name and logo. I needed to steer the situation back toward a workable rapport.

"If you'd taken a second to open the presentation my colleague prepared, you would've seen my research," I said.

Lori was staring at me openmouthed, still in shock at my hostility, but the HR guy sat back down, opened the deck, and began paging through it.

"Why didn't you say you did organizational mapping?" he said, pointing at the Bank of Switzerland research. "This is exactly what our sourcers need to hit the ground running. We're looking for a research provider who can work across industries and on a global basis. Is that something you could do?"

I scoffed. "I've been doing it for twenty years."

"For Global Search?"

"I have my own firm, RK Research."

"But it says here —"

"Global Search hired me as a recruiter, but they're in talks to buy my business." I shrugged, which was my way of saying it wasn't going to happen.

"As I've made quite clear, we're no longer hiring headhunters. It's a shame you're with Global Search. Otherwise, we might've been able to work together."

He stood again for us to leave. I glanced at the small stand on his desk that held his business cards. I'd rather have gone back to playing third fiddle to Daniel Baldwin than work with this jerk, this Lonnie Salvato, who hadn't even had the decency to introduce himself.

"Gimme back my deck."

For the second time, the guy looked stunned. He handed it to me, and I walked out.

$ $ $

"You're crazy," Lori said, hurrying to keep up with me as I hustled toward the elevator. I was so angry I was practically running. "You just trash-talked the head of human resources at Stanford Mutual."

I raised my hands as if to say *So what?*

"What's amazing is you turned him around. By the end, he wanted to hire you."

"He's an asshole," I said. "Working for him would be a nightmare."

"But it's Stanford Mutual!"

"I don't give a shit. They're not going to pay me any more for the research than Peter is. Why would I put up with that? Life's too short."

I banged on the elevator button and turned to Lori, expecting her to nod in agreement, but she was staring at me with what looked like pity.

"You might want to rethink that attitude. You may need that guy one day."

The elevator door opened, and Lori got in.

"What's that supposed to mean?" I asked, following.

"Nothing."

"Come on, spill it." When Lori hesitated, I reached to push the elevator's EMERGENCY STOP button. "Think I'm bluffing? Go ahead, make my day."

"Hey, I'm on your side. I think it's wrong what they're doing to you."

"Yeah, throwing me under the bus for the bonuses was a pretty dirty move."

Lori shook her head; there was something else.

"What, Martin?" I guessed feebly. "He's lucky he's not whale shit at the bottom of the ocean."

"They stole one of your researchers," she blurted.

The news hit me hard. It felt like the elevator had encountered turbulence. I leaned against the wall to brace myself.

"That's not possible," I said, thinking out loud. "My researchers wouldn't leave me. They're barely trained."

It took a solid year to make even a half-decent researcher. Chip, Ocean, and Strider were only eight months in.

"No, they got your friend."

"Pax?" I couldn't believe my lifelong friend would screw me like that. Though I remembered how quickly he'd been ready to turn state's evidence when investigators believed he was the infamous hacker Kevin Mitnick all those years ago.

"No, that's not his name," Lori said. "It's —"

"Shenanigans."

The elevator reached the lobby. When the doors opened, Lori took my elbow like I was in need of assistance, which I was. How the fuck had Peter stolen my best researcher? Perhaps Martin had come across Shen's contact information during his spy mission, or heard Suze or Angie on the phone with him. Even though he lived only half an hour away, I didn't make Shen come into the office since he'd been working from home for so long. It wasn't like he needed supervision. He'd become as good at the ruse as I was.

And now he was working for Peter and Jack?

Out on the sidewalk, Lori opened the door to the Town Car and guided me in. My brain scrambled to make sense of what had happened. I was no longer receiving as much research work from Global Search *because Shen was doing it.* He'd been telling me he was tied up with music projects and didn't have time to work for me. I figured good for him if he was making money from his art. I still got a thrill when I received residual checks from my acting days, even when the amounts were rarely more than ten bucks. I hadn't minded Shen taking a bit of a hiatus since work had slowed, but now I knew the reason for that was *Shen's own doing.* Of all the disreputable things I'd done, of all the lies I'd told, I'd never stolen a client from Leona. And Leona hadn't even taught me how to ruse, whereas I had taught Shen. It seemed the ultimate betrayal.

In the backseat of the car, I felt ill. As a kid, I'd been extremely susceptible to motion sickness. My dad's favorite activity was to take a Sunday drive to look at expensive houses. I never understood why he always seemed to be trying to find something better when our suburban home seemed plenty nice to me. I hated driving around like that, especially because it made me terribly nauseous. But I hadn't experienced bad motion sickness in years. The stop-and-go Manhattan traffic seemed to be a continuation of the elevator's shudder, as much a reflection of my emotional shakiness as a function of New York City gridlock.

When I remembered that the car was returning to the Global Search office, I rolled down the window, leaned out, and prepared for the worst.

$ $ $

As soon as the car dropped us, I ducked out and returned to my hotel to take a shower and change. Lori had promised she wouldn't say a word about spilling the secret, or my puking fit. She was worried about my saying something at the party that could expose her as my snitch, though I got the sense she was just as disgusted with working at Global Search as I was.

After I got dressed, I had a couple of drinks at the hotel bar. Then a few more. I briefly considered not attending the party, then remembered my mortgage payment. Global Search was still paying me a substantive salary as a recruiter, and if I quit I'd be ineligible for unemployment and couldn't imagine making up the lost income through rusing, not given the economic climate. I was more trapped than ever.

But there was another reason I wanted to go to the party: I needed to know if my hiring had been a giant ruse from the start. Had all the noise about buying my business been just a Trojan horse strategy to steal my methods and techniques? Had Peter tricked me into getting an office and hiring a team because he knew he needed massive amounts of research that I wouldn't have been able to deliver fast enough otherwise? Now that he had the bulk of the information, was the plan to poach my best researcher and cut me and the rest of the team loose? Had that been his plan all along?

Despite moaning hours earlier that he couldn't afford to buy my business, Jack MacDonald apparently had plenty of ducats lying around to reserve an entire three-star Michelin restaurant for the 2010 Christmas party. The nine-person Global Search team took up a single table in the otherwise unused restaurant — the servers outnumbered us. Vintage champagne and Napa Valley Cabs flowed. Former Federal Reserve Board chairman Alan Greenspan had blamed the dot-com bubble of the '90s on "irrational exuberance." Barely ten years after the bubble burst, and still in the hangover of another crash, one that had cratered the entire world economy, the Global Search folks inhaled Wagyu steak cooked tableside and shrimp larger than my fist as if none of it had ever happened. The self-serving amnesia that sustained Wall Street — and, one could argue, your average struggling actor — was on full display. If I hadn't been so demoralized by everything, I might have forgiven them taking one night to try to forget how bleak their futures were.

But no one fucking spoke to me, and I was not in a forgiving mood.

Jack and Peter gave another round of speeches focused on how great 2011 was going to be. It seemed pathetic to brag about how much people were *going* to make, but I guessed that's what the booze was for. I was too new to the bonus system to understand how badly they'd screwed the other recruiters who did not have a side income stream like mine for research. I just knew it was inappropriate to blame the situation on me. Even if I hadn't been an employee, Peter would have hired me to do his research. Global Search still would've had those expenses. It was just another con job.

"You're not cut out for this," said Beata, who'd taken the seat next to me when the meal began. This was the first we'd spoken since she'd tried to seduce me into starting our own firm. She finished the champagne in her flute, and before her glass hit the table a server hustled over to refill it.

"Because I didn't sleep with Jane Monahan?"

"You didn't even follow up with her. You wasted that opportunity."

I'd reached out to John Liu over and over, but it seemed obvious he'd been instructed to ignore me. I didn't even get a courtesy email that they'd chosen another search firm. Because I wouldn't go on a date with his boss's wife? There was a time when I would have thought that ludicrous.

"What if she just wanted a friend?" Beata kept after me.

"She was a lonely woman with a serious drinking problem in a bad marriage. Only a scumbag would try to take advantage of that," I retorted.

I thought of the letters my grandmother Shirley, pregnant with my uncle Jack, had written JK back in the 1930s. The hope he dangled in front of her that he would leave his wife for her. The Jane Monahan situation didn't rise to that level, but still, there was a special place in hell for men who engaged in that kind of manipulation.

All I wanted was to go home to California and back to the ruse, which seemed far more honorable than the world of executive recruiting.

"You're a resourceful guy. You could've finessed your way around the situation." Beata shook her head in disgust. "I know I would have."

Of that, I had zero doubt.

"I admire you being a good guy," she added. "But you're not cut out for this business."

For once we were in complete agreement.

$ $ $

After dinner, I was about to exit the restaurant's bathroom when Peter walked in.

"Funny meeting you here, Brad," he said. "I've been wanting to talk to you all night, but I needed to do so in private."

He leaned against the bathroom door as if to block anyone else from entering, slouching in a way that seemed unlike the Brit.

"I heard Stanford Mutual went well."

"It didn't. The guy was a prick."

"They're all pricks," he said, slurring slightly. He was soused, something I hadn't seen before. At past dinners, Peter had always maintained a certain decorum while the rest of us got rip-roaring drunk. "Stanford Mutual would be a good client for you. They're looking to replace headhunters like me with internal recruiters. They're hiring the zillion recruiters laid off during the crash. Without research like yours, though, they'll never pull it off. Remember that when you bill them."

Why the hell did he let me go to that meeting if he knew Stanford Mutual was never going to hire Global Search? He knew that meant I would only be of value to them as an independent researcher. Was it some sort of loyalty test? Or was he warning me to get a new job?

"Did you know that when I went to the meeting?" I asked.

"Of course I knew. This is my career. What I've done my whole life while you were running around onstage. There is nothing I don't know or can't find out."

Including the name of my top researcher, I almost added. I hadn't called Shen to let him know my opinion of him, either. What was I going to say, anyway? Shen hadn't been an employee with benefits — nor had he been a friend. He saw an opportunity to make more money and he took it. There was no honor among telephone thieves.

"When I hired you," Peter said, "I thought you were a risk-taker. You were an actor; you lied to get information on the phone. I was excited by that. Yet now you don't seem to want to get your hands dirty."

"Listen," I said. "I know everyone thinks I should've slept with Jane Monahan to make us all rich, but even if I had, what's the guarantee her husband would have hired us? I certainly wouldn't work with anyone my wife was sleeping with."

Peter chortled as if I'd said something stupid.

"You think Ken Monahan cares? You don't think he's doing the same thing? They have an *arrangement*. Maybe he wants to keep tabs on his wife's lover, so he hires him."

It was my turn to scoff as if he'd said something stupid. Admittedly, that kind of open marriage wasn't uncommon in Hollywood, but I didn't run in those circles. Gardia would've kicked me to the curb had I ever been foolish enough to sleep with another woman, even if it was for our personal financial gain.

"Anyway, that's why I let you go to the meeting," Peter said. "I wanted to see if you still were on my side."

"I'm working for Global Search, not Stanford Mutual," I said, wanting to make my allegiance clear, even though I felt Peter no longer deserved it.

"Well, I may not be," Peter said.

"Wait, what?"

"I got screwed on my bonus, too. I'm thinking about suing Jack."

The surprises just kept on coming. If Peter left, there was no way Jack would keep me around, since Peter was the one who'd brought me in and Jack seemed to think I should be arrested for overbilling. Without Peter, I was gone, too.

"Don't worry," he said, reading the panicked look on my face. "I have some other irons in the fire. I'm going to need lots of research there, too."

If Peter landed on his feet somewhere else — as he always had — there would be more work than Shen could handle. And while he was an excellent researcher, Shen was also a musician with a tendency to flake out at the most inopportune times. I'd been able to manage because I always had other researchers available to step in when he disappeared or messed up. I imagined Shen missing a critical deadline for Peter and putting him in a terrible position with a client. After one of these experiences, two at most, Peter would dump him. For all his flaws, Peter understood that paying a little more for research was an invaluable insurance policy against losing a major client.

"Don't say anything," Peter said in a whisper, though we were the only ones in the bathroom. "As soon as I'm set up I'll let you know."

He opened the door and walked out. I never saw him again.

CHAPTER TWENTY-SEVEN

Surviving the Long, Cold Malibu Winter

Visitors were often surprised by how cold it got in Malibu in the winter. I always carried extra sweatshirts and jackets in the trunk of my car, as invariably even locals sometimes forgot. The windchill from the air blowing hard off the ocean could be unexpectedly bracing. That January and February of 2011 felt particularly frigid to me. It wasn't just the weather that had turned; my life had, too.

I still went to the RK Research offices, though they were empty now. I'd let my researchers go since Global Search had stopped using us. My team hadn't seemed surprised — or all that disappointed. Ocean and Strider had carried their college diplomas straight into the worst economy since the Great Depression, so the idea of a business failing didn't come as a shock to them the way it did to me. And all Chip had carried before rusing was a surfboard. Besides, the ruse was hard work. I don't think any of them were sad not to have to lie for a living anymore.

At home at night I was drinking significantly more than I ever had. This was especially concerning since I came from a family with a history of alcohol issues. My maternal grandfather, George, had died from cirrhosis of the liver at age sixty. I feared I'd inherited the substance abuse gene. I rationalized that the red wine was warming me up during an unusually brisk winter, but really I was in denial of the failure of the Global Search experiment and the inevitability of closing my office. My son loved to play in the dolphin fountain when he came to visit, and I wanted him to be proud of me.

I didn't return to New York after the disastrous Christmas party. Peter never mentioned my coming east, though he peppered our conversations with talk of his huge new job opportunities, all of which were going to involve me. Each time we chatted about his plans to leave Global Search and use me for research again, I got my hopes up.

But nothing ever came of it.

Failure is an integral part of the acting life, but as a businessman I'd always been successful. I'd developed a lucrative business with the help of my wife, and it had been crushed through no fault of my own. The global economic crash that caused demand for my research to dry up wasn't my doing. I hadn't gambled away my earnings in Vegas or driven away clients. But the Global Search catastrophe was a different story.

I'd won no business despite sending out hundreds of emails. I'd obtained only a handful of meetings. I hadn't made a single placement beyond Stacey Warburton. Of course my ability to make additional placements had been hamstrung by the six-month mandatory delay between Stacey's hiring and when she could come on board. I had tried to circumvent her garden leave by sending her the résumés of individuals whom Jasmin liked, but Stacey hated every one of them. And Global Search couldn't risk having Stacey interview candidates directly for fear of it getting back to her former employers.

These were painful days. Every time I walked through the chilly sea wind and into the empty offices I was reminded of my son's excitement that first day. How he had likely seen me as this important business owner with the confidence and talent to commandeer all this space. Now it looked abandoned. It *was* abandoned. All of which made me think of my own father, and how it must have felt when he had to walk away from the dealership. Had he wondered what I thought about that, what I thought about him?

I was sulking alone in the office one morning when I got the impulse to call my old friend Pax. I hadn't spoken to him in a while since I no longer had any research for him.

"Kerbster," he said, "how's it hanging?"

I glanced out at the whitecapping Pacific. "Cold," I said.

"Please, it's twelve degrees in New York. What's it there, fifty-five? Sixty?"

Every single cross-coast friendship goes through this little routine every single winter, but I didn't have the spirit to play along. "Something like that."

"Dude, you don't sound good."

"I'm sitting in an empty office."

There was a pause. His tone turned somber.

"I guess that means you're not calling with work."

Before the crash, Pax had two apartments in Manhattan and a small home upstate. After the crash his clients disappeared and he took a job at a liquor store, which made me a little jealous given the amount of booze I was consuming. He'd lost the apartments and now lived full-time in the house upstate. His wife had a job that could support them both, but they were still struggling to pay the mortgage.

"I don't have work for anyone," I said, "including myself."

"I thought Global Search was going to buy your business."

"So did I."

"Well, you gotta get out of there."

I was thinking that Pax was right, but it wasn't even eleven. I doubted any of the Malibu restaurants with a liquor license were open yet.

"I should go surfing," I said, gazing longingly at the ocean. Though the wind was up, I knew spots where that wouldn't be an issue. But I hadn't surfed in ages, and I knew I didn't have the will. It was an empty suggestion.

"I'm not talking about going *outside*," Pax said. "I'm talking about getting out of that office. Permanently."

"I'm only partway through my lease. I'll lose my security deposit."

"Who cares? How much more money are you going to lose keeping it open?"

"What about the furniture?" I stared at the IKEA desks in the deserted bullpen, each one sporting a practically new Apple desktop. "What about the computers?"

"My friend, I know you. You don't sound right. You need to make a move."

I should've known Pax could hear the depression in my voice. We were professional telephone listeners. Could he hear how much I'd been drinking? Did he know the road I was heading down, the toll it was taking on my life? I certainly wasn't going to tell him. I was too ashamed. And it was getting worse. I'd recently caught myself sneaking home to drink wine at lunch — and not even good stuff; I was tipping Two-Buck Chuck. Combined with the stress, the alcohol made it difficult to sleep more than a few hours a night, which meant I was irritable all day. This had started to infect my dynamic with Gardia, whose eyes had taken on a wary look. I'd recently asked her to go back to work since money was getting tight, and she refused. Her rationale was that getting another low-paying job as an assistant in the music business wasn't going to put much of a dent in our bills anyway. She was correct, but her unwilling-ness created additional tension. Few things will test a marriage more than a lack of money, and my drinking was having a compounding effect. Losing my business was one thing, or even my home, but the thought of losing my wife was unfathomable.

"You still there?" Pax asked. "You jump off the ledge yet?"

My friend wasn't above going dark to get a laugh, which I appreciated in that moment. But he'd also pulled the bleakest of my thoughts into the light.

"I'm thinking about it," I said.

"Stop thinking and close that shit down."

I looked around at the phones and the staplers, paper clip holders, writing pads, and other office supplies on the desks. In my head, I counted up all the money wasted. The computers could be sold — at a significant loss — but who would want the office desks and equipment? No one in America was opening an office. In my building, the hollow shell of RK Research was the sole tenant. The other suites were completely vacant. It felt like everything was falling apart.

"Do it now," Pax said into my silence, "before it's too late."

$ $ $

A strange thing happened after our call. I felt pretty miserable and self-pitying, but I'd heard the truth in Pax's insistence and opened my laptop to start writing a letter to my landlord telling her I was breaking the lease. What came out was something entirely different. It was a letter, but it was written in the voice of a man planning to commit suicide. By jumping. Not from the relatively low ledge of a Malibu office building but from the railing of a cruise ship. He was despondent but had tripped into that mental space where the decision to jump had already been made, so his thoughts were flowing with a certain kind of fuck-it grandeur.

In a couple of hours I had a completed draft of a short story, the first piece of fiction I'd written since before I became an actor, when I was still an English major at Penn. Somehow, by looking at these dark thoughts from a critical distance, it relieved me of their burden. They were true, and they were mine, but I had handed them off to a character who carried them as far as he needed, or as far as I needed. It was strange and liberating and sparked some new possibility in me — a guy who'd already worked his way through three careers before he'd turned forty-eight.

I set it aside and wrote the letter to Dahlia letting her know I was moving out immediately. Over the next few days, Suze and Angie dismantled the office they'd put together only a year earlier. I gave each a lightly used Apple computer for their trouble. The office phones went into boxes, the conference table and desks into storage.

I grabbed the desk from my office and took it back to the shack, which we finally renovated. After my time in those luxurious offices in New York and Malibu, there was no way I could return to sitting in an uninsulated toolshed with fluorescent lighting. We hired a contractor who gave us a ridiculous deal since he was desperate for work. The bare paneling became painted walls. The plywood flooring became solid wood. The fluorescent lighting became track lights.

I was hardly set up for business again when a letter from Global Search arrived "inviting" me to merge with them — or be fired. There was no mention of any compensation for my business. Not that there was anything for them to buy now. I'd closed "their" Los Angeles office and let everyone go. I'd never been fired from a job, so the kiss-off stung. I tried to remain grateful, however. The income I'd earned from them had enabled me to keep up with my mortgage payments and kick the can down the road. The economy had to recover eventually, right?

I reached out to my old research clients to let them know I was back on the market, but none of them had any work for me. I spent my days watching the balance in our bank accounts drop lower and lower. But I began to do something else, too, something that kept me from drinking so much — or jumping off anything.

I started writing regularly.

The daily creative effort was at least mildly restorative, but of course it didn't solve our financial issues. Gardia and I discussed putting our home up for sale even though the housing market in Malibu, like everywhere else, had cratered. The pressure was debilitating. Something had to give, unless a miracle happened.

And then one did.

$ $ $

The email that landed in my inbox in April 2011 was from Stanford Mutual. I assumed we'd bounced a check since our bank accounts were with them now. We'd opened accounts with a different bank that had gone belly-up — another victim of the economic collapse — and Stanford Mutual had taken over. But the email wasn't telling me my balances were low. It was from a woman named Jennifer, who ran Stanford Mutual's internal sourcing group, their new headhunting division.

Her boss, Lonnie Salvato, the biggest asshole I'd met with during my time at Global Search, which was saying something, had recommended me. I couldn't imagine what he would want with me. It turned out that Jennifer had a project that required researching the major investment banks — or what was left of them — and wanted to know if my firm could handle it.

Hell. Yeah.

Did Stanford Mutual ask a single question about *how* I obtained my intelligence? Not a one. Did they know I employed illegal methods and impersonated major executives? You better believe it. One executive later told me that if they were allowed to ruse, they wouldn't need me — as if scoring corporate intelligence was as simple as scheduling a conference call. Part of me wished legitimate firms *would* try. Then perhaps they would stop busting my chops about my fees. But firms like Stanford Mutual didn't care how I got my intel. They were eliminating tens of millions, if not hundreds of millions, in recruitment search and placement fees. Every dollar saved was another dollar in some executive's bonus check. And that's all that mattered.

But a funny thing had happened. As LinkedIn grew in popularity, individuals had begun to list information in their profiles that in the past firms had paid me to obtain. "I'm a VP in the Financial Institutions investment banking group," one profile read, "part of a thirty-five-person team in three US locations." This used to be valuable private information. Companies always wanted to know the size of specific groups and teams at competing firms to ensure they weren't bloated or understaffed by comparison. But this VP didn't stop with publicizing the US headcount, he listed the *global* numbers, as well, followed by clients' names and the sizes of individual deals. The first few times I saw profiles like these, usually of younger employees, I couldn't believe it. I thought surely HR or the legal department would go ballistic and rein in this kind of corporate oversharing, but it just got worse.

Soon LinkedIn (and Apple and Google and Facebook and every other technology company) was collecting everyone's information, learning our likes and dislikes, even reading our emails, no matter how personal (and private) they were supposed to be. Overnight, formerly private information became not just public, but readily available. I mean, most of us just started offering it up eagerly. I'm sure that's why that Swiss investment bank and numerous other targets never came after me. It would be hard for them (or any of the firms I rused) to complain to the authorities about my stealing their information when their own employees were posting it on the internet for free.

Still, there were certain things firms like Stanford Mutual couldn't get on LinkedIn or anywhere else. I blew them away with the quality of my intelligence, as well as with the cheap price. Global Search had gotten rid of me because they thought my rate was too high. Stanford Mutual thought the *exact same rate* was the deal of the century. One of the guys in their internal sourcing group told me that my fees for an entire year wouldn't be enough to cover the cost of a single investment banker cocktail party. The experience reminded me (yet again!) that search firms treated researchers like redheaded stepchildren. A partner at a major search firm had once complained about my fees; later in the same call she bragged about her new Chris-Craft powerboat.

Regardless, what mattered was that I was back in business. I wasn't making anywhere near the money I'd made pre-crash, but I didn't care. I was in my cozy shack and had time to write, a creative outlet I was enjoying immensely.

One day that spring, my eight-year-old son, Davis, walked past and heard me rusing.

"Dad, are you a hacker?" he wanted to know after I hung up from the call.

I'm sure it wasn't the first time he'd heard me say I was calling from a regulator's office when I was actually in our backyard. I wasn't making any effort to hide what I did, and I was loud as hell on the phone. Perhaps because he was older now, he felt emboldened to call me out. I'd expected his questions and, in some sense, dreaded them. I feared he'd think I was a terrible person — as well as a crook. No one wants to go from being their child's hero to being the villain.

I explained that I wasn't a hacker, not even close, and that I'd never used my skills to get anything other than lists of employee names to help those people get better jobs. (Though I did once get David Geffen's private cell phone number, which was shockingly easy to obtain.) Davis nodded, listening to me as I defended what I've spent my time doing for more years than anything else. I imagined he was thinking that it wasn't so bad, that in the end there was a positive purpose.

Instead, he said, "But it's dishonest."

He gazed at me as if I'd lost sight of that simple fact. I most certainly had.

$ $ $

Around this time, I had what turned out to be a pivotal conversation with my old acting buddy Richie. We were on the phone when I mentioned the fictional suicide note I'd written, and he persuaded me to read it to him, though I was reluctant to be so vulnerable about both my dark moment and my new writing efforts. The piece was awful, but hearing it aloud made clear that there was something completely true about it, that I had channeled my pain into the language on the page. Richie encouraged me to continue writing the character, to explore the circumstances of his life crisis.

Over the next six months, I sat inside Big Daddy's and wrote a novel in the Notes app on my iPad. No punctuation. No grammar. Every other word misspelled. I didn't stop to correct a thing or to censor myself in any way. I knew I had to write it through to the end first. When I did, I realized the novel was terrible, as bad as a book could be, but the *story* was compelling. And I had become hooked on the process, on getting the words right.

I resolved to improve my prose and started a creative group called the Malibu Writers Circle. There were usually about eight of us, and we met every third Wednesday at a private library-like setting. At the same time, I started attending prestigious writing workshops and conferences such as Tin House and Bread Loaf. My short stories began to be published in literary journals, and three of them were nominated for a national literary award, the Pushcart Prize. A play I wrote, *Putin and the Snowman*, had two runs off-Broadway. I began to feel passionate again and hopped out of bed each morning.

It wasn't lost on me that this new avocation was connected to my earlier adventures in both acting and rusing. First there was the creative aspect: Writing fiction was akin to channeling the characters and story lines I'd developed on stage and on the phone. And, as with my previous pursuits, I dreamed that someday I might even make a living at it. But there was more to it than that. I had discovered something that meant the world to me. Sure, it involved making things up, but to me, it was *real*. A lifetime of lying had led me to the truth.

Last Call

So here we are. Fall 2020. Nine years beyond the implosion of my empire, such as it was, and I'm banging out these final pages back in my favorite spot: Big Daddy's Surf Shack. A story that, thankfully, I'm not writing from a French prison cell or some hidey-hole in a country without an extradition treaty. A lot has happened since I first took the elevator up to Leona's Upper East Side apartment in 1987. Since then, I've crossed paths with Yoko Ono, George Clooney, and Paul Newman; rubbed elbows with Wall Street titans; got hammered at a block party with the Yakuza; won some awards; and made quite a few million dollars as a corporate spy. I conned people and got conned in return.

We all face the same mysterious existential calculus. I strived to get a foothold in my dream career and struggled to make it work. I failed as much as I succeeded. The opportunity to pursue one's passions is its own privilege, and yet nearly everyone who tries is chasing a mirage. The promise of ultimately reaching a destination that's a place of professional fulfillment is, well, a lie.

Take my actor friend Richie, the one everyone thought was going to be a big star. Today he works as a DHL driver in Manhattan delivering packages to the same offices where he used to audition. When my acting career began to wane, this was exactly what I (and likely my father) feared happening to me.

As for my RK Research team, once I let them go they quickly found new paths. Chip opened a car wash, which turned into two, then three. I don't know how many he's up to now. Ocean became a realtor like everyone else in Los Angeles. Strider went on to a series of jobs as part of the gig economy.

Jasmin Shirazi still has the same job I demoted her to. Turns out she wanted to leave Bank of the World in LA as little as I wanted to leave Big Daddy's Surf Shack in Malibu.

Jack MacDonald was forced out of Global Search in Hong Kong. Apparently, he wasn't much more than an employee, either. His story of intending to buy my company had indeed been a ruse the entire time. Today, he's at a major recruiting firm in New York slinging the same bullshit he sold me.

Harold Sorrington got promoted again and is now Bank of the World's global head of private banking. One more step and he'll be the CEO of the largest financial institution in the world. I hope he's as happy in his new role as he was to receive an autographed picture of me as a Cardassian.

As far as I can tell, Jane Monahan is doing exactly what she was doing when I briefly met her: raising money for philanthropic causes, serving on community boards, and, presumably, looking for love in all the wrong seatmates. Today, her husband is the second most powerful person at Stadt Bank and, like Sorrington, one step away from becoming CEO.

And Peter McBee? He's at it with a new recruiting firm that specializes in — wait for it — corporate intelligence. The entire premise of the firm is its ability to find out anything. His website bio describes him as being at the forefront of an entirely new human capital development system that utilizes a state-of-the-art proprietary database to capture corporate intelligence on key leaders, trends, strategic challenges — basically anything a CEO or COO could ever want to know. Of course, I recognize the language as the same kind of gobbledygook bullshit Pax used in his transfer agency ploy.

The only differentiator Peter had was the second best researcher in the world, the one I'd trained: Shenanigans, he of the great Topanga drum circle tribe. After he'd jumped to the dark side with Peter, I never spoke to him again. Part of me was too disgusted by what Shen had done; another part of me wanted to tell him *Well played*. He did continue to send me invitations to see his band play. One of these days, I may hit a Renaissance Faire and check them out.

Oh, and O.J. made a brief reappearance in my life. In March 2016, the penultimate episode of FX's *The People v. O. J. Simpson: American Crime Story* opened with a re-creation of the exercise video I was part of in 1994. Oscar winner Cuba Gooding played the affably offensive Simpson, and they'd hired an actor to play me, complete with a red headband, which I would never have agreed to wear in real life. My wife had been watching the series and screamed at me to come when the scene came on. She ran it back, and I fell to the ground laughing watching the actor playing me jump up and down like a crazy person.

How many people can say someone was paid to pretend to be them on TV?

$ $ $

With the explosive growth of LinkedIn, there became less and less need for my intel since so much information was now available online for free. Right around the time the floor fell out from under my professional life in early 2011, LinkedIn completed an IPO and was publicly listed on the New York Stock Exchange. By the end of 2016, Microsoft had purchased it for $26 billion, and by the end of 2019, 660 million people were using it globally, with 90 million of those users considered "senior-level influencers." The company generated nearly $7 billion in revenue that year, much of it trafficking in the kind of corporate recruiting I first dove into more than thirty years earlier. As a result, with each project I now take on my rate drops lower and lower.

Soon I'll be getting $8 an hour.

In another unexpected life twist, I now make most of my money — wait, you'll love this — day-trading stocks. I like to think of it less as selling out than as continuing a family legacy, since it's exactly what my father did when his car business went south. And I'm surprisingly good at it. Or maybe that's not so surprising. Either way, I'm pretty sure the Wolf of Wall Street would approve of the size of my returns. I know my father would.

Mainly, though, I'm focused on my writing career. Oh, and my acting career. Wouldn't you know it, around 2015 a film director named Summer-Joy "SJ" Main Muñoz read one of my short stories in a literary journal and asked if she could make a film of it. I figured it was standard Hollywood bullshit — though she did have an impressive Wikipedia page — and said sure, go for it, never expecting anything to happen. We collaborated on the screenplay, and when it was time for casting I asked her to consider my son for the role of the teenage boy in the story since I'd based the character on him. SJ met with Davis and thought he would be perfect but then turned around and said she wanted me for the lead role of the father. I hadn't acted in a long time and didn't want to ruin her movie, but Davis begged me to do it. Against my better judgment I signed on.

To draw more attention to the film, SJ wanted to try to nab a celebrity to play the part of the elderly mother-in-law. Because it was difficult for older actresses to find quality roles, even Academy Award winners were often available for low-budget independent movies. SJ asked if I knew, of all people, Ellen Burstyn. Ah, the twists and turns of life. I said, sure, I would help reach out to her. What I didn't tell her was that the Oscar-winning star of Scorsese's *Alice Doesn't Live Here Anymore* would have booted me out of the Actors Studio all those years earlier if she'd had the power. Now she was co-president of the Studio along with Pacino and Alec Baldwin, and, to my shock, she offered kind words for the script and the project, though she ultimately passed. Can you guess who SJ's second choice was? Yep, Estelle Parsons, who was now the Studio's co-artistic-director. Instead, I suggested three-time Emmy Award–winner Barbara Bain, who'd played Cinnamon Carter in the original 1960s *Mission: Impossible* series, and she agreed. Kerry O'Malley from *Boardwalk Empire* and *Shameless* came aboard to play my wife, and we filmed from December 2016 into early 2017.

The film, *Reconnected*, was accepted at major film festivals all over the world and premiered in April 2018. It received multiple award nominations and even won Best Film at one festival. Even crazier, at the Madrid International Film Festival, fifteen years after I'd quit acting, I was nominated for Best Lead Actor along with Barbara for Best Lead Actress. Just goes to show ya, it's never too late.

But the best part by far was standing on the red carpet with Davis. I had unexpectedly been handed this wonderful opportunity to work with my son — in an aboveboard, satisfying way connected to my lifelong passion and not, thank God, via the ruse. We stood there taking on flash-bulbs together, dressed smart and smiling, and I thought for the first time in years of the joy my own father must have felt having me by his side on the car lot. This time it held a special resonance, and I squeezed Davis a little tighter. Honestly, it doesn't get any better than that.

Now Davis is about to turn eighteen. He's a senior in high school, busy applying to colleges on the East Coast and in the UK. Though he enjoyed his taste of the movie business, he's seen my struggles and is justifiably wary of taking the artist's path. So what does he want to study?

The law.

He wants to be a defense attorney. But he's determined to serve the less fortunate and not the type of white-collar criminal I've shuffled around the financial world for thirty-five years. Interestingly, Davis doesn't hold my ruse career against me. Perhaps that's because I never attempted to hide it from him. That would have been a ruse too far. The culture of secrets in which my father and Uncle Jack were raised made an indelible mark on my upbringing, too. Listening to the two brothers swap cryptic, coded stories of their childhood over Ping-Pong and in other settings, trying to piece those bits of information together into a meaningful mosaic, almost certainly set me on my path to a career in rusing. But that legacy ends here. And so I suppose it's possible, in an indirect way, that I influenced what Davis thinks he might want to do for his career.

And don't think for a second it hasn't occurred to me that having strong legal representation in my family may come in handy one day. Who knows? If I did get arrested and my own son defended me, what great material for a book that would be!

$$\$ \ \$ \ \$$

In terms of what I still call the ruse, two things have changed. I'm now truthful on the phone, something my father requested I do over twenty-five years earlier. I've become so skilled at working people, I just talk them into it, usually younger employees who want to see their names at the top of my lists. It's basically rusing without the ruse. And today I make my calls via the internet instead of over telephone lines. I still scribble my notes on a yellow pad, but then I take pictures of them to email to a woman off-site who types up my research and sends it back for editing. I then email the data to my clients in a fancy PowerPoint deck like I'm the CEO of a boutique firm in Beverly Hills rather than a one-man band working out of a remodeled surf shack up the coast.

I continue to be a cog — albeit a small one — in a dirty machine. The firms that hire me to ruse for them love the hear-no-evil approach. Recently, the privately held mega-company Bloomberg reached out to me for intelligence on diversity candidates at competitor organizations because they were woefully short on women, blacks, Latinos, and other minorities. After the police murder of George Floyd and the surge of Black Lives Matter protests in the spring of 2020, the entrenched whiteness was seriously problematic for a company founded by former New York mayor and presidential candidate Michael Bloomberg, especially since he was donating millions to the Democratic Party. Did the executive who called me ask a single question about how I would go about determining who the candidates were? Did they ask whether I would be lying to get the information they so desperately needed? *What do you think?* And I'm not picking on Bloomberg; trust me. All the companies that hire me want plausible deniability. In this world, lies are just as much currency as dollars.

The Wall Street Masters of the Universe and their ever-replenishing army of financial bro acolytes continue to flaunt their brazen duplicity unabated. Just to give one recent example, Goldman Sachs helped financier Jho Low steal $5 billion from an investment fund so he could purchase luxury real estate and throw champagne-drenched parties with celebrities such as Jamie Foxx and Paris Hilton. The 2018 book *Billion Dollar Whale* documented the story of how Low, a chubby Malaysian who attended my alma mater, bankrolled the 2013 movie version of *The Wolf of Wall Street* with buddy Leonardo DiCaprio *using those illicit funds.* Think about that for a moment: A film glorifying financial malfeasance was funded via financial malfeasance. No wonder voting members of the Academy of Motion Picture Arts and Sciences heckled director Martin Scorsese at a screening. They were sick of the romanticization of Wall

Street bankers whose outsized incomes seemed to be in inverse propor-
tion to their contributions to society.

Tim Leissner, the Goldman Sachs executive who orchestrated the
Low/1MDB scam, was all over my research for years. In December 2019,
the SEC barred him from working in the securities industry ever again
after he pleaded guilty to looting billions from Malaysia's sovereign
wealth fund. He admitted bribing high-ranking officials so that Goldman
could win lucrative business in a scandal that rocked the Asian political
scene as well as the giant Wall Street bank — the same giant Wall Street
bank that had eagerly accepted $10 billion in taxpayer-supplied bailout
funds from the government in 2008. Did Leissner go to jail? Of course
not. Did anyone else at Goldman face repercussions, since they most
certainly knew what Leissner was up to? Hell no. And Low? He hasn't
been caught.

Not that I have the right to any moral high ground.

I often think of my moles and how I deceived them over the years.
One call, in particular, over a decade ago, still haunts me. It was one of
the last lying ruse calls I ever made. I'd reached out to my long time mole,
Zoe, when I needed some intel.

"Hey, it's Kevin, how's it going?" I said when she picked up.

"Oh, hi, Kevin, this is Debbie," said a woman I didn't recognize, and
my stomach plunged. Before I could dwell too long on the likely reason
for Zoe's absence, Debbie added, "I'll get Zoe. She's right here."

Whew. But now I shifted to a different concern. No one else had ever
answered her line before. I prayed Zoe wasn't leaving the firm.

"You again," Zoe said when she came on the line.

"Missed me?"

"Not a bit." She laughed. "I have my own job, you know."

"Please. You love these calls."

"I do?"

"They make you realize *your* job isn't so crappy."

"That's true," she said. "I could never do what you do. I couldn't handle
the pressure."

"You don't want to do what I do, trust me."

It occurred to me that despite myself I had just uttered a factual statement.

Zoe got quiet, and all at once I knew she had bad news.

"The cancer's spread," she said, choking up. "It's in my bones, in my liver."

"Hey," I snapped. "You've had cancer since I've known you. That's close to twenty years. You're not going anywhere, so don't even think about it."

She seemed to regain her composure. "I'm on an experimental oral chemo now. The doctors say it's working."

"What did I tell you? Does Debbie there know?"

"Yes. She's kind of filling in. I've been missing a lot of work so they hired her to work with me."

"Oh."

It all came together. Here I was worried that Zoe was quitting and what that would mean for my easy access to her prime intel when she was actually training a replacement *because she was dying*.

"She knows about you," Zoe said, now trying to reassure me. "I told her you'd be calling now and then for information, that whenever she sees an anonymous number it's probably you. I said you're one of my favorite people at the firm."

It was my turn to choke up.

Zoe and I had never met. I'd never done a thing for her other than lend an ear to her struggles as she fought a terrible disease. How could she care so much about me? I was such a talented liar I'd somehow convinced Zoe that I was a person worthy of her friendship, her praise. But then I was also a professional listener, something I did earnestly and thoughtfully. Perhaps unlike others Zoe had confided in, I was actually present in our conversations, as if we were scene partners. I actively searched for ways to comfort her. I genuinely tried to help. I always made her laugh. I desperately wanted our play to have a happy ending, not this hackneyed third-act fatality.

"I'm going to give you her direct number," Zoe said. "In case I'm not here."

I mumbled something indecipherable. There were no words I could say this time. Zoe was getting her affairs in order. And part of that was supplying me with a new mole, a small gesture for her that would have great impact for me. Any comfort I would offer her now would ring as false as the name I'd given her all those years ago.

She read me Debbie's number. "I'm going to miss you, Kev."

"Please," I said. "I'm going to be pestering you for years to come."

We both knew that was a lie, though for different reasons. Zoe knew that, one way or another, she would not be around the next time I called. And I knew I wouldn't be calling her again anyway, no matter how much I wanted to. I'd be dialing Debbie's number, since I couldn't handle carrying the knowledge of Zoe's impending death — which I truly cared about — while pretending to be someone I wasn't.

It's hard to be sincere when you're lying about everything else.

"What do you need?" Zoe asked.

Since this was going to be my last call with her, I decided to go big.

"I need the names of every person in Investment Banking."

"US only?"

Might as well go out with a bang. "Globally."

This was likely close to — no joke — a *thousand* names. I waited for Zoe to freak out and say this was finally just too much, even for her.

"Well," she said, "we better get started then."

ACKNOWLEDGMENTS

*R*use would not have been possible without the help of the Malibu Writers Circle, especially members Bridget Crocker, Asher Sund, and Liz Ziemska. Nor would it have happened without the assistance of my Philly brother, Jay Fernandez, my writing brother, Michael Bland, or my PR brother, Michael Levine.

Special acknowledgments go to Brendan Spiegel at *Narratively*, which published a portion of chapter 9 as "My Acerbic Aerobics Class with O.J. Simpson," and to Sophie Beck at *The Normal School*, which published a portion of chapter 15 as "The King of Pong."

I'd also like to thank the Kerbeck family, Jess Walter, Sue William Silverman, Lee Martin, Bradley Hope, Rob Golenberg, Abby Wike, John Perkins, Valerie Plame, Rebel Steiner, Paul Vernet, William Boggess, Phil Parolisi, Tim Case, Matt Saver, Adam Rocke, Dan Bercu, Damon Skelton, Sam Kling, Jayson Orvis, Elle Gonzalez, and my agent, Dean Krystek, who has worked tirelessly on my behalf.

Like most authors, I've benefited from the help of many talented people during the process of finalizing this memoir, but after the publication of my first book, *Malibu Burning*, I learned that those involved with book promotion are equally smart, hard-working, and important. The following individuals got the word out about my first book, which led to the publication of this one: Lance Cleland and *Tin House*, Paul Morra, Patti Mehring, SJ Main, Sharan Street, Mikke Pierson, Laurel and Larry Thorne, *Exposition Review*, Vassil Pertchinkov, Yassen Tonev and V's Restaurant; Paul Kolsby, Soho House/Little Beach House Malibu, Kevin Dillon, Kolleen Carney Hoepfner, Claire Fullerton, Dawn Reiss, Melissa Curtin McDavitt, Jake White, Arnold and Karen York and *The Malibu Times*, Vivian Dorsel, Naomi Eagleson, Burt Ross,

Saladin Ambar, Khalil Rafati, Taylor Burns, Hali Norris and SunLife Organics, Marrie Stone, Maggie Luckerath and Vintage Grocers, Olandar Foundation, Erik Blackmore, Hollis Cadenhead and the Malibu Racquet Club, Morgan Runyon, and Tim Skogstrom and the Cornell Winery.

   Lastly, thank you to Chip Fleischer, Anthony LaSasso, Devin Wilkie, Helga Schmidt, David Goldberg, Peter Holm, Tom McKeveny, Laura Jorstad, Janet Jesso, and the entire team at Steerforth Press for giving *Ruse* such a wicked-cool home. And thanks to my wife, Gardia, and my daughter, Diana, for being my home.